Problem-Solving Exercises in Physics

Jennifer Bond Hickman

Prentice
Hall

Needham, Massachusetts
Upper Saddle River, New Jersey
Glenview, Illinois

To my grandfather, C. Lawrence Bond
When I was 10 years old, you paid me 10¢ to write a book for you.
I've finally finished it!

Illustrations by Jennifer Bond Hickman.

Cover Photograph: Motor Press Agent/Superstock, Inc.

Many of the designations used by manufacturers and sellers to distinguish their products are claimed as trademarks. Where such a designation appears in this book, and the publisher was aware of a trademark claim, the designations have been printed in initial caps (e.g., Macintosh).

ISBN 0-13-054275-X

5 6 7 8 9 10   05 04 03

Contents

Welcome to Physics!

Studying physics is exciting because it can help you answer many questions about how and why our world works. Your workbook is designed to take some "real-life" situations and examine them with the use of equations, a task often referred to as *problem solving*. Problem solving, however, is more than just solving numerical exercises by doing calculations. Using mathematics is only one way to obtain a solution. Another effective method of problem solving involves drawing on conceptual understanding to explain how the world works and applying those concepts in the laboratory. Like scientists, we perform experiments to test our hypotheses. Until we can understand the concepts and have the opportunity to make our own discoveries, the numbers and equations of physics are meaningless. In the words of Paul G. Hewitt, author of *Conceptual Physics*, "Formulas [should be used] as guides to thinking. . . . We [must] learn to conceptualize before we learn to compute."

This book is not meant to stand alone. It is not meant to replace your physics text, the laboratory work that you do, or your physics teacher. Its purpose is to reinforce the concepts that you have already learned in class and to give you the opportunity to try some calculations with your teacher's help. If you have had difficulty solving word problems in the past, rely on your conceptual understanding of the physics to reason out what should be happening before beginning your mathematical solution. The procedure outlined in the next section will lead you step-by-step through the exercises and make learning to do simple computations a little easier.

How to Use This Book

As you begin to use this book, you will discover that the word *problem* has been replaced with the word *exercise*. A physics exercise does not really become a problem until you accept the challenge it offers and attempt to solve it. Once you have chosen to make it *your* problem, you have a personal interest in finding the solution.

Each chapter of this workbook is divided into two or more topic sections that begin with some physics theory. This theory section provides a very brief review of the concepts and equations your teacher has discussed in class, and is *not* an introduction to new material. It is presumed that you have already learned everything in the theory section before beginning the exercises. This review is simply a reminder and a place to find all the equations you need.

Following the theory, there is a section called Solved Examples, where the theory is applied to exercises similar to those you will be expected to solve later. Solutions are organized to make it easy to follow a calculation from beginning to end. Most solved examples are in the following format.

Given: States the known values in the exercise.

Unknown: Lists the unknown you are looking for.

Original equation: Shows the equation in its original form.

Solve: Shows the equation set up in terms of the unknown, substitutes the numerical values, and solves for the unknown. The answer is then written with the correct units and shown in boldface type for easy identification.

A section of Practice Exercises allows you to apply some of the skills you have learned to new situations.

For more practice, at the end of each chapter there is a section of Additional Exercises, which require the same level of understanding as the Practice Exercises. The final section, called Challenge Exercises for Further Study, contains exercises requiring more complex calculations. Challenge Exercises are intended for you to use after you have mastered the skills used in earlier exercises and are anxious to take on some more rigorous computations.

At the end of the workbook, some Selected Answers will allow you to check your progress.

Using the Right Recipe

Solving physics exercises is much like baking a cake. The first time you try to do it, you must read the recipe very carefully and use exactly the ingredients listed. The next time, you are a little less nervous about how well the cake will turn out. Pretty soon you can make the cake without having to read the recipe at all. You eventually become so comfortable making cakes that you are able to experiment by adding ingredients in a different order or changing the recipe slightly to make the cake even better. When solving physics exercises, you will find it easy to follow the prescribed "recipe" shown in the Solved Examples. After trying a few exercises, you will have started to develop a strategy for constructing your solution that you can retain throughout the entire book. As you get better and better at doing calculations and you develop a greater conceptual understanding of the physics involved, you may even come up with an alternative method of solving an exercise that is different from the one used in this book. If so, congratulations! You have done just what the physicist does when he or she tries to find a solution. Be sure to show your teacher and classmates your alternative approach. It is valuable to look at many different solutions to the same exercise.

An Alternative to Counting on Your Fingers

Early scientists had to make all of their calculations by hand. Later, the slide rule made calculations a little quicker. Today's tool is the hand-held pocket calculator. To save time, you are encouraged to do your calculations with the use of a calculator, but be sure that you first understand *why* you are doing them. Remember, it's important to know how to operate without a calculator as well. Many students rely so heavily on their calculator that they begin to lose the skill of doing calculations by hand. It is extremely important to be able to add, subtract, multiply, divide, and square numbers. You should practice working with exponents (called *scientific notation*) and estimating answers to the nearest power of ten because you may not always have a calculator handy!

How Much is Too Much?

When making measurements, you may have measurement tools that allow you only a certain degree of precision. For example, you may be able to measure your friend's height to the nearest millimeter, but estimating it any closer is difficult. You may say his height is 1536 mm or, in other words, 1.536 m. Since we don't know what comes after the 6, we say that this number contains 4 significant figures. Each one can be accurately measured. When adding, subtracting, multiplying, and dividing numbers, it is important to keep significant figures in mind. The invention of the calculator has made this task difficult, because the calculator customarily carries out our calculations to 8 figures or more, many of which are probably not significant. The rules for the correct use of significant figures can be found in Appendix A. You will find that all of the solved examples in this book and the selected answers in the back adhere to these rules on significant figures and you should too, whenever possible.

You Can't Add Apples and Oranges

When solving numerical exercises, it is always important to include the proper units with any number you are using. Not only will this help you determine the units in the final answer, but it will also help you with your numerical solution as well. If the units in an exercise do not combine to give the correct units in your final answer, then you may have made a mistake in setting up the original equation. In other words, using the correct units is a way of double-checking all of your work.

In this book we will use the units of the *Système International* (SI), the standard system of units in the physics community. Any units not written in the SI form should be converted to the SI system before beginning your calculations. See Appendix A for a review of some important prefixes that you will see when working in the SI system.

A Word of Thanks

I would like to thank the physics students at Boston University Academy, Phillips Academy, and Belmont High School for their input in writing, editing and solving exercises in this book.

Finally, I give my heartfelt thanks to my husband, Paul Hickman, for his countless hours proofreading, editing, and problem solving, and for his unending support and encouragement throughout my work on this book.

Jennifer Bond Hickman

1 Motion

1-1 Speed, Velocity, and Acceleration

Speed vs. Velocity

Vocabulary   **Distance:** How far something travels.

Vocabulary   **Displacement:** How far something travels in a given direction.

Notice that these two terms are very similar. **Distance** is an example of what we call a *scalar* quantity. In other words, it has magnitude, but no direction. **Displacement** is an example of a *vector* quantity because it has both magnitude and direction.

The SI (Système International) unit for distance and displacement is the **meter (m).**

Displacements smaller than a meter may be expressed in units of centimeters (cm) or millimeters (mm). Displacements much larger than a meter may be expressed in units of kilometers (km). See Appendix A for the meanings of these and other common prefixes.

Vocabulary   **Speed:** How fast something is moving.

$$\textbf{average speed} = \frac{\textbf{distance traveled}}{\textbf{elapsed time}} \quad \text{or} \quad v_{av} = \frac{d}{\Delta t}$$

Vocabulary   **Velocity:** How fast something is moving in a given direction.

$$\textbf{average velocity} = \frac{\textbf{displacement}}{\textbf{elapsed time}} \quad \text{or} \quad v_{av} = \frac{\Delta d}{\Delta t} = \frac{d_f - d_o}{t_f - t_o}$$

where d_f and t_f are the final position and time respectively, and d_o and t_o are the initial position and time. The symbol "Δ" (delta) means "change" so Δd is the change in position, or the displacement, while Δt is the change in time.

In this book all vector quantities will be introduced in an equation with **bold type** while all scalar quantities will be introduced in an equation in regular type. Note that speed is a scalar quantity while velocity is a vector quantity.

1

The SI unit for both speed and velocity is the **meter per second (m/s)**.

When traveling in any moving vehicle, you rarely maintain the same velocity throughout an entire trip. If you did, you would travel at a constant speed in a straight line. Instead, speed and direction usually vary during your time of travel.

If you begin and end at the same location but you travel for a great distance in getting there (for example, when you travel in a circle), you have a measurable average speed. However, since your total displacement for such a trip is zero, your average velocity is also zero. In this chapter, both average speed and average velocity will be written as v_{av}. The "av" subscript will be dropped in later chapters.

Acceleration

Vocabulary **Acceleration:** The rate at which the velocity changes during a given amount of time.

$$\text{acceleration} = \frac{\text{change in velocity}}{\text{elapsed time}} \quad \text{or} \quad a = \frac{\Delta v}{\Delta t} = \frac{v_f - v_o}{t_f - t_o}$$

where the terms v_f and v_o mean final velocity and initial velocity, respectively.

The SI unit for acceleration is the **meter per second squared (m/s²)**.

If the final velocity of a moving object is smaller than its initial velocity, the object must be slowing down. A slowing object is sometimes said to have *negative acceleration* because the magnitude of the acceleration is preceded by a negative sign.

Solved Examples

Example 1: Benjamin watches a thunderstorm from his apartment window. He sees the flash of a lightning bolt and begins counting the seconds until he hears the clap of thunder 10. s later. Assume that the speed of sound in air is 340 m/s. How far away was the lightning bolt a) in m? b) in km? (Note: The speed of light, 3.0×10^8 m/s, is considerably faster than the speed of sound. That is why you see the lightning flash so much earlier than you hear the clap of thunder. In actuality, the lightning and thunder clap occur almost simultaneously.)

a. *Given:* $v_{av} = 340$ m/s   *Unknown:* $\Delta d = ?$
$\quad\qquad \Delta t = 10.0$ s   *Original equation:* $v_{av} = \dfrac{\Delta d}{\Delta t}$

Solve: $\Delta d = v_{av}\Delta t = (340 \text{ m/s})(10. \text{ s}) = \textbf{3400 m}$

b. For numbers this large you may wish to express the final answer in km rather than in m. Because "kilo" means 1000, then 1.000 km = 1000. m.

$$3400 \text{ m} \frac{(1.000 \text{ km})}{1000. \text{ m}} = \textbf{3.4 km}$$

The lightning bolt is 3.4 km away, which is just a little over two miles for those of you who think in English units!

Example 2: On May 28, 2000, Juan Montoya became the first Colombian citizen to win the Indianapolis 500. Montoya completed the race in a time of 2.98 h. What was Montoya's average speed during the 500.-mi race? (Note: Generally the unit "miles" is not used in physics exercises. However, the Indianapolis 500 is a race that is measured in miles, so the mile is appropriate here. Don't forget, the SI unit for distance is the meter.)

Given: d = 500. mi $\qquad$ *Unknown:* v_{av} = ?
$\qquad \quad \Delta t$ = 2.98 h $\qquad \qquad$ *Original equation:* $\Delta t = \dfrac{\Delta d}{v}$

Solve: $\Delta t = \dfrac{\Delta d}{v} = \dfrac{500. \text{ mi}}{2.98 \text{ h}} = 168 \text{ mi/h}$

Example 3: The slowest animal ever discovered was a crab found in the Red Sea. It traveled with an average speed of 5.70 km/y. How long would it take this crab to travel 100. km?

Given: Δd = 100. km $\qquad$ *Unknown:* Δt = ?
$\qquad \quad v_{av}$ = 5.70 km/y $\qquad$ *Original equation:* $\Delta t = \dfrac{\Delta d}{v_{av}}$

Solve: $\Delta t = \dfrac{\Delta d}{v_{av}} = \dfrac{100. \text{ km}}{5.70 \text{ km/y}} = \textbf{17.5 y}$ A long time!

Example 4: Tiffany, who is opening in a new Broadway show, has some limo trouble in the city. With only 8.0 minutes until curtain time, she hails a cab and they speed off to the theater down a 1000.-m-long one-way street at a speed of 25 m/s. At the end of the street the cab driver waits at a traffic light for 1.5 min and then turns north onto a 1700.-m.-long traffic-filled avenue on which he is able to travel at a speed of only 10.0 m/s. Finally, this brings them to the theater. a) Does Tiffany arrive before the theater lights dim? b) Draw a distance vs. time graph of the situation.

Solution: First, break this exercise down into segments and solve each segment independently.

Segment 1: (one-way street)

Given: Δd = 1000. m $\qquad$ *Unknown:* Δt = ?
$\qquad \quad v_{av}$ = 25 m/s $\qquad \qquad$ *Original equation:* $v_{av} = \dfrac{\Delta d}{\Delta t}$

Solve: $\Delta t = \dfrac{\Delta d}{v_{av}} = \dfrac{1000. \text{ m}}{25 \text{ m/s}} = \textbf{40. s}$

Segment 2: (traffic light)

Given: $\Delta t = 1.5$ min $\qquad (1.5 \text{ min})\dfrac{(60. \text{ s})}{(1.0 \text{ min})} = 90. \text{ s}$

Segment 3: (traffic-filled avenue)

Given: $\Delta d = 1700.$ m $\qquad\qquad$ Unknown: $\Delta t = ?$
$\qquad v_{av} = 10.0$ m/s $\qquad\qquad$ Original equation: $v_{av} = \dfrac{\Delta d}{\Delta t}$

Solve: $\Delta t = \dfrac{\Delta d}{v_{av}} = \dfrac{1700. \text{ m}}{10.0 \text{ m/s}} = 170. \text{ s}$

total time $= 40. \text{ s} + 90. \text{ s} + 170. \text{ s} = 300. \text{ s}$ $\quad (300. \text{ s})\dfrac{(1.0 \text{ min})}{(60. \text{ s})} = \textbf{5.0 min}$

Yes, she not only makes it to the show in time, but she even has 3.0 minutes to spare to put on her costume and make-up.

b. The motion of the cab can be described by the following graph.

In Segment 1, the distance of 1000. m was covered in a fairly short amount of time, which means that the cab was traveling quickly. This high speed can be seen as a steep slope on the graph.

In Segment 2, the cab was at rest. Notice that even though the cab did not move, time continued on, resulting in a horizontal line on the graph.

In Segment 3, the distance of 1700. m was covered in a much longer amount of time so the cab was traveling slowly. This low speed is indicated by a slope that is not as steep as that in segment 1.

Remember, all graphs should have titles and the axes should be labeled with the correct units.

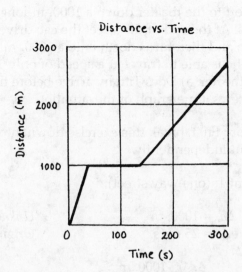

Example 5: Grace is driving her sports car at 30 m/s when a ball rolls out into the street in front of her. Grace slams on the brakes and comes to a stop in 3.0 s. What was the acceleration of Grace's car?

Given: $v_o = 30$ m/s
$v_f = 0$ m/s
$\Delta t = 3.0$ s

Unknown: $a = ?$
Original equation: $a = \dfrac{v_f - v_o}{\Delta t}$

Solve: $a = \dfrac{v_f - v_o}{\Delta t} = \dfrac{0 \text{ m/s} - 30 \text{ m/s}}{3.0 \text{ s}} = -10 \text{ m/s}^2$

The negative sign means the car was slowing down.

Practice Exercises

Exercise 1: Hans stands at the rim of the Grand Canyon and yodels down to the bottom. He hears his yodel echo back from the canyon floor 5.20 s later. Assume that the speed of sound in air is 340.0 m/s. How deep is the canyon at this location?

Answer: ⎯⎯⎯⎯⎯⎯⎯⎯⎯⎯⎯⎯

Exercise 2: The world speed record on water was set on October 8, 1978 by Ken Warby of Blowering Dam, Australia. If Ken drove his motorboat a distance of 1000. m in 7.045 s, how fast was his boat moving a) in m/s? b) in mi/h?

Answer: **a.** ⎯⎯⎯⎯⎯⎯⎯⎯⎯⎯⎯⎯

Answer: **b.** ⎯⎯⎯⎯⎯⎯⎯⎯⎯⎯⎯⎯

Exercise 3: According to the World Flying Disk Federation, on April 8, 2000, Jennifer Griffin of Fredericksburg, Virginia threw a Frisbee for a distance of 138.56 m to capture the women's record. If the Frisbee was thrown horizontally with a speed of 13.0 m/s, how long did the Frisbee remain aloft?

Answer: _____

Exercise 4: It is now 10:29 a.m., but when the bell rings at 10:30 a.m. Suzette will be late for French class for the third time this week. She must get from one side of the school to the other by hurrying down three different hallways. She runs down the first hallway, a distance of 35.0 m, at a speed of 3.50 m/s. The second hallway is filled with students, and she covers its 48.0-m length at an average speed of 1.20 m/s. The final hallway is empty, and Suzette sprints its 60.0-m length at a speed of 5.00 m/s. a) Does Suzette make it to class on time or does she get detention for being late again? b) Draw a distance vs. time graph of the situation.

Answer: **a.** _____

Exercise 5: A jumbo jet taxiing down the runway receives word that it must return to the gate to pick up an important passenger who was late to his connecting flight. The jet is traveling at 45.0 m/s when the pilot receives the message. What is the acceleration of the plane if it takes the pilot 5.00 s to bring the plane to a halt?

Answer: _____

Exercise 6:   While driving his sports car at 20.0 m/s down a four-lane highway, Eddie comes up behind a slow-moving dump truck and decides to pass it in the left-hand lane. If Eddie can accelerate at 5.00 m/s², how long will it take for him to reach a speed of 30.0 m/s?

Answer: _____

Exercise 7:   Vivian is walking to the hairdresser's at 1.3 m/s when she glances at her watch and realizes that she is going to be late for her appointment. Vivian gradually quickens her pace at a rate of 0.090 m/s². a) What is Vivian's speed after 10.0 s? b) At this speed, is Vivian walking, jogging, or running very fast?

Answer: **a.** _____

Answer: **b.** _____

Exercise 8:   A torpedo fired from a submerged submarine is propelled through the water with a speed of 20.00 m/s and explodes upon impact with a target 2000.0 m away. If the sound of the impact is heard 101.4 s after the torpedo was fired, what is the speed of sound in water? (Because the torpedo is held at a constant speed by its propeller, the effect of water resistance can be neglected.)

Answer: _____

1-2 Free Fall

Vocabulary

Free Fall: The movement of an object in response to a gravitational attraction.

When an object is released, it falls toward the earth due to the gravitational attraction the earth provides. As the object falls, it will accelerate at a constant rate of 9.8 m/s^2 regardless of its mass. However, to make calculations more expedient and easier to do without a calculator, this number will be written as $g = 10.0$ m/s^2 throughout this book.

There are many different ways to solve free fall exercises. The sign convention used may be chosen by you or your teacher. In this book, the downward direction will be positive, and anything falling downward will be written with a positive velocity and position; anything moving upward will be represented with a negative velocity and position. Remember: Gravity *always* acts to pull an object down, so the gravitational acceleration, g, will always be written as a positive number regardless of which direction the object is moving.

The displacement of a falling object in a given amount of time is written as

$$\Delta d = v_o \Delta t + \left(\frac{1}{2}\right) g \Delta t^2$$

The final velocity of a falling object can be represented by the equation

$$v_f^2 = v_o^2 + 2g\Delta d$$

or by the earlier equation, $a = (v_f - v_o)/\Delta t$, rewritten as $v_f = v_o + a\Delta t$, or

$$v_f = v_o + g\Delta t$$

Note that the term "g" in all of these exercises can be written as "a" if you use a constant acceleration other than gravity. Therefore, these equations can be used for objects moving horizontally as well as vertically.

It is common to neglect air resistance in most free fall exercises (including those in this book), although in real life, air resistance is a factor that must be taken into account. This book will also assume that the initial speed of all objects in free fall is zero, unless otherwise specified.

Solved Examples

Example 6:

King Kong carries Fay Wray up the 321-m-tall Empire State Building. At the top of the skyscraper, Fay Wray's shoe falls from her foot. How fast will the shoe be moving when it hits the ground?

$$\text{Given: } v_o = 0 \text{ m/s} \qquad\qquad \text{Unknown: } v_f = ?$$
$$\qquad\qquad g = 10.0 \text{ m/s}^2 \qquad\qquad \text{Original equation: } v_f^2 = v_o^2 + 2g\Delta d$$
$$\qquad\qquad \Delta d = 321 \text{ m}$$

$$\text{Solve: } v_f = \sqrt{v_o^2 + 2g\Delta d} = \sqrt{0 + 2(10.0 \text{ m/s}^2)(321 \text{ m})} = \sqrt{6420 \text{ m}^2/\text{s}^2}$$
$$= \textbf{80.1 m/s}$$

Example 7: The Steamboat Geyser in Yellowstone National Park, Wyoming is capable of shooting its hot water up from the ground with a speed of 48.0 m/s. How high can this geyser shoot?

Solution: Remember, the geyser is shooting **up**; therefore it must have a negative initial velocity.

$$\text{Given: } v_o = -48.0 \text{ m/s} \qquad\qquad \text{Unknown: } \Delta d = ?$$
$$\qquad\qquad v_f = 0 \text{ m/s} \qquad\qquad\qquad \text{Original equation: } v_f^2 = v_o^2 + 2g\Delta d$$
$$\qquad\qquad g = 10.0 \text{ m/s}^2$$

$$\text{Solve: } \Delta d = \frac{v_f^2 - v_o^2}{2g} = \frac{(0 \text{ m/s})^2 - (-48.0 \text{ m/s})^2}{2(10.0 \text{ m/s}^2)} = \textbf{-115 m}$$

As you might expect, the final answer has a negative displacement. This means that the total distance the water has traveled is measured up from the ground.

Example 8: A baby blue jay sits in a tall tree awaiting the arrival of its dinner. As the mother lands on the nest, she drops a worm toward the hungry chick's mouth, but the worm misses and falls from the nest to the ground in 1.50 s. How high up is the nest?

$$\text{Given: } v_o = 0 \text{ m/s} \qquad\qquad \text{Unknown: } \Delta d = ?$$
$$\qquad\qquad g = 10.0 \text{ m/s}^2 \qquad\qquad \text{Original equation: } \Delta d = v_o \Delta t + \left(\frac{1}{2}\right)g\Delta t^2$$
$$\qquad\qquad t = 1.50 \text{ s}$$

$$\text{Solve: } \Delta d = v_o \Delta t + \left(\frac{1}{2}\right)g\Delta t^2 = 0 + \left(\frac{1}{2}\right)(10.0 \text{ m/s}^2)(1.50 \text{ s})^2 = \textbf{11.3 m}$$

Example 9: A giraffe, who stands 6.00 m tall, bites a branch off a tree to chew on the leaves, and he lets the branch fall to the ground. How long does it take the branch to hit the ground?

$$\text{Given: } \Delta d = 6.00 \text{ m} \qquad\qquad \text{Unknown: } \Delta t = ?$$
$$\qquad\qquad g = 10.0 \text{ m/s}^2 \qquad\qquad \text{Original equation: } \Delta d = v_o \Delta t + \left(\frac{1}{2}\right)g\Delta t^2$$
$$\qquad\qquad v_o = 0 \text{ m/s}$$

$$\text{Solve: } \Delta t = \sqrt{\frac{2\Delta d}{g}} = \sqrt{\frac{2(6.00 \text{ m})}{10.0 \text{ m/s}^2}} = \sqrt{1.20 \text{ s}^2} = \textbf{1.10 s}$$

Practice Exercises

Exercise 9:   Billy, a mountain goat, is rock climbing on his favorite slope one sunny spring morning when a rock comes hurtling toward him from a ledge 40.0 m above. Billy ducks and avoids injury. a) How fast is the rock traveling when it passes Billy? b) How does this speed compare to that of a car traveling down the highway at the speed limit of 25 m/s (equivalent to 55 mi/h)?

Answer: **a.** _____

Answer: **b.** _____

Exercise 10:   Reverend Northwick climbs to the church belfry one morning to determine the height of the church. From an outside balcony he drops a book and observes that it takes 2.00 s to strike the ground below. a) How high is the balcony of the church belfry? b) Why would it be difficult to determine the height of the belfry balcony if the Reverend dropped only one page out of the book?

Answer: **a.** _____

Answer: **b.** _____

Exercise 11:   How long is Tina, a ballerina, in the air when she leaps straight up with a speed of 1.8 m/s?

Answer: _____

Exercise 12: In order to open the clam it catches, a seagull will drop the clam repeatedly onto a hard surface from high in the air until the shell cracks. If a seagull flies to a height of 25 m, how long will the clam take to fall?

Answer: _____

Exercise 13: At Six Flags Great Adventure Amusement Park in New Jersey, a popular ride known as "Free Fall" carries passengers up to a height of 33.5 m and drops them to the ground inside a small cage. How fast are the passengers going at the bottom of this exhilarating journey?

Answer: _____

Exercise 14: A unique type of basketball is played on the planet Zarth. During the game, a player flies above the basket and drops the ball in from a height of 10 m. If the ball takes 5.0 s to fall, find the acceleration due to gravity on Zarth.

Answer: _____

Additional Exercises

A-1: During an Apollo moon landing, reflecting panels were placed on the moon. This allowed earth-based astronomers to shoot laser beams at the moon's surface to determine its distance. The reflected laser beam was observed 2.52 s after the laser pulse was sent. If the speed of light is 3.00×10^8 m/s, what was the distance between the astronomers and the moon?

A-2: The peregrine falcon is the world's fastest known bird and has been clocked diving downward toward its prey at constant vertical velocity of 97.2 m/s. If the falcon dives straight down from a height of 100. m, how much time does this give a rabbit below to consider his next move as the falcon begins his descent?

A-3: The Kentucky Derby, the first of three horse races for the triple crown, was won on May 7, 2000 by Fusaichi Pegasus with a time of 121.1 s. If the race covers 2011.25 m, what was Fusaichi Pegasus' average speed in a) m/s? b) mi/h?

A-4: For years, the posted highway speed limit was 88.5 km/h (55 mi/h) but now some rural stretches of highway have posted speed limits of 104.6 km/h (65 mi/h). In Maine, the distance from Portland to Bangor is 215 km. How much time can be saved in traveling from Portland to Bangor at this higher speed limit?

A-5: A tortoise and a hare are in a road race to defend the honor of their breeds. The tortoise crawls the entire 1000.-m distance at a speed of 0.2000 m/s while the rabbit runs the first 200.0 m at 2.000 m/s. The rabbit then stops to take a nap for 1.300 h and awakens to finish the last 800.0 m with an average speed of 3.000 m/s. a) Who wins the race and by how much time? b) Draw a graph of distance vs. time for the situation.

A-6: Two physics professors challenge each other to a 100.-m race across the football field. The loser will grade the winner's physics labs for one month. Dr. Nelson runs the race in 10.40 s. Dr. Bray runs the first 25.0 m with an average speed of 10.0 m/s, the next 50.0 m with an average speed of 9.50 m/s, and the last 25.0 m with an average speed of 11.1 m/s. Who gets stuck grading physics labs for the next month?

A-7: A caterpillar crawling up a leaf slows from 0.75 cm/s to 0.50 cm/s at a rate of -0.05 cm/s^2. How long does it take the caterpillar to make the change?

A-8: In the Wizard of Oz, Dorothy awakens in Munchkinland where her house has been blown by a tornado. If the house fell from a height of 3000. m, with what speed did it hit the Wicked Witch of the East when it landed?

A-9: The Tambora volcano on the island of Sumbawa, Indonesia has been known to throw ash into the air with a speed of 625 m/s during an eruption. a) How high could this volcanic plume have risen? b) On Venus, where the acceleration due to gravity is slightly less than on Earth, would this volcanic plume rise higher or not as high as it does on Earth?

A-10: Chief Boolie, the jungle dweller, is out hunting for dinner when a coconut falls from a tree and lands on his toe. If the nut fell for 1.4 s, how fast was it traveling when it hit Chief Boolie's toe?

A-11: Here is a bet that you are almost sure to win! Try dropping a dollar bill through a friend's fingers and offer to let her keep it if she can catch it. The bill should be started just at the finger level and your friend shouldn't have any advanced warning when it is going to drop. A dollar bill has a length of 15.5 cm and human reaction time is rarely less than 0.20 s. Do the necessary calculations—why is this almost a sure bet?

A-12: While repairing a defective radio transmitter located 410 m up on the Skydeck of Chicago's Sears Tower, Lyle drops his hammer that falls all the way to the ground below. a) How long will it take for Lyle's hammer to fall? b) With what speed will the hammer hit the pavement? c) How far will the hammer have fallen after 1.50 s when a janitor watches it pass outside an office window?

A-13: On July 31, 1994, Sergey Bubka of the Ukraine broke his own world pole-vaulting record by attaining a height of 6.14 m. a) How long did it take Bubka to return to the ground from the highest part of his vault? b) Describe how this time compares to the time it took him to go from the ground to the highest point.

A-14: A Christmas tree ball will break if dropped on a hardwood floor with a speed of 2.0 m/s or more. Holly is decorating her Christmas tree when her cat, Trickor, taps a ball, causing it to fall 15 cm from a tree branch to the floor. Does the ball break?

A-15: Perhaps sometime in the future, NASA will develop a program to land a human being on Mars. If you were the first Mars explorer and discovered that when you dropped a hammer it took 0.68 s to fall 0.90 m to the ground, what would you calculate for the gravitational acceleration on Mars?

Challenge Exercises for Further Study

B-1: Seth is doing his student driving with the "Give-Me-A-Brake" driving school and is traveling down the interstate with a speed of 9.0 m/s. Mack is driving his "18-wheeler" down the fast lane at 27.0 m/s when he notices Seth 30.0 m ahead of him in the right lane. a) If Mack and Seth maintain their speeds, how far must Mack travel before he catches up to Seth? b) How long will this take?

B-2: At the 2000 summer Olympics in Sydney Australia, the women's 400-m medley swimming relay was won by the United States. The four U.S. women swam the 100.0-m leg of the race with the following average speeds: Barbara Bedford (backstroke) at 1.6289 m/s, Megan Quann (breaststroke) at 1.5085 m/s, Jenny Thompson (fly) at 1.7467 m/s and Dara Torres (freestyle) at 1.8737 m/s. a) How far was the team's final time from the world record time of 4.028 min. set by the Chinese in 1994? b) Did the American women break the world record, or miss it? c) What was the U.S. team's average speed for the 400.0-m race?

B-3:   In 1945, the *Enola Gay*, a B-29 bomber, dropped the atomic bomb from a height of 9450 m over Hiroshima, Japan. If the plane carrying the bomb were traveling with a horizontal velocity of 67.0 m/s, how far horizontally would the bomb have traveled between the point of release and the point where it exploded 513 m above the ground? (To avoid being above the bomb when it exploded, the Enola Gay turned sharply away after the bomb's release.)

B-4:   Pepe, the clown, is jumping on a trampoline as Babette, the tightrope walker, above him suddenly loses her balance and falls off the tightrope straight toward Pepe. Pepe has just started upward at 15 m/s when Babette begins to fall. Pepe catches her in midair after 1.0 s. a) How far has Babette fallen when she is caught by Pepe? b) What is Babette's velocity at the time of contact? c) What is Pepe's velocity at the time of contact? d) How far above the trampoline was Babette before she fell?

B-5:   Mr. DeFronzo has just learned that he won the Presidential Award for Excellence in Science Teaching. He runs to the open window and throws his red marking pen into the air with an initial upward speed of 5.00 m/s. a) If the window is 12.0 m above the ground, what is the velocity of the pen 1.0 s after it is thrown? b) How far has the pen fallen from its starting position after 2.0 s? c) How long does it take the pen to hit the ground?

B-6:   On October 24, 1901 Annie Edson Taylor, a school teacher from Michigan, became the first person to successfully ride over Niagara Falls in a wooden barrel. Assume Annie began her journey at Goat Island, 240. m from the falls, where the water current started her down the Niagara River at 8.00 m/s. During her journey, the current reached 15.0 m/s as it carried Annie over Horseshoe Falls, a drop of 51.0 m. How long was Annie's trip from start to finish?

2 Vectors and Projectiles

2-1 Vectors and Scalars

Vocabulary **Vector:** A quantity with magnitude (size) and direction.

Some examples of vectors are displacement, velocity, acceleration, and force.

Vocabulary **Scalar:** A quantity with magnitude only.

Some examples of scalars are distance, speed, mass, time, and volume.

Vectors are represented by arrows. They can be added by placing the arrows head to tail. The arrow that extends from the tail of the first vector to the head of the last vector is called the **resultant.** It indicates both the magnitude and direction of the vector sum.

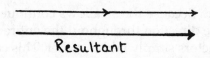

Resultant

Remember, vectors don't always have to be in a straight line but may be oriented at angles to each other, such as

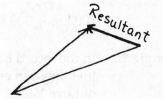

Resultant vectors can be determined by a number of different methods. Here you will solve vector addition exercises both **graphically** and with **vector components.**

Graphical addition of vectors: Using a ruler, draw all vectors to scale and connect them head to tail. The resultant is the vector that connects the tail of the first vector with the head of the last. (Hint: Using graph paper makes this method even easier!)

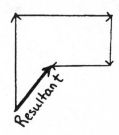

Resultant

Vector Components: Because a vector has both magnitude and direction, you can separate it into horizontal (or x) and vertical (or y) components. To do this, draw a rectangle with horizontal and vertical sides and a diagonal equal to the vector. Draw arrow heads on one horizontal and one vertical side to make the original vector the resultant of the horizontal and vertical components.

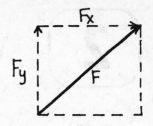

After you have drawn the components, you can find their lengths by using simple trigonometry. If you are not familiar with trigonometry or need a quick refresher, refer to Appendix A.

Solved Examples

Example 1:   Every March, the swallows return to San Juan Capistrano, California after their winter in the south. If the swallows fly due north and cover 200 km on the first day, 300 km on the second day, and 250 km on the third day, draw a vector diagram of their trip and find their total displacement for the three-day journey.

Solution: Because the swallows continue to fly in the same direction throughout the entire trip, these vectors simply add together. This can be shown by placing the displacement vectors head to tail.

200 km + 300 km + 250 km = **750 km north**

Example 2:   In the record books, there are men who claim that they have such strong teeth that they can even use them to move cars, trains, and helicopters. Joe Ponder of Love Valley, North Carolina is one such man. Suppose a car pulling forward with a force of 20 000 N was pulled back by a rope that Joe held in his teeth. Joe pulled the car with a force of 25 000 N. Draw a vector diagram of the situation and find the resultant force.

Solution: In this exercise, the vectors are pointing in opposite directions, so the situation would look like this.

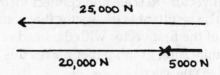

25 000 N − 20 000 N = **5000 N in the direction Joe is pulling.** Strong teeth!

Example 3: If St. Louis Cardinals homerun king, Mark McGwire, hit a baseball due west with a speed of 50.0 m/s, and the ball encountered a wind that blew it north at 5.00 m/s, what was the resultant velocity of the baseball?

Solution: Begin by drawing a vector diagram of the situation.

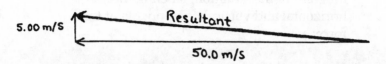

Solve using the Pythagorean theorem:

$$a^2 + b^2 = c^2$$
$$(50.0 \text{ m/s})^2 + (5.00 \text{ m/s})^2 = c^2$$
$$c = \sqrt{2500 \text{ m}^2/\text{s}^2 + 25.0 \text{ m}^2/\text{s}^2} = \textbf{50.2 m/s toward the northwest}$$

For those of you who understand trigonometry, you can find the exact angle at which the ball travels by saying:

$$\tan \theta = \frac{\text{opp}}{\text{adj}} = \frac{5.00 \text{ m/s}}{50.0 \text{ m/s}} = 0.100 \qquad \text{so } \tan^{-1} 0.100 = \textbf{5.71°}$$

However, don't worry. If you are not familiar with trigonometry, you can simply write the answer as 50.2 m/s to the north of west. For a brief review of trigonometry, see Appendix A.

Example 4: The Maton family begins a vacation trip by driving 700 km west. Then the family drives 600 km south, 300 km east, and 400 north. Where will the Matons end up in relation to their starting point? Solve graphically.

Solution: First, draw the appropriate diagram to scale using a relationship such as 1 cm = 1 km, and you will see a space remaining between where the Matons began their trip and where they ended. Because you are solving this exercise graphically, measure with a ruler the length of the remaining space and convert your measurement back into km. This is the resultant displacement. (Hint: You may find it easier to use graph paper for your drawing so that you can have 1 km equal to a certain number of squares.)

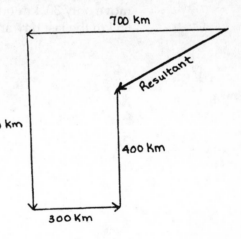

Answer is **450 km,** as measured with a ruler.

Example 5: Ralph is mowing the back yard with a push mower that he pushes downward with a force of 20.0 N at an angle of 30.0° to the horizontal. What are the horizontal and vertical components of the force exerted by Ralph?

Solution: Begin solving by drawing a diagram of the situation, labeling the horizontal and vertical components of the force.

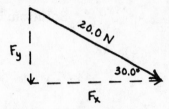

Horizontal component: The hypotenuse in this exercise is the 20.0-N force. The horizontal component is the one going in the x direction. This is the side adjacent to the 30.0° angle so you use the equation for the cosine of an angle.

$$\cos \theta = \frac{F_x}{F} \qquad F_x = F \cos \theta = (20.0 \text{ N}) \cos 30.0° = \mathbf{17.3 \text{ N}}$$

Vertical component: Again, the 20.0-N force is the hypotenuse of the triangle. The vertical component is the one going in the y direction. This is the side opposite the 30.0° angle so you use the equation for the sine of an angle.

$$\sin \theta = \frac{F_y}{F} \qquad F_y = F \sin \theta = (20.0 \text{ N}) \sin 30.0° = \mathbf{10.0 \text{ N}}$$

Practice Exercises

Exercise 1: Some Antarctic explorers heading due south toward the pole travel 50. km during the first day. A sudden snow storm slows their progress and they move only 30. km on the second day. With plenty of rest they travel the final 65 km the last day and reach the pole. What was the explorers' displacement?

Answer: _____

Exercise 2: Erica and Tory are out fishing on the lake on a hot summer day when they both decide to go for a swim. Erica dives off the front of the boat with a force of 45 N, while Tory dives off the back with a force of 60. N. a) Draw a vector diagram of the situation. b) Find the resultant force on the boat.

Answer: **b.** ————————————

Exercise 3: Young thoroughbreds are sometimes reluctant to enter the starting gate for their first race. Astro Turf is one such horse, and it takes two strong men to get him set for the race. Derek pulls Astro Turf's bridle from the front with a force of 200. N and Dan pushes him from behind with a force of 150. N, while the horse pushes back against the ground with a force of 300. N. a) Draw a vector diagram of the situation. b) What is the resultant force on Astro Turf?

Answer: **b.** ————————————

Exercise 4: Shareen finds that when she drives her motorboat upstream she can travel with a speed of only 8 m/s, while she moves with a speed of 12 m/s when she heads downstream. What is the current of the river on which Shareen is traveling?

Answer: ————————————

Exercise 5: Rochelle is flying to New York for her big Broadway debut. If the plane heads out of Los Angeles with a velocity of 220. m/s in a northeast direction, relative to the ground, and encounters a wind blowing head-on at 45 m/s, what is the resultant velocity of the plane, relative to the ground?

Answer: _____

Exercise 6: While Dexter is on a camping trip with his boy scout troop, the scout leader hands each boy a compass and map. The directions on Dexter's map read as follows: "Walk 500.0 m north, 200.0 m east, 300.0 m south, and 400.0 m west." If he follows the map, what is Dexter's displacement? Solve graphically.

Answer: _____

Exercise 7: Amit flies due east from San Francisco to Washington, D.C., a displacement of 5600. km. He then flies from Washington to Boston, a displacement of 900. km at an angle of 55.0° east of north. What is Amit's total displacement?

Answer: _____

Exercise 8: Marcie shovels snow after a storm by exerting a force of 30.0 N on her shovel at an angle of 60.0° to the vertical. What are the horizontal and vertical components of the force exerted by Marcie?

Answer: _____

Answer: _____

Exercise 9: Ivan pulls a sled loaded with logs to his cabin in the woods. If Ivan pulls with a force of 800. N in a direction 20.0° above the horizontal, what are the horizontal and vertical components of the force exerted by Ivan?

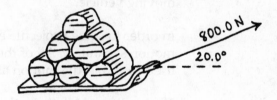

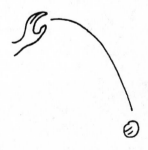

Answer: _____

Answer: _____

2-2 Projectile Motion

Vocabulary **Projectile:** An object that moves through space acted upon only by the earth's gravity.

A projectile may start at a given height and move toward the ground in an arc. For example, picture the path a rock makes when it is tossed straight out from a cliff.

A projectile may also start at a given level and then move upward and downward again as does a football that has been thrown.

Regardless of its path, a projectile will always follow these rules:

1. Projectiles always maintain a constant horizontal velocity (neglecting air resistance).

2. Projectiles always experience a constant vertical acceleration of 10.0 m/s^2 downward (neglecting air resistance).

3. Horizontal and vertical motion are completely independent of each other. Therefore, the velocity of a projectile can be separated into horizontal and vertical components.

4. For a projectile beginning and ending at the same height, the time it takes to rise to its highest point equals the time it takes to fall from the highest point back to the original position.

5. Objects dropped from a moving vehicle have the same velocity as the moving vehicle.

In order to solve projectile exercises, you *must* consider horizontal and vertical motion separately. All of the equations for linear motion in Chapter 1 can be used for projectile motion as well. You don't need to learn any new equations!

To simplify calculations, the term for initial vertical velocity, v_{yo}, will be left out of all equations in which an object is projected horizontally. For example, $\Delta d_y = v_{yo}\Delta t + \left(\frac{1}{2}\right)g\Delta t^2$ will be written as $\Delta d_y = \left(\frac{1}{2}\right)g\Delta t^2$.

Solved Examples

Example 6:

In her physics lab, Melanie rolls a 10-g marble down a ramp and off the table with a horizontal velocity of 1.2 m/s. The marble falls in a cup placed 0.51 m from the table's edge. How high is the table?

Solution: The first thing you should notice about projectile exercises is that you do not need to consider the mass of the object projected. Remember, if you ignore air resistance, all bodies fall at exactly the same rate regardless of their mass.

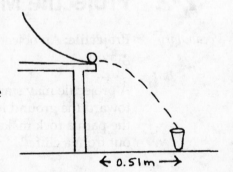

← 0.51m →

Before you can find the height of the table, you must first determine how long the marble is in the air. The horizontal distance traveled equals the constant horizontal velocity times the travel time.

Given: $\Delta d_x = 0.51$ m   Unknown: $\Delta t = ?$
$\qquad\quad v_x = 1.2$ m/s   Original equation: $v_x = \dfrac{\Delta d_x}{\Delta t}$

Solve: $\Delta t = \dfrac{\Delta d_x}{v_x} = \dfrac{0.51 \text{ m}}{1.2 \text{ m/s}} = 0.43$ s

Now that you know the time the marble takes to fall, you can find the vertical distance it traveled.

Given: $g = 10.0$ m/s²   Unknown: $\Delta d_y = ?$
$\qquad\quad \Delta t = 0.43$ s   Original equation: $\Delta d_y = \left(\dfrac{1}{2}\right)g\Delta t^2$

Solve: $\Delta d_y = \left(\dfrac{1}{2}\right)(10.0 \text{ m/s}^2)(0.43 \text{ s})^2 = \textbf{0.92 m}$

Example 7:   Bert is standing on a ladder picking apples in his grandfather's orchard. As he pulls each apple off the tree, he tosses it into a basket that sits on the ground 3.0 m below at a horizontal distance of 2.0 m from Bert. How fast must Bert throw the apples (horizontally) in order for them to land in the basket?

Solution: Before you can find the horizontal component of the velocity, you must first find the time that the apple is in the air.

Given: $\Delta d_y = 3.0$ m   Unknown: $\Delta t = ?$
$\qquad\quad g = 10.0$ m/s²   Original equation: $\Delta d_y = \left(\dfrac{1}{2}\right)g\Delta t^2$

Solve: $t = \sqrt{\dfrac{2\Delta d_y}{g}} = \sqrt{\dfrac{2(3.0 \text{ m})}{10.0 \text{ m/s}^2}} = \textbf{0.77 s}$

Now that you know the time, you can use it to find the horizontal component of the velocity.

Given: $\Delta d_x = 2.0$ m   Unknown: $v_x = ?$
$\qquad\quad \Delta t = 0.77$ s   Original equation: $\Delta d_x = v_x \Delta t$

Solve: $v_x = \dfrac{\Delta d_x}{\Delta t} = \dfrac{2.0 \text{ m}}{0.77 \text{ s}} = \textbf{2.6 m/s}$

Example 8:   Emanuel Zacchini, the famous human cannonball of the Ringling Bros. and Barnum & Bailey Circus, was fired out of a cannon with a speed of 24.0 m/s at an angle of 40.0° to the horizontal. If he landed in a net 56.6 m away at the same height from which he was fired, how long was Zacchini in the air?

Solution: Because Zacchini was in the air for the same amount of time vertically that he was horizontally, you can find his horizontal time and this will be the answer. First, you need the horizontal velocity component.

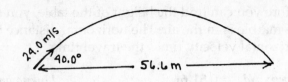

$$\cos \theta = \frac{v_x}{v} \qquad v_x = v \cos \theta = (24.0 \text{ m/s}) \cos 40.0° = 18.4 \text{ m/s}$$

Now you have the horizontal velocity component and the horizontal displacement, so you can find the time.

Given: $v_x = 18.4 \text{ m/s}$ *Unknown:* $\Delta t = ?$
           $\Delta d_x = 56.6 \text{ m}$ *Original equation:* $\Delta d_x = v_x \Delta t$

Solve: $\Delta t = \dfrac{\Delta d_x}{v_x} = \dfrac{56.6 \text{ m}}{18.4 \text{ m/s}} = $ **3.08 s**

Example 9: On May 20, 1999, 37-year old Robbie Knievel, son of famed daredevil Evel Knievel, successfully jumped 69.5 m over a Grand Canyon gorge. Assuming that he started and landed at the same level and was airborne for 3.66 s, what height from his starting point did this daredevil achieve?

Solution: Because 3.66 s is the time for the entire travel through the air, Robbie spent half of this time reaching the height of the jump. The motorcycle took 1.83 s to go up, and another 1.83 s to come down. To find the height the motorcycle achieved, look only at its downward motion as measured from the highest point.

Given: $\Delta t = 1.83 \text{ s}$ *Unknown:* $\Delta d_y = ?$
           $g = 10.0 \text{ m/s}^2$ *Original equation:* $\Delta d_y = \left(\dfrac{1}{2}\right) g \Delta t^2$

Solve: $\Delta d_y = \left(\dfrac{1}{2}\right) g \Delta t^2 = \left(\dfrac{1}{2}\right)(10.0 \text{ m/s}^2)(1.83 \text{ s})^2 = $ **16.7 m**

Practice Exercises

Exercise 10: Billy-Joe stands on the Talahatchee Bridge kicking stones into the water below. a) If Billy-Joe kicks a stone with a horizontal velocity of 3.50 m/s, and it lands in the water a horizontal distance of 5.40 m from where Billy-Joe is standing, what is the height of the bridge? b) If the stone had been kicked harder, how would this affect the time it would take to fall?

Answer: **a.** _____

Answer: **b.** _____

Exercise 11: The movie "The Gods Must Be Crazy" begins with a pilot dropping a bottle out of an airplane. It is recovered by a surprised native below, who thinks it is a message from the gods. If the plane from which the bottle was dropped was flying at an altitude of 500. m, and the bottle lands 400. m horizontally from the initial dropping point, how fast was the plane flying when the bottle was released?

Answer: ─────────────

Exercise 12: Tad drops a cherry pit out the car window 1.0 m above the ground while traveling down the road at 18 m/s. a) How far, horizontally, from the initial dropping point will the pit hit the ground? b) Draw a picture of the situation. c) If the car continues to travel at the same speed, where will the car be in relation to the pit when it lands?

Answer: **a.** ─────────────

Answer: **c.** ─────────────

Exercise 13: Ferdinand the frog is hopping from lily pad to lily pad in search of a good fly for lunch. If the lily pads are spaced 2.4 m apart, and Ferdinand jumps with a speed of 5.0 m/s, taking 0.60 s to go from lily pad to lily pad, at what angle must Ferdinand make each of his jumps?

Answer: ─────────────

Exercise 14: At her wedding, Jennifer lines up all the single females in a straight line away from her in preparation for the tossing of the bridal bouquet. She stands Kelly at 1.0 m, Kendra at 1.5 m, Mary at 2.0 m, Kristen at 2.5 m, and Lauren at 3.0 m. Jennifer turns around and tosses the bouquet behind her with a speed of 3.9 m/s at an angle of 50.0° to the horizontal, and it is caught at the same height 0.60 s later. a) Who catches the bridal bouquet? b) Who might have caught it if she had thrown it more slowly?

Answer: **a.** _____

Answer: **b.** _____

Exercise 15: At a meeting of physics teachers in Montana, the teachers were asked to calculate where a flour sack would land if dropped from a moving airplane. The plane would be moving horizontally at a constant speed of 60.0 m/s at an altitude of 300. m. a) If one of the physics teachers neglected air resistance while making his calculation, how far horizontally from the dropping point would he predict the landing? b) Draw a sketch that shows the path the flour sack would take as it falls to the ground (from the perspective of an observer on the ground and off to the side.)

Answer: **a.** _____

Exercise 16: Jack be nimble, Jack be quick, Jack jumped over the candlestick with a velocity of 5.0 m/s at an angle of 30.0° to the horizontal. Did Jack burn his feet on the 0.25-m-high candle?

Answer: _____

Additional Exercises

A-1: A flock of Canada geese is flying south for the winter. On the first day the geese fly due south a distance of 800. km. On the second day they fly back north 100. km and pause for a couple of days to graze on a sod farm. The last day the geese continue their journey due south, covering a distance of 750. km. a) Draw a vector diagram of the journey and find the total displacement of the geese during this time. b) How does this value differ from the total distance traveled?

A-2: A seal swims toward an inlet with a speed of 5.0 m/s as a current of 1.0 m/s flows in the opposite direction. How long will it take the seal to swim 100. m?

A-3: In Moncton, New Brunswick, each high tide in the Bay of Fundy produces a large surge of water known as a tidal bore. If a riverbed fills with this flowing water that travels north with a speed of 1.0 m/s, what is the resultant velocity of a puffin who tries to swim east across the tidal bore with a speed of 4.0 m/s?

A-4: Lynn is driving home from work and finds that there is road construction being done on her favorite route, so she must take a detour. Lynn travels 5 km north, 6 km east, 3 km south, 4 km west, and 2 km south. a) Draw a vector diagram of the situation. b) What is her displacement? Solve graphically. c) What total distance has Lynn covered?

A-5: Avery sees a UFO out her bedroom window and calls to report it to the police. She says, "The UFO moved 20.0 m east, 10.0 m north, and 30.0 m west before it disappeared." What was the displacement of the UFO while Avery was watching? Solve graphically.

A-6: Eli finds a map for a buried treasure. It tells him to begin at the old oak and walk 21 paces due west, 41 paces at an angle 45° south of west, 69 paces due north, 20 paces due east, and 50 paces at an angle of 53° south of east. How far from the oak tree is the buried treasure? Solve graphically.

A-7: Dwight pulls his sister in her wagon with a force of 65 N at an angle of 50.0° to the vertical. What are the horizontal and vertical components of the force exerted by Dwight?

A-8: Esther dives off the 3-m springboard and initially bounces up with a velocity of 8.0 m/s at an angle of 80.° to the horizontal. What are the horizontal and vertical components of her velocity?

A-9: In many locations, old abandoned stone quarries have become filled with water once excavating has been completed. While standing on a 10.0-m-high quarry wall, Clarence tosses a piece of granite into the water below. If Clarence throws the rock horizontally with a velocity of 3.0 m/s, how far out from the edge of the cliff will it hit the water?

A-10: While skiing, Ellen encounters an unexpected icy bump, which she leaves horizontally at 12.0 m/s. How far out, horizontally, from her starting point will Ellen land if she drops a distance of 7.00 m in the fall?

A-11: The Essex county sheriff is trying to determine the speed of a car that slid off a small bridge on a snowy New England night and landed in a snow pile 4.00 m below the level of the road. The tire tracks in the snow show that the car landed 12.0 m measured horizontally from the bridge. How fast was the car going when it left the road?

A-12: Superman is said to be able to "leap tall buildings in a single bound." How high a building could Superman jump over if he were to leave the ground with a speed of 60.0 m/s at an angle of 75.0° to the horizontal?

A-13: Len is running to school and leaping over puddles as he goes. From the edge of a 1.5-m-long puddle, Len jumps 0.20 m high off the ground with a horizontal velocity component of 3.0 m/s in an attempt to clear it. Determine whether or not Len sits in school all day with wet socks on.

Challenge Exercises for Further Study

B-1: Veronica can swim 3.0 m/s in still water. While trying to swim directly across a river from west to east, Veronica is pulled by a current flowing southward at 2.0 m/s. a) What is the magnitude of Veronica's resultant velocity? b) If Veronica wants to end up exactly across stream from where she began, at what angle to the shore must she swim upstream?

B-2: Solve Practice Exercise A-6 using vector components.

B-3: Mubarak jumps and shoots a field goal from the far end of the court into the basket at the other end, a distance of 27.6 m. The ball is given an initial velocity of 17.1 m/s at an angle of 40.0° to the horizontal from a height of 2.00 m above the ground. What is its velocity as it hits the basket 3.00 m off the ground?

B-4: Drew claims that he can throw a dart at a dartboard from a distance of 2.0 m and hit the 5.0-cm-wide bulls-eye if he throws the dart horizontally with a speed of 15 m/s. He starts the throw at the same height as the top of the bulls-eye. See if Drew is able to hit the bulls-eye by calculating how far his shot falls from the bulls-eye's lower edge.

B-5: Caitlin is playing tennis against a wall. She hits the tennis ball from a height of 0.5 m above the ground with a velocity of 20.0 m/s at an angle of 15.0° to the horizontal toward the wall that is 6.00 m away. a) How far off the ground is the ball when it hits the wall? b) Is the ball still traveling up or is it on its way down when it hits the wall?

B-6: From Chapter 1, Exercise B-6, determine how far from the base of Niagara Falls Annie Taylor landed in her wooden barrel.

3 Forces

3-1 Forces and Acceleration

Vocabulary **Force:** A push or a pull.

When an unbalanced force is exerted on an object, the object accelerates in the direction of the force. The acceleration is proportional to the force and inversely proportional to the mass of the object. This is Newton's second law and it can be represented with an equation that says

$$\text{force} = (\text{mass})(\text{acceleration}) \quad \text{or} \quad F = ma$$

The unbalanced force is called the **net force,** or resultant of all the forces acting on the system.

The SI unit for force is the **newton,** which equals one **kilogram meter per second squared** ($\text{N} = \text{kg} \cdot \text{m/s}^2$).

You can think of a newton as being about equivalent to the weight of a stick of butter.

Mass, or the amount of matter in an object, does not change regardless of where an object is located. It is a constant property of any object. However, do not confuse mass with **weight!** The weight of an object is simply the gravitational force acting on the object. Therefore, if an object is moved away from Earth to a location where g is no longer 10.0 m/s^2, the object will no longer have the same weight as it did on Earth. The equation for weight is just a specific case of $F = ma$.

$$\text{weight} = (\text{mass})(\text{acceleration due to gravity}) \quad \text{or} \quad w = mg$$

Because of its weight, an object pushes against a surface on which it lies. By Newton's third law, the surface pushes back on the object. This push, which is called the **normal force,** is always perpendicular to the surface on which the object rests.

Some of the exercises you will do in this chapter require the use of some basic trigonometry. If you would like a review of trigonometry, refer to Appendix A.

Solved Examples

Example 1: Felicia, the ballet dancer, has a mass of 45.0 kg. a) What is Felicia's weight on Earth? b) What is Felicia's mass on Jupiter, where the acceleration due to gravity is 25.0 m/s^2? c) What is Felicia's weight on Jupiter?

Solution: a. Felicia's weight on Earth depends upon the gravitational pull of the earth on Felicia's mass.

Given: $m = 45.0$ kg   *Unknown:* $w = ?$
         $g = 10.0$ m/s^2 *Original equation:* $w = mg$

Solve: $w = mg = (45.0 \text{ kg})(10.0 \text{ m/s}^2) = $ **450. N**

b. The mass of an object remains the same whether the object is on Earth, in space, or on another planet. Therefore, on Jupiter, Felicia's mass is still 45.0 kg.

c. The acceleration due to gravity on Jupiter is 25.0 m/s^2.

Given: $m = 45.0$ kg   *Unknown:* $w = ?$
         $g = 25.0$ m/s^2 *Original equation:* $w = mg$

Solve: $w = mg = (45.0 \text{ kg})(25.0 \text{ m/s}^2) = $ **1130 N**

Since a newton is equivalent to 0.22 pounds, little Felicia would weigh about 260 lb on Jupiter. It should be noted, however, that it would be impossible to stand on Jupiter due to its entirely gaseous surface.

Example 2: Butch, the 72.0-kg star quarterback of Belmont High School's football team, collides with Trask, a stationary left tackle, and is brought to a stop with an acceleration of −20.0 m/s^2. a) What force does Trask exert on Butch? b) What force does Butch exert on Trask?

Solution: a. The force depends upon the rate at which Butch's mass is brought to rest.

Given: $m = 72.0$ kg   *Unknown:* $F = ?$
         $g = -20.0$ m/s^2 *Original equation:* $F = ma$

Solve: $F = ma = (72.0 \text{ kg})(-20.0 \text{ m/s}^2) = $ **−1440 N**

The negative sign in the answer implies that the direction of the force is opposite that of Butch's original direction of motion.

b. Newton's third law states that for every action there is an equal and opposite reaction. Therefore, if Trask exerts a force of −1440 N on Butch, Butch will exert the same **1440 N** force back on Trask, but in the opposite direction.

Example 3: A 20-g sparrow flying toward a bird feeder mistakes the pane of glass in a window for an opening and slams into it with a force of 2.0 N. What is the bird's acceleration?

Solution: Since the sparrow exerts 2.0 N of force on the window, the window must provide −2.0 N back in the opposite direction. Don't forget to convert grams into kilograms before beginning.

$$20 \text{ g} = 0.02 \text{ kg}$$

For a review of unit conversions, see Appendix A.

Given: $m = 0.02$ kg   Unknown: $a = ?$
       $F = -2.0$ N   Original equation: $F = ma$

Solve: $a = \dfrac{F}{m} = \dfrac{-2.0 \text{ N}}{0.02 \text{ kg}} = \textbf{−100 m/s}^2$ (about 10 g's!)

Therefore, the bird experiences a very rapid negative acceleration, as the window brings the bird to a sudden stop. Ouch!

Example 4: A 30.0-g arrow is shot by William Tell through an 8.00-cm-thick apple sitting on top of his son's head. If the arrow enters the apple at 30.0 m/s and emerges at 25.0 m/s in the same direction, with what force has the apple resisted the arrow?

Solution: First, convert g to kg and cm to m.

$$30.0 \text{ g} = 0.0300 \text{ kg} \qquad 8.00 \text{ cm} = 0.0800 \text{ m}$$

Next, find the acceleration of the arrow before finding the force.

Given: $v_o = 30.0$ m/s   Unknown: $a = ?$
       $v_f = 25.0$ m/s   Original equation: $v_f^2 = v_o^2 + 2a\Delta d$
       $\Delta d = 0.0800$ m

Solve: $a = \dfrac{v_f^2 - v_o^2}{2\Delta d} = \dfrac{(25.0 \text{ m/s})^2 - (30.0 \text{ m/s})^2}{2(0.0800 \text{ m})} = \dfrac{625 \text{ m}^2/\text{s}^2 - 900. \text{ m}^2/\text{s}^2}{0.160 \text{ m}}$

$= -1720 \text{ m/s}^2$

The negative sign before the answer implies that the apple was causing the arrow to slow down. Now solve for the force exerted by the apple.

Given: $m = 0.0300$ kg   Unknown: $F = ?$
       $a = -1720$ m/s^2 Original equation: $F = ma$

Solve: $F = ma = (0.0300 \text{ kg})(-1720 \text{ m/s}^2) = \textbf{−51.6 N}$

This is the force that the apple exerts on the arrow. It is negative because its direction is opposite to the arrow's direction of motion.

Example 5: Rose is sledding down an ice-covered hill inclined at an angle of 15° with the horizontal. If Rose and the sled have a combined mass of 54.0 kg, what is the force pulling them down the hill?

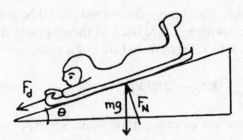

Solution: This exercise is a bit more complex than the preceding examples. Before beginning the solution, look at all the forces on the sled.

a. First, there is the **gravitational force,** which always acts downward. This is the weight of the sled. It is labeled *mg*.

b. The next force to be considered is the **normal force.** This force always acts perpendicular to the surface, so it pushes against the bottom of the sled. It is labeled F_N.

c. The resultant of these forces is a **component of the gravitational force** that goes in the direction of the motion of the sled, or down the slope. It is labeled F_d.

You can redraw these three forces as a right triangle. The angle of the slope corresponds to the angle between *mg* and F_N. Now with the use of trigonometry, you can solve for the force down the incline, F_d.

Given: $m = 54.0$ kg
$g = 10.0$ m/s^2
$\theta = 15°$

Unknown: $F_d = ?$
Original equation: $\sin \theta = \dfrac{\text{opp}}{\text{hyp}} = \dfrac{F_d}{mg}$

Solve: $F_d = mg \sin \theta = (54.0 \text{ kg})(10.0 \text{ m/s}^2) \sin 15° = 140$ N

Practice Exercises

Exercise 1: You can find your own mass in kg with the following information: 1.0 kg weighs about 2.2 lb on Earth. a) What is your mass in kg? b) What is your weight in newtons?

Answer: **a.** _____

Answer: **b.** _____

Exercise 2: Gunter the weightlifter can lift a 230.0-kg barbell overhead on Earth. The acceleration due to gravity on the sun is 274 m/s^2. a) Would the barbells be heavier on the sun or on Earth? b) How much (in newtons) would the barbells weigh on the sun (if it were possible to stand on the sun without melting)?

Answer: **a.** _____

Answer: **b.** _____

Exercise 3: Sammy Sosa swings at a 0.15 kg baseball and accelerates it at a rate of 3.0×10^4 m/s^2. How much force does Sosa exert on the ball?

Answer: _____

Exercise 4:   Claudia stubs her toe on the coffee table with a force of 100. N. a) What is the acceleration of Claudia's 1.80-kg foot? b) What is the acceleration of the table if it has a mass of 20.0 kg? (Ignore any frictional effects.) c) Why would Claudia's toe hurt less if the table had less mass?

Answer: **a.** _____

Answer: **b.** _____

Answer: **c.** _____

Exercise 5:   While chopping down his father's cherry tree, George discovered that if he swung the axe with a speed of 25 m/s, it would embed itself 2.3 cm into the tree before coming to a stop. a) If the axe head had a mass of 2.5 kg, how much force was the tree exerting on the axe head upon impact? b) How much force did the axe exert back on the tree?

Answer: **a.** _____

Answer: **b.** _____

Exercise 6:   Carter's favorite ride at Playland Amusement Park is the rollercoaster. The rollercoaster car and passengers have a combined mass of 1620 kg, and they descend the first hill at an angle of 45.0° to the horizontal. With what force is the rollercoaster pulled down the hill?

Answer: _____

3-2 Friction

Friction: The force that acts to oppose the motion between two materials moving past each other.

There are many types of friction between surfaces. They include

Static friction: The resistance force that must be overcome to start an object in motion.

Kinetic or sliding friction: The resistance force between two surfaces already in motion.

Rolling friction: The resistance force between a surface and a rolling object.

Fluid friction: The resistance force of a gas or a liquid as an object passes through. One example of fluid friction is air resistance.

In this chapter, we will deal only with kinetic or sliding friction.

The force of sliding friction between two surfaces depends on the normal force pressing the surfaces together, and on the types of surfaces that are in contact with each other. The magnitude of this force is written as

force of sliding friction = (coefficient of sliding friction)(normal force)

or $F_f = \mu F_N$

If an object is sitting on a horizontal surface, the normal force is equal to the weight of the object. The symbol μ (pronounced "mu") is called the **coefficient of sliding friction.** A high coefficient of friction (in other words, a large number for μ) means that the object is not likely to slide easily, while a low coefficient of friction (or a small μ) is found between very slippery surfaces. Because the coefficient of sliding friction is simply a ratio of the force of sliding friction to the normal force, it has no units.

Solved Examples

Example 6:   Brian is walking through the school cafeteria but does not realize that the person in front of him has just spilled his glass of chocolate milk. As Brian, who weighs 420 N, steps in the milk, the coefficient of sliding friction between Brian and the floor is suddenly reduced to 0.040. What is the force of sliding friction between Brian and the slippery floor?

Solution: In order to find the force of sliding friction, you need to know the normal force, or the force the ground exerts upward on Brian. On a horizontal surface this normal force is equivalent to the object's weight, which in this case is 420 N.

Given: F_N = 420 N   Unknown: F_f = ?
         μ = 0.040   Original equation: $F_f = \mu F_N$

Solve: $F_f = \mu F_N = (0.040)(420 \text{ N}) = \textbf{17 N}$

Example 7: While redecorating her apartment, Kitty slowly pushes an 82-kg china cabinet across the wooden dining room floor, which resists the motion with a force of friction of 320 N. What is the coefficient of sliding friction between the china cabinet and the floor?

Solution: As in the previous exercise, the normal force is equivalent to the weight of the china cabinet because the cabinet is sitting on a horizontal surface.

Given: m = 82 kg   Unknown: w = ?
         g = 10.0 m/s^2 Original equation: $w = mg$

Solve: $w = mg = (82 \text{ kg})(10.0 \text{ m/s}^2) = 820 \text{ N}$ so F_N is also 820 N.

Given: F_N = 820 N   Unknown: μ = ?
         F_f = 320 N   Original equation: $F_f = \mu F_N$

Solve: $\mu = \dfrac{F_f}{F_N} = \dfrac{320 \text{ N}}{820 \text{ N}} = \textbf{0.39}$ Remember, μ has no units!

Example 8: At Sea World, a 900.-kg polar bear slides down a wet slide inclined at an angle of 25.0° to the horizontal. The coefficient of friction between the bear and the slide is 0.0500. What frictional force impedes the bear's motion down the slide?

Solution: In this example, unlike the previous ones in this section, the polar bear is inclined at an angle to the horizontal so you must find the normal force on the polar bear by using the cosine of this angle. Remember, the normal force, F_N, always acts perpendicular to the surface on which the object is moving.

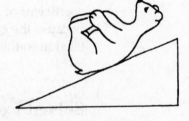

Given: m = 900. kg   Unknown: F_N = ?
         g = 10.0 m/s^2 Original equation: $\cos\theta = \dfrac{\text{adj}}{\text{hyp}} = \dfrac{F_N}{mg}$
         θ = 25.0°

Solve: $F_N = mg \cos\theta = (900. \text{ kg})(10.0 \text{ m/s}^2) \cos 25.0° = 8160 \text{ N}$

Given: F_N = 8160 N   Unknown: F_f = ?
         μ = 0.0500   Original equation: $F_f = \mu F_N$

Solve: $F_f = \mu F_N = (0.0500)(8160 \text{ N}) = \textbf{408 N}$

Practice Exercises

Exercise 7: Unbeknownst to the students, every time the school floors are waxed, Mr. Tracy, the principal, likes to slide down the hallway in his socks. Mr. Tracy weighs 850. N and the coefficient of sliding friction between his socks and the floor is 0.120. What is the force of friction that opposes Mr. Tracy's motion down the hall?

Answer: _____

Exercise 8: Skye is trying to make her 70.0-kg Saint Bernard go out the back door but the dog refuses to walk. If the coefficient of sliding friction between the dog and the floor is 0.50, how hard must Skye push in order to move the dog with a constant speed?

Answer: _____

Exercise 9: Rather than taking the stairs, Martin gets from the second floor of his house to the first floor by sliding down the banister that is inclined at an angle of 30.0° to the horizontal. a) If Martin has a mass of 45 kg and the coefficient of sliding friction between Martin and the banister is 0.20, what is the force of friction impeding Martin's motion down the banister? b) If the banister is made steeper (inclined at a larger angle), will this have any effect on the force of friction? If so, what?

Answer: **a.** _____

Answer: **b.** _____

Exercise 10: As Alan is taking a shower, the soap falls out of the soap dish and Alan steps on it with a force of 500 N. If Alan slides forward and the frictional force between the soap and the tub is 50 N, what is the coefficient of friction between these two surfaces?

Answer: _____

Exercise 11: Howard, the soda jerk at Bea's diner, slides a 0.60-kg root beer from the end of the counter to a thirsty customer. A force of friction of 1.2 N brings the drink to a stop right in front of the customer. a) What is the coefficient of sliding friction between the glass and the counter? b) If the glass encounters a sticky patch on the counter, will this spot have a higher or lower coefficient of friction?

Answer: **a.** _____

Answer: **b.** _____

3-3 Statics

Vocabulary   **Statics:** The study of forces in equilibrium.

When forces are in **equilibrium,** all the forces acting on a body are balanced, and the body is not accelerating. In order to solve statics exercises, you must study all the forces acting on an object in the horizontal or x-direction separately from all the forces acting in the vertical or y-direction. This means that you must take the horizontal and vertical components of these forces. Because the object is not accelerating, the sum of all the horizontal components must equal zero and the sum of all the vertical components must equal zero. Rules for finding horizontal and vertical components are found in Appendix A.

A few hints: In statics exercises, you may frequently see the term **tension.** Tension is the force that is exerted by a rope or a wire, or any object that pulls on another. It has the same units as any other force.

You will notice that there are several exercises here that involve objects hanging from wires. Whenever this situation occurs, the sum of the vertical components of the tension in each wire is equal to the object's weight. If the object hangs in the middle of two equal-length wires, the weight is shared equally by each wire.

Solved Examples

Example 9: Flip, an exhausted gymnast, hangs from a bar by both arms in an effort to catch his breath. If Flip has a mass of 65.0 kg, what is the tension in each of Flip's arms as he hangs in place?

Solution: First find Flip's weight.

Given: m = 65.0 kg   *Unknown: w* = ?
        g = 10.0 m/s^2 *Original equation: w = mg*

Solve: w = mg = (65.0 kg)(10.0 m/s^2) = 650. N

Since Flip is pulling down on the bar with a force of 650. N, his arms must be holding him up by sharing an upward force of 650. N. If each of Flip's arms shares the force equally, then each must provide a tension of **325 N**.

Example 10: At an art auction, Whitney has acquired a painting that now hangs from a nail on her wall, as shown in the figure. If the painting has a mass of 12.6 kg, what is the tension in each side of the wire supporting the painting?

Solution: The weight of the painting is shared equally by two wires, so each wire must support only half of the weight. However, in this example the wires do not hang vertically, but instead act at an angle with the painting. Therefore, you must use trigonometry to find the actual tension in the wire.

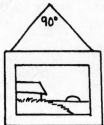

Given: m = 12.6 kg   *Unknown: w* = ?
        g = 10.0 m/s^2 *Original equation: w = mg*

Solve: w = mg = (12.6 kg)(10.0 m/s^2) = 126 N

Therefore, each of the wires equally shares 63 N. Call this value F_y, and use trigonometry to find the angle.

$$\cos \theta = \frac{\text{adj}}{\text{hyp}} = \frac{F_y}{F} \qquad F = \frac{F_y}{\cos \theta} = \frac{63 \text{ N}}{\cos 45°} = \frac{63 \text{ N}}{0.71} = \textbf{89 N}$$

Therefore, each wire holds the painting with a tension or force of 89 N.

Example 11: Michelle likes to swing on a tire tied to a tree branch in her yard, as in the figure. a) If Michelle and the tire have a combined mass of 82.5 kg, and Elwin pulls Michelle back far enough for her to make an angle of 30.0° with the vertical, what is the tension in the rope supporting Michelle and the tire?

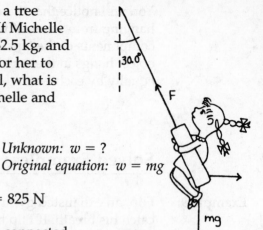

Given: $m = 82.5$ kg   *Unknown:* $w = ?$
          $g = 10.0$ m/s^2 *Original equation:* $w = mg$

Solve: $w = mg = (82.5 \text{ kg})(10.0 \text{ m/s}^2) = 825$ N

First, redraw the forces so that they are connected head to tail in a triangle. This allows you to use rules of trigonometry to solve for the tension, *F*.

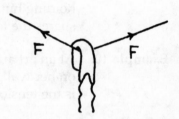

$$\cos \theta = \frac{\text{adj}}{\text{hyp}} = \frac{mg}{F}$$

$$F = \frac{mg}{\cos \theta} = \frac{825 \text{ N}}{\cos 30.0°} = \frac{825 \text{ N}}{0.866} = \textbf{953 N}$$

Example 12: After returning home from the beach, Samantha hangs her wet 0.20-kg bathing suit in the center of the 6.0-m-long clothesline to dry. This causes the clothesline to sag 4.0 cm. What is the tension in the clothesline?

Solution: First, convert cm to m.

$$4.0 \text{ cm} = 0.040 \text{ m}$$

Because the bathing suit is hung in the center of the clothesline, the tension in each side of the line is the same. You must find the downward force on the clothesline, which is simply the weight of the bathing suit.

Given: $m = 0.20$ kg   *Unknown:* $w = ?$
          $g = 10.0$ m/s^2 *Original equation:* $w = mg$

Solve: $w = mg = (0.20 \text{ kg})(10.0 \text{ m/s}^2) = 2.0$ N

Half of this force, 1.0 N, will pull on the left side of the clothesline and half will pull on the right, *only* because the bathing suit hangs in the middle of the line.

Before you can calculate the tension, F, in the rope, you need to determine the angle the clothesline makes with the horizontal. To do this, use the known distances of 3.0 m and 0.040 m as shown in the diagram. This diagram is not drawn to scale.

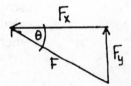

(Not drawn to scale)

$$\tan \theta = \frac{\text{opp}}{\text{adj}} = \frac{d_y}{d_x} = \frac{0.040 \text{ m}}{3.0 \text{ m}} = 0.013$$

Taking the inverse of the tangent gives the angle,

$$\tan^{-1} 0.013 = \theta \qquad \text{so} \qquad \theta = 0.74°$$

The angle is 0.74° and the bathing suit causes the clothesline to pull up with a force of 1.0 N. Now find the tension in the line. Again, this is done using trigonometry, because the angle and the vertical component of the force are known.

$$\sin \theta = \frac{\text{opp}}{\text{hyp}} = \frac{F_y}{F}$$

$$F = \frac{F_y}{\sin \theta} = \frac{1.0 \text{ N}}{\sin 0.74°} = \frac{1.0 \text{ N}}{0.013} = \textbf{77 N}$$

The tension in each side of the clothesline is 77 N.

Practice Exercises

Exercise 12: While moving out of her dorm room, Bridget carries a 12-kg box to her car, holding it in both arms. a) How much force must be exerted by each of her arms to support the box? b) How will this force change if Bridget holds the box with only one arm?

Answer: **a.** ——————————————

Answer: **b.** ——————————————

Exercise 13: A flower pot of mass 4.20 kg is hung above a window by three ropes, each making an angle of 15.0° with the vertical, as shown. What is the tension in each rope supporting the flower pot?

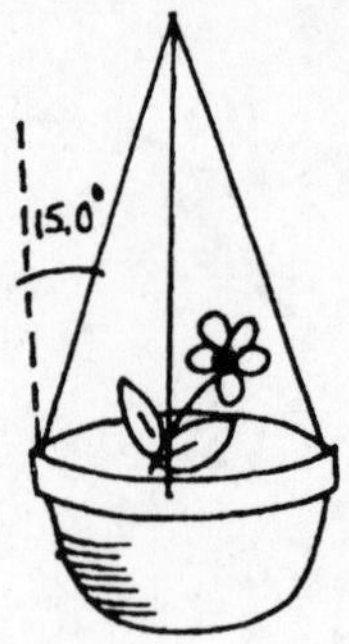

15.0°

Answer: _____

Exercise 14: Luke Skywalker must swing Princess Leia across a large chasm in order to escape the Storm Troopers. If Luke and Leia's combined mass is 145 kg, calculate the tension in the rope just before Luke and Leia start their swing, when the pair makes an angle of 30.0° with the vertical.

Answer: _____

Exercise 15: The ACE towing company tows a disabled 1050-kg automobile off the road at a constant speed. If the tow line makes an angle of 10.0° with the vertical as shown, what is the tension in the line supporting the car?

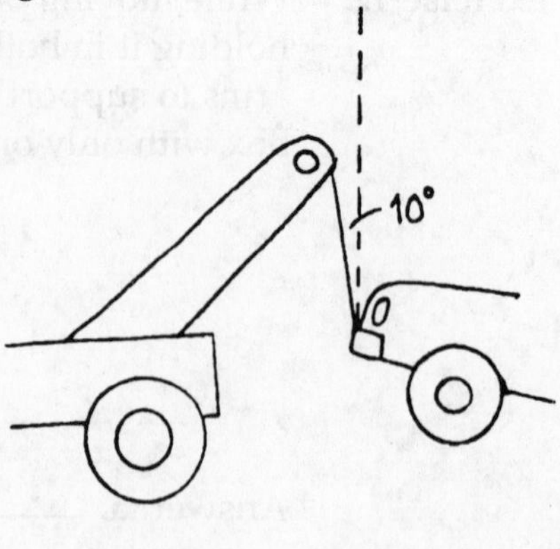

10°

Answer: _____

Exercise 16: Yvette hangs a 2.4-kg bird feeder in the middle of a rope tied between two trees. The feeder creates a tension of 480 N in each side of the the rope.
a) If the two trees are 4.0 m apart, how much will the rope sag in the center?
b) If a bird lands on the feeder, will this have any effect on the tension in the rope? Explain.

Answer: **a.** ──────────────

Answer: **b.** ──────────────

Exercise 17: After pulling his car off to the side of the road during a rainstrom, Travis is dismayed to find that the car has become stuck in the mud. Travis ties one end of a rope to the front of the car and the other end to a tree 12.00 m away as shown. a) If Travis can exert a force of 610 N on the rope, moving it 1.00 m in the direction shown, how much force will the rope exert on the car? b) Why is this method better than simply tying a rope to the front of the car and pulling the car straight out?

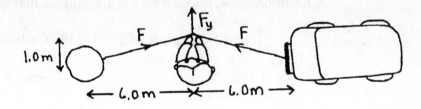

Answer: **a.** ──────────────

Answer: **b.** ──────────────

3-4 Pressure

Vocabulary   **Pressure:** The force per unit area.

$$\text{pressure} = \frac{\text{force}}{\text{area}} \quad \text{or} \quad P = \frac{F}{A}$$

The SI unit for pressure is the **pascal,** which equals one **newton per square meter** ($P = N/m^2$).

It is very easy to confuse pressure with force. While force is a push or a pull, pressure is a push or pull on a certain area. For a given force, the pressure due to that force is inversely proportional to the area on which the force is exerted. Therefore, if the area of contact is small, the amount of pressure between two surfaces is much greater than if the force were exerted over a larger area.

For example, place a pencil between the palms of your hands with the pointed end pushing against one palm and the eraser end against the other. As you squeeze your hands together, you will feel a much more unpleasant sensation at the pencil tip than at the eraser! The eraser has a larger area, so the force is spread out more evenly over the nerve endings of your hand.

Solved Examples

Example 13: Brooke comes home from school and puts her books down on the kitchen table while she goes to grab a snack. The books have a combined weight of 25 N and the area of contact is 0.19 m by 0.24 m. What pressure do the books apply on the table?

Solution: First, find the area of the surface that is pressing down on the table.

$$\text{area} = \text{length} \times \text{width} = 0.19 \text{ m} \times 0.24 \text{ m} = 0.046 \text{ m}^2$$

Given: $F = 25$ N   *Unknown:* $P = ?$
             $A = 0.046 \text{ m}^2$ *Original equation:* $P = \dfrac{F}{A}$

Solve: $P = \dfrac{F}{A} = \dfrac{25 \text{ N}}{0.046 \text{ m}^2} = 540 \ \dfrac{\text{N}}{\text{m}^2}$

Example 14: A full coffee mug has a mass of 0.60 kg and an empty mug has a mass of 0.30 kg. a) Which mug, the full one or the empty one, applies a greater pressure on the table? b) If the full mug applies a pressure of 1200. N/m^2, what is the area inside a circular ring of coffee left on the table by the bottom of the mug? c) What is the radius of the ring of coffee?

a. The full mug applies more pressure because a larger force is spread over the given area.

b. The force exerted by the full mug is its weight.

$$w = mg = (0.60 \text{ kg})(10.0 \text{ m/s}^2) = 6.0 \text{ N}$$

Given: $F = 6.0$ N   *Unknown:* $A = ?$
       $P = 1200. \text{ N/m}^2$ *Original equation:* $P = \dfrac{F}{A}$

Solve: $A = \dfrac{F}{P} = \dfrac{6.0 \text{ N}}{1200. \text{ N/m}^2} = \textbf{0.0050 m}^2$

c. To find the radius, use the equation for the area of a circle.

Given: $A = 0.0050 \text{ m}^2$ *Unknown:* $r = ?$
       $\pi = 3.14$ *Original equation:* $A = \pi r^2$

Solve: $r = \sqrt{\dfrac{A}{\pi}} = \sqrt{\dfrac{0.0050 \text{ m}^2}{3.14}} = \textbf{0.040 m}$

Practice Exercises

Exercise 18:   a) Which exerts a greater force on a table, a 1.70-kg physics book lying flat on the table, or a 1.70-kg physics book standing on end on the table? b) Which applies a greater pressure? c) If each book measures 0.260 m × 0.210 m × 0.040 m, calculate the pressure applied in each of these two drawings.

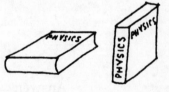

Answer: **a.** ─────────────────

Answer: **b.** ─────────────────

Answer: **c.** ─────────────────

Exercise 19: Miss Culp, a high school English teacher, marches next to Miss Vance, a physics teacher, in the graduation procession across the football field. Each woman has a mass of 60.0 kg, but Miss Culp is wearing spike heels that have an area of 0.40 cm^2 while Miss Vance wears wide heels with an area of 6.0 cm^2. a) Calculate how much pressure each woman will apply on the ground. b) What could Miss Culp do, while she walks, to help her sink less into the ground?

Answer: **a.** _____

Answer: **b.** _____

Exercise 20: Morgan has a mass of 85 kg and is on top of a bed in such a position that she can apply a pressure of 9530 N/m^2 on the mattress. Would you calculate that Morgan is standing, sitting, or lying on the bed?

Answer: _____

Exercise 21: Caleb is filling up water balloons for the Physics Olympics balloon toss competition. Caleb sets a 0.50-kg spherical water balloon on the kitchen table and notices that the bottom of the balloon flattens until the pressure on the bottom is reduced to 630 N/m^2. a) What is the area of the flat spot on the bottom of the balloon? b) What is the radius of the flat spot?

Answer: **a.** _____

Answer: **b.** _____

Additional Exercises

A-1: What is the minimal force a mother must exert to lift her 5.0-kg baby out of its crib?

A-2: On the moon, the gravity is 1/6 that of Earth. While on the moon, Buzz Aldrin carried on his back a support system that would weigh over 1760 N on Earth. a) What did the backpack weigh on the moon? b) What was its mass on the moon?

A-3: A common malady in runners who run on too hard a surface is shin splints. If a runner's 7.0-kg leg hits the pavement so that it comes to rest with an acceleration of -200.0 m/s^2 on each hit, how much force must the runner's leg withstand on each step?

A-4: In the district soccer championship finals, Elizabeth kicks a 0.600-kg soccer ball with a force of 80.0 N. How much does she accelerate the soccer ball from rest in the process?

A-5: Barker is unloading 20-kg bottles of water from this delivery truck when one of the bottles tips over and slides down the truck ramp that is inclined at an angle of 30° to the ground. What amount of force moves the bottle down the ramp?

A-6: Sarah, whose mass is 40.0 kg, is on her way to school after a winter storm when she accidentally slips on a patch of ice whose coefficient of sliding friction is 0.060. What force of friction will eventually bring Sarah to a stop?

A-7: In her physics lab, Molly puts a 1.0-kg mass on a 2.0-kg block of wood. She pulls the combination across another wooden board with a constant speed to determine the coefficient of sliding friction between the two surfaces. If Molly must pull with a force of 6.0 N, what coefficient of sliding friction does she calculate for wood on wood?

A-8: A 1250-kg slippery hippo slides down a mud-covered hill inclined at an angle of 18.0° to the horizontal. a) If the coefficient of sliding friction between the hippo and the mud is 0.0900, what force of friction impedes the hippo's motion down the hill? b) If the hill were steeper, how would this affect the coefficient of sliding friction?

A-9: Erma receives a 5.00-kg package in the mail tied with a string that goes around each side of the box, as shown. If Erma lifts the box by the string in the center so that each piece of string makes an angle of 45.0° with the vertical, what is the tension in each piece of string?

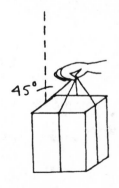

A-10: To make extra money during the summer, Mr. Garber, a 66.0-kg physics teacher, paints the outside of houses while sitting on a 4.0-kg plank suspended by two vertical cables. What is the tension in each of the two cables?

A-11: While camping in Denali National Park in Alaska, a wise camper hangs his pack of food from a rope tied between two trees, to keep the food away from the bears. If the 5.0-kg bag of food hangs from the center of a rope that is 3.0 m long, and the rope sags 6.0 cm in the middle, what is the tension in the rope?

A-12: In the figure, a 1240-kg wrecking ball is pulled back with a horizontal force of 5480 N before being swung against the side of a building. a) What angle does the wrecking ball make with the vertical when it is pulled back? b) What is the tension in the ball's supporting cable when it is at this angle?

A-13: What force must you exert on a ball point pen in order to apply a pressure of 0.067 N/mm^2 on a piece of paper, if the ball of the pen has a surface area of 1.2 mm^2 touching the paper?

A-14: Asad cuts his knee in a fall while chasing a soccer ball. If a 6-N force is exerted on Asad's knee during the fall, applying a pressure of 1000 N/m^2 on an area of his skin, what is the area of the cut that results from the impact?

A-15: The amazing Gambini walks across a 30.0-m-long tightrope high above a 3-ring circus. a) If the 75.0-kg Gambini pushes the tightrope down 15.0 cm in the center, find the tension in the tightrope. b) If a 10-cm^2 area of Gambini's foot presses on the rope, how much pressure does Gambini apply on this area?

A-16: In the TV show, *The Addams Family*, Uncle Fester found it quite comfortable to sleep on a bed of nails. Though this doesn't sound like the most pleasant way to take a nap, it is not too painful if many nails are placed fairly close together. a) If Uncle Fester has a mass of 53 kg and his body covers 700 nails, each with a surface area of 1.00 mm^2, what is the pressure exerted on his body? b) What would be the pressure if Uncle Fester napped on a bed made of only 1 nail?

Challenge Exercises for Further Study

Example 15: Linc, the 65.0-kg lifeguard, slides down a water slide that is inclined at an angle of 35.0° to the horizontal, into the community swimming pool. If the coefficient of friction of the slide is 0.050, what is Linc's rate of acceleration as he slides down?

Solution: Start by constructing a triangle showing all the forces acting on the lifeguard. Then find the normal force acting on Linc when he is inclined at an angle to the horizontal. Because the normal force always acts perpendicular to the surface on which the object sits, find this force with the use of trigonometry.

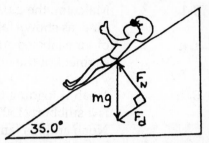

$$\cos\theta = \frac{\text{adj}}{\text{hyp}} = \frac{F_N}{mg}$$

$$F_N = mg\cos\theta = (65.0\text{ kg})(10.0\text{ m/s}^2)\cos 35.0° = 532\text{ N}$$

Now use this normal force to find the force of friction.

Given: $F_N = 532$ N   *Unknown:* $F_f = ?$
      $\mu = 0.050$ *Original equation:* $F_f = \mu F_N$

Solve: $F_f = \mu F_N = (0.050)(532\text{ N}) = 27$ N

Next, return to the original triangle to find the downward component of the weight, which pulls Linc down the slide.

$$\sin\theta = \frac{\text{opp}}{\text{hyp}} = \frac{F_d}{mg}$$

$$F_d = mg\sin\theta = (65.0\text{ kg})(10.0\text{ m/s}^2)\sin 35.0° = 373\text{ N}$$

The exercise asks for Linc's acceleration at the bottom of the slide. Because friction opposes Linc's motion, subtract its effect from F_d. The net force acting on Linc is

$$F_{net} = F_d - F_f = 373\text{ N} - 27\text{ N} = 346\text{ N}$$

Now solve for the rate of acceleration.

Given: $F = 346$ N   *Unknown:* $a = ?$
      $m = 65.0$ kg   *Original equation:* $F = ma$

Solve: $a = \dfrac{F}{m} = \dfrac{346\text{ N}}{65.0\text{ kg}} = \textbf{5.32 m/s}^2$

B-1: Malcolm, the 20.0-kg monkey, hangs from a jungle vine, as shown. a) What is the tension in the segment of vine labeled AB? b) What is the tension in the segment of the vine labeled BC?

B-2: Noah is loading the ark and the last animal on board is a stubborn 1500-kg elephant who refuses to budge. Noah and his family pull the elephant at a constant speed up the 10° incline with a force of 10 000 N. What is the coefficient of sliding friction between the elephant and the loading platform?

B-3: Blythe lies in a hospital bed with her foot in traction, as shown. How much tension will the traction device exert on her foot?

B-4: Madison, whose mass is 35.0 kg, climbs the ladder on the slide in her back yard, and slides to the ground at an angle of 30.0° to the horizontal. If the coefficient of sliding friction is 0.15, what is Madison's acceleration down the slide? Ignore the initial effects of starting friction.

B-5: A chunk of rock of mass 50.0 kg slides down the side of a volcano that slopes up at an angle of 30.0° to the horizontal. If the rock accelerates at a rate of 3.0 m/s², what is the coefficient of sliding friction between the rock and the side of the volcano?

B-6: While waterskiing behind her father's boat, Cheryl is pulled at a constant speed with a force of 164 N by a rope that makes an angle of 10.0° with the horizontal. If Cheryl has a mass of 65.0 kg, what is the coefficient of sliding friction between Cheryl and the water?

B-7: Gooluk, the Inuit, is pulling a 62.0-kg sled through the snow on his way home from ice fishing. On the back of the sled is his 50.0-kg sack of fishing tackle. The coefficient of sliding friction between the sled and the snow is 0.0700 and the coefficient of sliding friction between the sled and the sack is 0.100. While pulling, the fishing rod sticking out of his sack catches on a tree branch, but Gooluk doesn't notice and keeps walking. What force does Gooluk need to exert to keep the sled moving with a constant speed while the sack is pulled back across it?

4 Momentum

4-1 Impulse and Momentum

Vocabulary **Momentum:** A measure of how difficult it is to stop a moving object.

$$\text{momentum} = \text{(mass)(velocity)} \quad \text{or} \quad p = mv$$

If the momentum of an object is changing, as it is when a force is exerted to start it or stop it, the change in momentum can be found by looking at the change in mass and velocity during the interval.

$$\text{change in momentum} = \text{change in [(mass)(velocity)]} \quad \text{or} \quad \Delta p = \Delta(mv)$$

For all the exercises in this book, assume that the mass of the object remains constant, and consider only the change in velocity, Δv, which is equal to $v_f - v_0$. Momentum is a vector quantity. Its direction is in the direction of the object's velocity.

The SI unit for momentum is the **kilogram·meter/second (kg·m/s)**.

Vocabulary **Impulse:** The product of the force exerted on an object and the time interval during which it acts.

$$\text{impulse} = \text{(force)(elapsed time)} \quad \text{or} \quad J = F\Delta t$$

The SI unit for impulse is the **newton·second (N·s)**.

The impulse given to an object is equal to the change in momentum of the object.

$$F\Delta t = m\Delta v$$

The same change in momentum may be the result of a large force exerted for a short time, or a small force exerted for a long time. In other words, impulse is the thing that you *do*, while change in momentum is the thing that you *see*.

The units for impulse and momentum are equivalent. Remember, $1\,\text{N} = 1\,\text{kg·m/s}^2$. Therefore, $1\,\text{N·s} = 1\,\text{kg·m/s}$.

Solved Examples

Example 1: Tiger Woods hits a 0.050-kg golf ball, giving it a speed of 75 m/s. What impulse does he impart to the ball?

Solution: Because the impulse equals the change in momentum, you can reword this exercise to read, "What was the ball's change in momentum?" It is understood that the ball was initially at rest, so its initial speed was 0 m/s.

Given: $m = 0.050$ kg   Unknown: $\Delta p = ?$
$\quad\quad\quad\Delta v = 75$ m/s   Original equation: $\Delta p = m\Delta v$

Solve: $\Delta p = (0.050$ kg$)(75$ m/s$) = $ **3.8 kg·m/s**

Example 2: Wayne hits a stationary 0.12-kg hockey puck with a force that lasts for 1.0×10^{-2} s and makes the puck shoot across the ice with a speed of 20.0 m/s, scoring a goal for the team. With what force did Wayne hit the puck?

Given: $m = 0.12$ kg   Unknown: $F = ?$
$\quad\quad\quad\Delta v = 20.0$ m/s   Original equation: $F\Delta t = m\Delta v$
$\quad\quad\quad\Delta t = 1.0 \times 10^{-2}$ s

Solve: $F = \dfrac{m\Delta v}{\Delta t} = \dfrac{(0.12 \text{ kg})(20.0 \text{ m/s})}{1.0 \times 10^{-2} \text{ s}} = 240 \text{ kg·m/s}^2 = $ **240 N**

Example 3: A tennis ball traveling at 10.0 m/s is returned by Venus Williams. It leaves her racket with a speed of 36.0 m/s in the opposite direction from which it came. a) What is the change in momentum of the tennis ball? b) If the 0.060-kg ball is in contact with the racket for 0.020 s, with what average force has Venus hit the ball?

Solution: In this exercise, the tennis ball is coming toward Venus with a speed of 10.0 m/s in one direction, but she hits it back with a speed of 36.0 m/s in the opposite direction. Therefore, you must think about velocity vectors and call one direction positive and the opposite direction negative.

a. Given: $v_o = -10.0$ m/s   Unknown: $\Delta p = ?$
$\quad\quad\quad\quad v_f = 36.0$ m/s   Original equation: $\Delta p = m\Delta v = m(v_f - v_o)$
$\quad\quad\quad\quad m = 0.060$ kg

Solve: $\Delta p = m(v_f - v_o) = (0.060$ kg$)[36.0$ m/s $- (-10.0$ m/s$)] = $ **2.8 kg·m/s**

b. Given: $m = 0.060$ kg   Unknown: $F = ?$
$\quad\quad\quad\quad\Delta v = 46.0$ m/s   Original equation: $F\Delta t = m\Delta v$
$\quad\quad\quad\quad\Delta t = 0.020$ s

Solve: $F = \dfrac{m\Delta v}{\Delta t} = \dfrac{(0.060 \text{ kg})(46.0 \text{ m/s})}{(0.020 \text{ s})} = $ **140 N**

Example 4: To demonstrate his new high-speed camera, Flash performs an experiment in the physics lab in which he shoots a pellet gun at a pumpkin to record the moment of impact on film. The 1.0-g pellet travels at 100. m/s until it embeds itself 2.0 cm into the pumpkin. What average force does the pumpkin exert to stop the pellet?

Solution: First, convert g to kg and cm to m.

$$1.0 \text{ g} = 0.0010 \text{ kg} \qquad 2.0 \text{ cm} = 0.020 \text{ m}$$

Before you can solve for the force in the exercise, you must first know how long the force is being exerted. Remember, in order to find the time, you must use the average velocity, v_{av}.

$$v_{av} = \frac{v_f + v_o}{2} = \frac{0 \text{ m/s} + 100. \text{ m/s}}{2} = 50.0 \text{ m/s}$$

Given: $v = 50.0$ m/s   *Unknown:* $\Delta t = $?
　　　　$\Delta d = 0.020$ m   *Original equation:* $\Delta d = v\Delta t$

Solve: $\Delta t = \dfrac{\Delta d}{v} = \dfrac{0.020 \text{ m}}{50.0 \text{ m/s}} = 0.00040$ s

Now we can solve for the force the pumpkin exerts to stop the pellet.

Given: $m = 0.0010$ kg   *Unknown:* $F = $?
　　　　$\Delta v = 100.$ m/s   *Original equation:* $F\Delta t = m\Delta v$
　　　　$\Delta t = 0.0040$ s

Solve: $F = \dfrac{m\Delta v}{\Delta t} = \dfrac{(0.0010 \text{ kg})(100. \text{ m/s})}{(0.00040 \text{ s})} = $ **250 N**

Practice Exercises

Exercise 1: On April 15, 1912, the luxury cruiseliner *Titanic* sank after running into an iceberg. a) What momentum would the 4.23×10^8-kg ship have imparted to the iceberg if it had hit the iceberg head-on with a speed of 11.6 m/s? (Actually, the impact was a glancing blow.) b) If the captain of the ship had seen the iceberg a kilometer ahead and had tried to slow down, why would this have been a futile effort?

Answer: **a.** ——————————

Answer: **b.** ——————————

Exercise 2: Auto companies frequently test the safety of automobiles by putting them through crash tests to observe the integrity of the passenger compartment. If a 1000.-kg car is sent toward a cement wall with a speed of 14 m/s and the impact brings it to a stop in 8.00×10^{-2} s, with what average force is it brought to rest?

Answer: _____

Exercise 3: Rhonda, who has a mass of 60.0 kg, is riding at 25.0 m/s in her sports car when she must suddenly slam on the brakes to avoid hitting a dog crossing the road. She is wearing her seatbelt, which brings her body to a stop in 0.400 s. a) What average force did the seatbelt exert on her? b) If she had not been wearing her seatbelt, and the windshield had stopped her head in 1.0×10^{-3} s, what average force would the windshield have exerted on her? c) How many times greater is the stopping force of the windshield than the seatbelt?

Answer: **a.** _____

Answer: **b.** _____

Answer: **c.** _____

Exercise 4: If 270 million people in the United States jumped up in the air simultaneously, pushing off Earth with an average force of 800. N each for a time of 0.10 s, what would happen to the 5.98×10^{24} kg Earth? Show a calculation that justifies your answer.

Answer: _____

Exercise 5: In Sharkey's Billiard Academy, Maurice is waiting to make his last shot. He notices that the cue ball is lined up for a perfect head-on collision, as shown. Each of the balls has a mass of 0.0800 kg and the cue ball comes to a complete stop upon making contact with the 8 ball. Suppose Maurice hits the cue ball by exerting a force of 180. N for 5.00×10^{-3} s, and it knocks head-on into the 8 ball. Calculate the resulting velocity of the 8 ball.

Answer: _____

Exercise 6: During an autumn storm, a 0.012-kg hail stone traveling at 20.0 m/s made a 0.20-cm-deep dent in the hood of Darnell's new car. What average force did the car exert to stop the damaging hail stone?

Answer: _____

4-2 Conservation of Momentum

According to the **law of conservation of momentum,** the total momentum in a system remains the same if no external forces act on the system. Consider the two types of collisions that can occur.

Vocabulary **Elastic collision:** A collision in which objects collide and bounce apart with no energy loss.

In an elastic collision, because momentum is conserved, the *mv* before a collision for each of the two objects must equal the *mv* after the collision for each of the two objects. This is written as

$$m_1 v_{1o} + m_2 v_{2o} = m_1 v_{1f} + m_2 v_{2f}$$

The subscripts 1 and 2 refer to objects 1 and 2, respectively.

Vocabulary   **Inelastic collision:** A collision in which objects collide and some mechanical energy is transformed into heat energy.

A common kind of inelastic collision is one in which the colliding objects stick together, or start out stuck together and then separate. However, in an inelastic collision the objects need not remain stuck together but may instead deform in some way.

Because momentum is also conserved in an inelastic collision, the *mv* before the collision for each of the two objects must equal the *mv* after the collision for each of the two objects. When objects are stuck together after the collision (assuming mass does not change), this equation becomes

$$m_1v_{1o} + m_2v_{2o} = (m_1 + m_2)v_f$$

where v_f is the combined final velocity of the two objects.

Solved Examples

Example 5:   Tubby and his twin brother Chubby have a combined mass of 200.0 kg and are zooming along in a 100.0-kg amusement park bumper car at 10.0 m/s. They bump Melinda's car, which is sitting still. Melinda has a mass of 25.0 kg. After the elastic collision, the twins continue ahead with a speed of 4.12 m/s. How fast is Melinda's car bumped across the floor?

Solution: Notice that you must add the mass of the bumper car to the mass of the riders.

Given: $m_1 = 300.0$ kg   Unknown: $v_{2f} = ?$
         $m_2 = 125.0$ kg   *Original equation:*
         $v_{1o} = 10.0$ m/s $m_1v_{1o} + m_2v_{2o} = m_1v_{1f} + m_2v_{2f}$
         $v_{2o} = 0$ m/s
         $v_{1f} = 4.12$ m/s

Solve: $v_{2f} = \dfrac{m_1v_{1o} + m_2v_{2o} - m_1v_{1f}}{m_2}$

$$= \frac{(300.0 \text{ kg})(10.0 \text{ m/s}) + (125.0 \text{ kg})(0 \text{ m/s}) - (300.0 \text{ kg})(4.12 \text{ m/s})}{125.0 \text{ kg}}$$

$$= \frac{3000 \text{ kg·m/s} + 0 \text{ kg·m/s} - 1236 \text{ kg·m/s}}{125.0 \text{ kg}} = \frac{1764 \text{ kg·m/s}}{125.0 \text{ kg}}$$

$$= \textbf{14.1 m/s}$$

Example 6: Sometimes the curiosity factor at the scene of a car accident is so great that it actually produces secondary accidents as a result, while people watch to see what is going on. If an 800.-kg sports car slows to 13.0 m/s to check out an accident scene and the 1200.-kg pick-up truck behind him continues traveling at 25.0 m/s, with what velocity will the two move if they lock bumpers after a rear-end collision?

Solution: Since the two vehicles lock bumpers, both objects have the same final velocity.

Given: $m_1 = 800.$ kg   Unknown: $v_f = ?$
$\qquad m_2 = 1200.$ kg   Original equation:
$\qquad v_{1o} = 13.0$ m/s $m_1 v_{1o} + m_2 v_{2o} = (m_1 + m_2)v_f$
$\qquad v_{2o} = 25.0$ m/s

Solve: $v_f = \dfrac{m_1 v_{1o} + m_2 v_{2o}}{(m_1 + m_2)} = \dfrac{(800.\ \text{kg})(13.0\ \text{m/s}) + (1200.\ \text{kg})(25.0\ \text{m/s})}{(800.\ \text{kg} + 1200.\ \text{kg})}$

$\qquad = \dfrac{10\ 400\ \text{kg} \cdot \text{m/s} + 30\ 000\ \text{kg} \cdot \text{m/s}}{2000.\ \text{kg}} = \textbf{20.2 m/s forward}$

Example 7: Charlotte, a 65.0-kg skin diver, shoots a 2.0-kg spear with a speed of 15 m/s at a fish who darts quickly away without getting hit. How fast does Charlotte move backwards when the spear is shot?

Solution: To start, Charlotte and the spear are together and both are at rest.

Given: $m_1 = 65.0$ kg   Unknown: $v_{1f} = ?$
$\qquad m_2 = 2.0$ kg   Original equation:
$\qquad v_o = 0$ m/s $(m_1 + m_2)v_o = m_1 v_{1f} + m_2 v_{2f}$
$\qquad v_{2f} = 15.0$ m/s

Solve: $v_{1f} = \dfrac{(m_1 + m_2)v_o - m_2 v_{2f}}{m_1}$

$\qquad = \dfrac{(65.0\ \text{kg} + 2.0\ \text{kg})(0\ \text{m/s}) - (2.0\ \text{kg})(15\ \text{m/s})}{65.0\ \text{kg}}$

$\qquad = \dfrac{-30.\text{kg} \cdot \text{m/s}}{65.0\ \text{kg}} = \textbf{-0.46 m/s}$

Remember, the minus sign here is indicating direction. Therefore, Charlotte would travel with a speed of 0.46 m/s in a direction opposite to that of the spear.

Practice Exercises

Exercise 7: Jamal is at the state fair playing some of the games. At one booth he throws a 0.50-kg ball forward with a velocity of 21.0 m/s in order to hit a 0.20-kg bottle sitting on a shelf, and when he makes contact the bottle goes flying forward at 30.0 m/s. a) What is the velocity of the ball after it hits the bottle? b) If the bottle were more massive, how would this affect the final velocity of the ball?

Answer: **a.** ⎯⎯⎯⎯⎯⎯⎯⎯⎯⎯

Answer: **b.** ⎯⎯⎯⎯⎯⎯⎯⎯⎯⎯

Exercise 8: Jeanne rolls a 7.0-kg bowling ball down the alley for the league championship. One pin is still standing, and Jeanne hits it head-on with a velocity of 9.0 m/s. The 2.0-kg pin acquires a forward velocity of 14.0 m/s. What is the new velocity of the bowling ball?

Answer: ⎯⎯⎯⎯⎯⎯⎯⎯⎯⎯

Exercise 9: Running at 2.0 m/s, Bruce, the 45.0-kg quarterback, collides with Biff, the 90.0-kg tackle, who is traveling at 7.0 m/s in the other direction. Upon collision, Biff continues to travel forward at 1.0 m/s. How fast is Bruce knocked backwards?

Answer: ⎯⎯⎯⎯⎯⎯⎯⎯⎯⎯

Exercise 10: Anthony and Sissy are participating in the "Roll-a-Rama" rollerskating dance championship. While 75.0-kg Anthony rollerskates backwards at 3.0 m/s, 60.0-kg Sissy jumps into his arms with a velocity of 5.0 m/s in the same direction. a) How fast does the pair roll backwards together? b) If Anthony is skating toward Sissy when she jumps, would their combined final velocity be larger or smaller than your answer to part a? Why?

Answer: **a.** _____

Answer: **b.** _____

Exercise 11: To test the strength of a retainment wall designed to protect a nuclear reactor, a rocket-propelled F-4 Phantom jet aircraft was crashed head-on into a concrete barrier at high speed in Sandia, New Mexico on April 19, 1988. The F-4 phantom had a mass of 19100 kg, while the retainment wall's mass was 469000 kg. The wall sat on a cushion of air that allowed it to move during impact. If the wall and F-4 moved together at 8.41 m/s during the collision, what was the initial speed of the F-4 Phantom?

Answer: _____

Exercise 12: Valentina, the Russian Cosmonaut, goes outside her ship for a spacewalk, but when she is floating 15 m from the ship, her tether catches on a sharp piece of metal and is severed. Valentina tosses her 2.0-kg camera away from the spaceship with a speed of 12 m/s a) How fast will Valentina, whose mass is now 68 kg, travel toward the spaceship? b) Assuming the spaceship remains at rest with respect to Valentina, how long will it take her to reach the ship?

Answer: **a.** _____

Answer: **b.** _____

Exercise 13: A 620.-kg moose stands in the middle of the railroad tracks, frozen by the lights of an oncoming 10 000.-kg locomotive that is traveling at 10.0 m/s. The engineer sees the moose but is unable to stop the train in time and the moose rides down the track sitting on the cowcatcher. What is the new combined velocity of the locomotive and the moose?

Answer: _____

Exercise 14: Lee is rolling along on her 4.0-kg skateboard with a constant speed of 3.0 m/s when she jumps off the back and continues forward with a velocity of 2.0 m/s relative to the ground. This causes the skateboard to go flying forward with a speed of 15.5 m/s relative to the ground. What is Lee's mass?

Answer: _____

Additional Exercises

A-1:   Bernie, whose mass is 70.0 kg, leaves a ski jump with a velocity of 21.0 m/s. What is Bernie's momentum as he leaves the ski jump?

A-2:   Ethel is sitting on a park bench feeding the pigeons when a child's ball rolls toward her across the grass. Ethel returns the ball to the child by hitting it with her 2.0-kg pocketbook with a speed of 20 m/s. If the impact lasts for 0.4 s, with what force does Ethel hit the ball?

A-3:   When Reggie stepped up to the plate and hit a 0.150-kg fast ball traveling at 36.0 m/s, the impact caused the ball to leave his bat with a velocity of 45.0 m/s in the opposite direction. If the impact lasted for 0.002 s, what force did Reggie exert on the baseball?

A-4:   The U.S. Army's parachuting team, the Golden Knights, are on a routine jumping mission over a deserted beach. On a jump, a 65-kg Knight lands on the beach with a speed of 4.0 m/s, making a 0.20-m deep indentation in the sand. With what average force did the parachuter hit the sand?

A-5:   The late news reports the story of a shooting in the city. Investigators think that they have recovered the weapon and they run ballistics tests on the pistol at the firing range. If a 0.050-kg bullet were fired from the handgun with a speed of 400 m/s and it traveled 0.080 m into the target before coming to rest, what force did the bullet exert on the target?

A-6:   About 50 000 years ago, in an area located outside Flagstaff, Arizona, a giant 4.5×10^7-kg meteor fell and struck the earth, leaving a 180-m-deep hole now known as Barringer crater. If the meteor was traveling at 20 000 m/s upon impact, with what average force did the meteor hit the earth?

A-7:   Astronaut Pam Melroy, history's third woman space shuttle pilot, flew the space shuttle *Discovery* to the International Space Station to complete construction in October of 2000. To undock from the space station Pilot Melroy released hooks holding the two spacecraft together and the 68 000-kg shuttle pushed away from the space station with the aid of four large springs. a) If the 73 000-kg space station moved back at a speed of 0.50 m/s, how fast and in what direction did the space shuttle move? b) What was the relative speed of the two spacecraft as they separated?

A-8:   Tyrrell throws his 0.20-kg football in the living room and knocks over his mother's 0.80-kg antique vase. After the collision, the football bounces straight back with a speed of 3.9 m/s, while the vase is moving at 2.6 m/s in the opposite direction. a) How fast did Tyrrell throw the football? b) If the football continued to travel at 3.9 m/s in the same direction it was thrown, would the vase have to be more or less massive than 0.80 kg?

A-9:   A 300.-kg motorboat is turned off as it approaches a dock and it coasts in toward the dock at 0.50 m/s. Isaac, whose mass is 62.0 kg, jumps off the front of the boat with a speed of 3.0 m/s relative to the boat. What is the velocity of the boat after Isaac jumps?

A-10: Miguel, the 72.0-kg bullfighter, runs toward an angry bull at a speed of 4.00 m/s. The 550.-kg bull charges toward Miguel at 12.0 m/s and Miguel must jump on the bull's back at the last minute to avoid being run over. What is the new velocity of Miguel and the bull as they move across the arena?

A-11: A space shuttle astronaut is sent to repair a defective relay in a 600.00-kg satellite that is traveling in space at 17 000.0 m/s. Suppose the astronaut and his Manned Maneuvering Unit (MMU) have a mass of 400.00 kg and travel at 17 010.0 m/s toward the satellite. What is the combined velocity when the astronaut grabs hold of the satellite?

A-12: The U.S.S. *Constitution*, the oldest fully commissioned war ship in the world, is docked in Boston, Massachusetts. Also known as "Old Ironsides" for her seemingly impenetrable hull, the frigate houses 56 pieces of heavy artillery. Mounted on bearings that allow them to recoil at a speed of 1.30 m/s are 20 carronades, each with a mass of 1000. kg. If a carronade fires a 14.5-kg cannonball straight ahead, with what muzzle velocity does the cannonball leave the cannon?

Challenge Exercises for Further Study

B-1: On a hot sumer afternoon, Keith and Nate are out fishing in their rowboat when they decide to jump into the water and go for a swim. Keith, whose mass is 65.0 kg, jumps straight off the front of the boat with a speed of 2.00 m/s relative to the boat, while Nate propels his 68.0-kg body simultaneously off the back of the boat at 4.00 m/s relative to the boat. If the 100.-kg boat is initially traveling forward at 3.00 m/s, what is its velocity after both boys jump?

B-2: Lilly, whose mass is 45.0 kg, is ice skating with a constant speed of 7.00 m/s when she hits a rough patch of ice with a coefficient of friction of 0.0800. How long will it take before Lilly coasts to a stop?

B-3: In a train yard, train cars are rolled down a long hill in order to link them up with other cars as shown. A car of mass 4000. kg starts to roll from rest at the top of a hill 5.0 m high, and inclined at an angle of 5.0° to the horizontal. The coefficient of rolling friction between the train and the track is 0.050. What velocity would the car have if it linked up with 3 identical cars sitting on flat ground at the bottom of the track? (Hint: The equation for rolling friction is just like the one for sliding friction.)

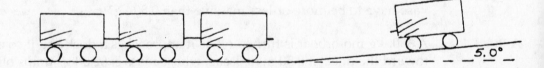

5 Energy and Machines

5-1 Work and Power

Vocabulary **Work:** The product of the component of the force exerted on an object in the direction of displacement and the magnitude of the displacement.

$$\textbf{work} = \textbf{(force)(displacement)} \quad \text{or} \quad W = F\Delta d$$

The SI unit for work is the **joule (J)**, which equals one **newton·meter (N·m)**.

For maximum work to be done, the object *must* move in the direction of the force. If the object is moving at an angle to the force, determine the component of the force in the direction of motion. Remember, if the object does not move, or moves perpendicular to the direction of the force, no work has been done.

Vocabulary **Power:** The rate at which work is done.

$$\textbf{power} = \frac{\textbf{work}}{\textbf{elapsed time}} \quad \text{or} \quad P = \frac{W}{\Delta t}$$

The SI unit for power is the **watt (W),** which equals one **joule per second (J/s).** One person is more powerful than another if he or she can do more work in a given amount of time, or can do the same amount of work in less time.

Solved Examples

Example 1: Bud, a very large man of mass 130 kg, stands on a pogo stick. How much work is done as Bud compresses the spring of the pogo stick 0.50 m?

Solution: First, find Bud's weight, which is the force with which he compresses the pogo stick spring.

Given: $m = 130 \text{ kg}$
$ g = 10.0 \text{ m/s}^2$

Unknown: $w = ?$
Original equation: $w = mg$

Solve: $w = mg = (130 \text{ kg})(10.0 \text{ m/s}^2) = 1300 \text{ N}$

Now use this weight to solve for the work done to compress the spring.

63

Given: F = 1300 N   *Unknown: W = ?*
        Δd = 0.050 m   *Original equation: W = FΔd*

Solve: W = FΔd = (1300 N)(0.050 m) = **65 J**

Don't get confused here by the two *W*'s you see in this example. The *w* in *w = mg* means *weight* while the *W* in *W = FΔd* means *work*. There are many ways to tell them apart, the most important of which is to understand how they are used in the context of the exercise. Also, the units used for each are quite different: weight is measured in newtons, and work is measured in joules. Last of all, weight is a vector and work is a scalar.

Example 2: After finishing her physics homework, Sherita pulls her 50.0-kg body out of the living room chair and climbs up the 5.0-m-high flight of stairs to her bedroom. How much work does Sherita do in ascending the stairs?

Solution: First find Sherita's weight. Her muscles exert a force to carry her weight up the stairs.

Given: m = 50.0 kg   *Unknown: w = ?*
        g = 10.0 m/s^2   *Original equation: w = mg*

Solve: w = mg = (50.0kg)(10.0 m/s^2) = 500. N

Now use Sherita's weight (or force) to determine the amount of work done. It is important to note that when you are solving for the work done, you need know only the displacement of the body moved. The number of stairs climbed or their steepness is irrelevant. All that is important is the *change* in position.

Given: F = 500. N   *Unknown: W = ?*
        Δd = 5.0 m   *Original equation: W = FΔd*

Solve: W = FΔd = (500. N)(5.0 m) = **2500 J**

Example 3: In the previous example, Sherita slowly ascends the stairs, taking 10.0 s to go from bottom to top. The next evening, in a rush to catch her favorite TV show, she runs up the stairs in 3.0 s. a) On which night does Sherita do more work? b) On which night does Sherita generate more power?

a) Sherita does the same amount of work on both nights because the force she exerts and her displacement are the same each time.

b) Sherita's power output varies because the time taken to do the same amount of work varies.

First night:

Given: W = 2500 J   *Unknown: P = ?*
        Δt = 10.0 s   *Original equation: $P = \dfrac{W}{\Delta t}$*

Solve: $P = \dfrac{W}{\Delta t} = \dfrac{2500 \text{ J}}{10.0 \text{ s}} = \mathbf{250 \text{ W}}$

Second night:

Given: $W = 2500$ J
$\quad\quad\quad \Delta t = 3.0$ s

Unknown: $P = ?$
Original equation: $P = \dfrac{W}{\Delta t}$

Solve: $P = \dfrac{W}{\Delta t} = \dfrac{2500 \text{ J}}{3.0 \text{ s}} = \mathbf{830 \text{ W}}$

Sherita generates more power on the second night.

Practice Exercises

Exercise 1: On his way off to college, Russell drags his suitcase 15.0 m from the door of his house to the car at a constant speed with a horizontal force of 95.0 N. a) How much work does Russell do to overcome the force of friction? b) If the floor has just been waxed, does he have to do more work or less work to move the suitcase? Explain.

Answer: **a.** _____

Answer: **b.** _____

Exercise 2: Katie, a 30.0-kg child, climbs a tree to rescue her cat who is afraid to jump 8.0 m to the ground. How much work does Katie do in order to reach the cat?

Answer: _____

Exercise 3: Marissa does 3.2 J of work to lower the window shade in her bedroom a distance of 0.8 m. How much force must Marrisa exert on the window shade?

Answer: _____

Exercise 4: Atlas and Hercules, two carnival sideshow strong men, each lift 200.-kg barbells 2.00 m off the ground. Atlas lifts his barbells in 1.00 s and Hercules lifts his in 3.00 s. a) Which strong man does more work? b) Calculate which man is more powerful.

Answer: **a.** _____

Answer: **b.** _____

5-2 Energy

Potential and Kinetic Energy

Vocabulary   **Energy:** The ability to do work.

There are many different types of energy. This chapter will focus on only mechanical energy, or the energy related to position (**potential energy**) and motion (**kinetic energy**).

Vocabulary   **Potential Energy:** Energy of position, or stored energy.

An object gains gravitational potential energy when it is lifted from one level to a higher level. Therefore, we generally refer to the *change* in potential energy or ΔPE, which is proportional to the change in height, Δ*h*.

Δ gravitational potential energy = (mass)(acceleration due to gravity)(Δ height)

$$\text{or} \qquad \Delta PE = mg\Delta h$$

It is important to remember that gravitational potential energy relies *only* upon the vertical change in height, Δh, and not upon the path taken.

In addition to gravitational potential energy, there are other forms of stored energy. For example, when a bow is pulled back and before it is released, the energy in the bow is equal to the work done to deform it. This stored or potential energy is written as $\Delta PE = F\Delta d$. Springs possess elastic potential energy when they are displaced from the equilibrium position. The equation for elastic potential energy will not be used in this chapter.

Vocabulary   **Kinetic Energy:** Energy of motion.

The kinetic energy of an object varies with the square of the speed.

$$\textbf{kinetic energy} = \left(\frac{1}{2}\right)\textbf{(mass)(speed)}^2 \qquad \text{or} \qquad KE = \left(\frac{1}{2}\right)mv^2$$

The SI unit for energy is the **joule.** Notice that this is the same unit used for work. When work is done on an object, energy is transformed from one form to another. The sum of the changes in potential, kinetic, and heat energy is equal to the work done on the object. Mechanical energy is transformed into heat energy when work is done to overcome friction.

Conservation of Energy

According to the **law of conservation of energy,** energy cannot be created or destroyed. The total amount of mechanical energy in a system remains constant if no work is done by any force other than gravity.

In an isolated system where there are no mechanical energy losses due to friction

$$\Delta KE = \Delta PE$$

In other words, all the kinetic and potential energy before an interaction equals all the kinetic and potential energy after the interaction.

$$KE_o + PE_o = KE_f + PE_f \quad \text{or} \quad \left(\frac{1}{2}\right)mv_o^2 + mgh_o = \left(\frac{1}{2}\right)mv_f^2 + mgh_f$$

As a reminder, the terms with the subscript $_o$ are the initial conditions, while those with the subscript $_f$ are final conditions.

Energy and Machines   67

Solved Examples

Example 4: Legend has it that Isaac Newton "discovered" gravity when an apple fell from a tree and hit him on the head. If a 0.20-kg apple fell 7.0 m before hitting Newton, what was its change in PE during the fall?

Solution: For a given object, the change in PE depends only upon the change in position. The apple does not need to fall all the way to the ground to experience an energy change.

Given: $m = 0.20$ kg $\qquad\qquad$ Unknown: $\Delta PE = ?$
$\quad\quad\quad g = 10.0$ m/s^2 $\qquad\qquad$ Original equation: $\Delta PE = mg\Delta h$
$\quad\quad\quad \Delta h = 7.0$ m

Solve: $\Delta PE = mg\Delta h = (0.20$ kg$)(10.0$ m/s$^2)(7.0$ m$) = $ **14 J**

Example 5: A greyhound at a race track can run at a speed of 16.0 m/s. What is the KE of a 20.0-kg greyhound as it crosses the finish line?

Given: $m = 20.0$ kg $\qquad\qquad$ Unknown: $KE = ?$
$\quad\quad\quad v = 16.0$ m/s $\qquad\qquad$ Original equation: $KE = \left(\dfrac{1}{2}\right)mv^2$

Solve: $KE = \left(\dfrac{1}{2}\right)mv^2 = \left(\dfrac{1}{2}\right)(20.0$ kg$)(16.0$ m/s$)^2 = $ **2560 J**

Example 6: In a wild shot, Bo flings a pool ball of mass m off a 0.68-m-high pool table, and the ball hits the floor with a speed of 6.0 m/s. How fast was the ball moving when it left the pool table? (Use the law of conservation of energy.)

Given: $v_f = 6.0$ m/s $\qquad\qquad$ Unknown: $v_o = ?$
$\quad\quad\quad g = 10.0$ m/s^2 $\qquad\qquad$ Original equation: $\Delta KE = \Delta PE$
$\quad\quad\quad h_o = 0.68$ m
$\quad\quad\quad h_f = 0$ m

Solve: $KE_o + PE_o = KE_f + PE_f$ or $\left(\dfrac{1}{2}\right)mv_o^2 + mgh_o = \left(\dfrac{1}{2}\right)mv_f^2 + mgh_f$

Notice that mass is contained in each of these equations. Therefore, it cancels out and does not need to be included in the calculation.

$$v_o = \sqrt{\dfrac{\left(\dfrac{1}{2}\right)mv_f^2 + mgh_f - mgh_o}{\left(\dfrac{1}{2}\right)m}} = \sqrt{\dfrac{\left(\dfrac{1}{2}\right)v_f^2 + gh_f - gh_o}{\dfrac{1}{2}}}$$

$$= \sqrt{\dfrac{\left(\dfrac{1}{2}\right)(6.0 \text{ m/s})^2 + (10.0 \text{ m/s}^2)(0 \text{ m}) - (10.0 \text{ m/s}^2)(0.68 \text{ m})}{\dfrac{1}{2}}}$$

$$= \sqrt{\dfrac{18 \text{ m}^2/\text{s}^2 - 6.8 \text{ m}^2/\text{s}^2}{\dfrac{1}{2}}} = \textbf{4.7 m/s}$$

Example 7: Frank, a San Francisco hot dog vender, has fallen asleep on the job. When an earthquake strikes, his 300-kg hot-dog cart rolls down Nob Hill and reaches point A at a speed of 8.00 m/s. How fast is the hot-dog cart going at point B when Frank finally wakes up and starts to run after it?

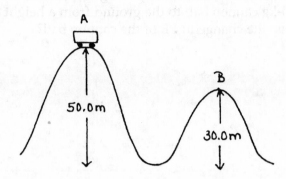

Solution: Because mass is contained in each of these equations, it cancels out and does not need to be included in the calculation. Also, the inclination of the hill makes no difference. All that matters is the change in height.

Given: $v_o = 8.00$ m/s   *Unknown:* $v_f = ?$
       $g = 10.0$ m/s^2 *Original equation:* $\Delta KE = \Delta PE$
       $h_o = 50.0$ m
       $h_f = 30.0$ m

Solve: $KE_o + PE_o = KE_f + PE_f$ or $\left(\dfrac{1}{2}\right)mv_o^2 + mgh_o = \left(\dfrac{1}{2}\right)mv_f^2 + mgh_f$

$$v_f = \sqrt{\frac{\left(\dfrac{1}{2}\right)mv_o^2 + mgh_o - mgh_f}{\left(\dfrac{1}{2}\right)m}} = \sqrt{\frac{\left(\dfrac{1}{2}\right)v_o^2 + gh_o - gh_f}{\dfrac{1}{2}}}$$

$$= \sqrt{\frac{\left(\dfrac{1}{2}\right)(8.00 \text{ m/s})^2 + (10.0 \text{ m/s}^2)(50.0 \text{ m}) - (10.0 \text{ m/s}^2)(30.0 \text{ m})}{\dfrac{1}{2}}}$$

$$= \sqrt{\frac{32.0 \text{ m}^2/\text{s}^2 + 500. \text{ m}^2/\text{s}^2 - 300. \text{ m}^2/\text{s}^2}{\dfrac{1}{2}}}$$

$$= \sqrt{464 \text{ m}^2/\text{s}^2} = \textbf{21.5 m/s}$$

Practice Exercises

Exercise 5: It is said that Galileo dropped objects off the Leaning Tower of Pisa to determine whether heavy or light objects fall faster. If Galileo had dropped a 5.0-kg cannon ball to the ground from a height of 12 m, what would have been the change in PE of the cannon ball?

Answer: _____

Exercise 6: The 2000 Belmont Stakes winner, Commendable, ran the horse race at an average speed of 15.98 m/s. If Commendable and jockey Pat Day had a combined mass of 550.0 kg, what was their KE as they crossed the finish line?

Answer: _____

Exercise 7: Brittany is changing the tire of her car on a steep hill 20.0 m high. She trips and drops the 10.0-kg spare tire, which rolls down the hill with an initial speed of 2.00 m/s. What is the speed of the tire at the top of the next hill, which is 5.00 m high? (Ignore the effects of rotation KE and friction.)

Answer: _____

Exercise 8:   A Mexican jumping bean jumps with the aid of a small worm that lives inside the bean. a) If a bean of mass 2.0 g jumps 1.0 cm from your hand into the air, how much potential energy has it gained in reaching its highest point. b) What is its speed as the bean lands back in the palm of your hand?

Answer: **a.** —————————————

Answer: **b.** —————————————

Exercise 9:   A 500.-kg pig is standing at the top of a muddy hill on a rainy day. The hill is 100.0 m long with a vertical drop of 30.0 m. The pig slips and begins to slide down the hill. What is the pig's speed at the bottom of the hill? Use the law of conservation of energy.

Answer: —————————————

Exercise 10:   While on the moon, the Apollo astronauts enjoyed the effects of a gravity much smaller than that on Earth. If Neil Armstrong jumped up on the moon with an initial speed of 1.51 m/s to a height of 0.700 m, what amount of gravitational acceleration did he experience?

Answer: —————————————

5-3 Machines and Efficiency

Vocabulary   **Machine:** A device that helps do work by changing the magnitude or direction of the applied force.

Three common machines are the **lever, pulley,** and **incline.**

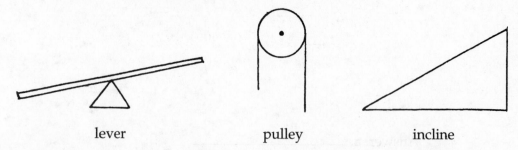

lever   pulley   incline

In an ideal situation, where frictional forces are negligible, work input equals work output.

$$F_{in}\Delta d_{in} = F_{out}\Delta d_{out}$$

However, situations are never ideal. The **actual mechanical advantage,** or **AMA,** of the machine is a ratio of the magnitude of the force out (resistance) to the magnitude of the force in (effort).

$$\textbf{actual mechanical advantage} = \frac{\textbf{force out (resistance)}}{\textbf{force in (effort)}} \quad \text{or} \quad AMA = \frac{F_{out}}{F_{in}}$$

On the other hand, the theoretical or **ideal mechanical advantage, IMA,** is based only on the geometry of the system and does not take frictional effects into account.

$$\textbf{ideal mechanical advantage} = \frac{\textbf{distance in (effort distance)}}{\textbf{distance out (resistance distance)}}$$

$$\text{or} \quad IMA = \frac{\Delta d_{in}}{\Delta d_{out}}$$

Because no machine is perfect and because you will always get out less work than you put in, you need to consider the efficiency of the machine that you are using. The more efficient the machine, the greater work output you will get for your work input. The efficiency will always be less than 100%.

Vocabulary   **Efficiency:** The ratio of the work output to the work input.

$$\text{efficiency} = \frac{\text{work output}}{\text{work input}} = \frac{F_{out}\Delta d_{out}}{F_{in}\Delta d_{in}} = \frac{\text{AMA}}{\text{IMA}}$$

Efficiency has no units and is usually expressed as a percent.

Solved Examples

Example 8:   A crate of bananas weighing 3000. N is shipped from South America to New York, where it is unloaded by a dock worker who lifts the crate by pulling with a force of 200. N on the rope of a pulley system. What is the actual mechanical advantage of the pulley system?

Given: F_{out} = 3000. N   *Unknown:* AMA = ?
           F_{in} = 200. N   *Original equation:* AMA $= \dfrac{F_{out}}{F_{in}}$

Solve: AMA $= \dfrac{F_{out}}{F_{in}} = \dfrac{3000.\text{ N}}{200.\text{ N}} =$ **15.0**

The pulley exerts 15.0 times more force on the crate than the dock worker exerts to pull the rope. Notice that mechanical advantage has no units.

Example 9:   Two clowns, of mass 50.0 kg and 70.0 kg respectively, are in a circus act performing a stunt with a trampoline and a seesaw. The smaller clown stands on the lower end of the seesaw while the larger clown jumps from the trampoline onto the raised side of the seesaw, propelling his friend into the air. a) what is the ideal mechanical advantage of the seesaw? b) If the larger clown exerts a force of 850. N on the seesaw as he jumps, how much force is exerted on the smaller clown?

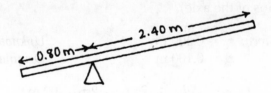

a. The seesaw acts as a lever with the fulcrum 0.80 m from the left side. The ideal mechanical advantage is found by comparing the two distances.

Given: Δd_{in} = 2.40 m   *Unknown:* IMA = ?
         Δd_{out} = 0.80 m   *Original equation:* IMA $= \dfrac{\Delta d_{in}}{\Delta d_{out}}$

Solve: IMA $= \dfrac{\Delta d_{in}}{\Delta d_{out}} = \dfrac{2.40\text{ m}}{0.80\text{ m}} =$ **3.0**

b. To answer this question, assume that the seesaw is 100% efficient and the work out equals the work in (which is highly unlikely!).

Given: F_{in} = 850. N
Δd_{in} = 2.40 m
Δd_{out} = 0.80 m

Unknown: F_{out} = ?
Original equation: $F_{in}\Delta d_{in} = F_{out}\Delta d_{out}$

Solve: $F_{out} = \dfrac{F_{in}\Delta d_{in}}{\Delta d_{out}} = \dfrac{(850.\ N)(2.40\ m)}{0.80\ m}$ = **2550 N**

Example 10: A jackscrew with a handle 30.0 cm long is used to lift a car sitting on the jack. The car rises 2.0 cm for every full turn of the handle. What is the ideal mechanical advantage of the jack?

Solution: For a screw, IMA $= \dfrac{\Delta d_{in}}{\Delta d_{out}} = \dfrac{2\pi r}{\Delta h}$ where $2\pi r$ is the circumference of the circle through which the handle turns, and height, Δh, refers to the amount the jack (and hence the automobile) is raised.

Given: r = 30.0 cm
Δh = 2.0 cm

Unknown: IMA = ?
Original equation: IMA $= \dfrac{\Delta d_{in}}{\Delta d_{out}}$

Solve: IMA $= \dfrac{\Delta d_{in}}{\Delta d_{out}} = \dfrac{2\pi r}{\Delta h} = \dfrac{2\pi(30.0\ cm)}{2.0\ cm}$ = **94**

Example 11: Jack and Jill went up the hill to fetch a pail of water. At the well, Jill used a force of 20.0 N to turn a crank handle of radius 0.400 m that rotated an axle of radius 0.100 m, so she could raise a 60.0-N bucket of water. a) What is the ideal mechanical advantage of the wheel? b) What is the actual mechanical advantage of the wheel? c) What is the efficiency of the wheel?

Solution: Since the crank handle and the axle both turn in a circle, $\Delta d_{in} = 2\pi r_c$ (where r_c is the radius of the crank handle) and $\Delta d_{out} = 2\pi r_a$ (where r_a is the radius of the axle).

a. Given: r_c = 0.400 m
r_a = 0.100 m

Unknown: IMA = ?
Original equation: IMA $= \dfrac{\Delta d_{in}}{\Delta d_{out}}$

Solve: IMA $= \dfrac{\Delta d_{in}}{\Delta d_{out}} = \dfrac{2\pi r_c}{2\pi r_a} = \dfrac{2\pi(0.400\ m)}{2\pi(0.100\ m)}$ = **4.00**

b. The force on the bucket of water is F_{out} and the force exerted by Jill is F_{in}.

Given: F_{out} = 60.0 N
F_{in} = 20.0 N

Unknown: AMA = ?
Original equation: AMA $= \dfrac{F_{out}}{F_{in}}$

Solve: AMA $= \dfrac{F_{out}}{F_{in}} = \dfrac{60.0\ N}{20.0\ N}$ = **3.00**

c. *Given:* AMA = 3.00
        IMA = 4.00

Unknown: Eff = ?
Original equation: Eff = $\dfrac{\text{AMA}}{\text{IMA}}$

Solve: Eff = $\dfrac{\text{AMA}}{\text{IMA}} = \dfrac{3.00}{4.00} = 0.750 = \mathbf{75.0\%}$

Example 12: Clyde, a stubborn 3500-N mule, refuses to walk into the barn, so Farmer MacDonald must drag him up a 5.0-m ramp to his stall, which stands 0.50 m above ground level. a) What is the ideal mechanical advantage of the ramp? b) If Farmer MacDonald needs to exert a 450-N force on the mule to drag him up the ramp with a constant speed, what is the actual mechanical advantage of the ramp? c) What is the efficiency of the ramp?

Solution: For a ramp, ramp length is Δd_{in} and ramp height is Δd_{out}.

a. *Given:* Δd_{in} = 5.0 m
        Δd_{out} = 0.50 m

Unknown: IMA = ?
Original equation: IMA = $\dfrac{\Delta d_{in}}{\Delta d_{out}}$

Solve: IMA = $\dfrac{\Delta d_{in}}{\Delta d_{out}} = \dfrac{5.0 \text{ m}}{0.50 \text{ m}} = \mathbf{10.}$

b. *Given:* F_{out} = 3500 N
        F_{in} = 450 N

Unknown: AMA = ?
Original equation: AMA = $\dfrac{F_{out}}{F_{in}}$

Solve: AMA = $\dfrac{F_{out}}{F_{in}} = \dfrac{3500 \text{ N}}{450 \text{ N}} = \mathbf{7.8}$

c. *Given:* IMA = 10.
        AMA = 7.8

Unknown: Eff = ?
Original equation: Eff = $\dfrac{\text{AMA}}{\text{IMA}}$

Solve: Eff = $\dfrac{\text{AMA}}{\text{IMA}} = \dfrac{7.8}{10.} = 0.78 = \mathbf{78\%}$

Practice Exercises

Exercise 11: Cathy, a 460-N actress playing Peter Pan, is hoisted above the stage in order to "fly" by a stagehand pulling with a force of 60. N on a rope wrapped around a pulley system. What is the actual mechanical advantage of the pulley system?

Answer: ─────────────────

Exercise 12: A windmill uses sails blown by the wind to turn an axle that allows a grind-stone to grind corn into meal with a force of 90. N. The windmill has sails of radius 6.0 m blown by a wind that exerts a force of 15 N on the sails, and the axle of the grindstone has a radius of 0.50 m. a) What is the ideal mechanical advantage of the wheel? b) What is the actual mechanical advantage of the wheel? c) What is the efficiency of the wheel?

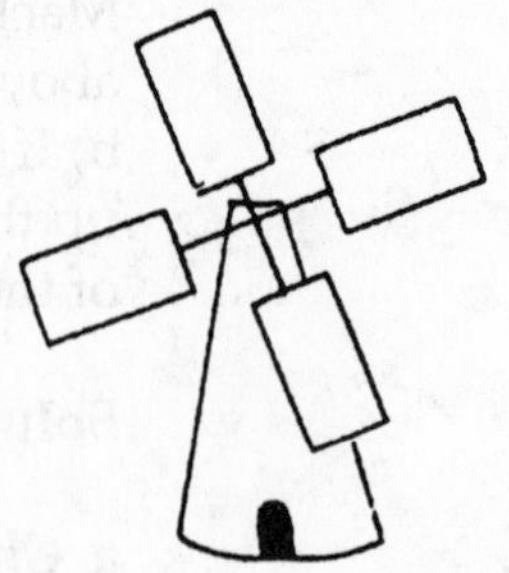

Answer: **a.** _____

Answer: **b.** _____

Answer: **c.** _____

Exercise 13: Winnie, a waitress, holds in one hand a 5.0-N tray stacked with twelve 3.5-N dishes. The length of her arm from her hand to her elbow is 30.0 cm and her biceps muscle exerts a force 5.0 cm from her elbow, which acts as a fulcrum. How much force must her biceps exert to allow her to hold the tray?

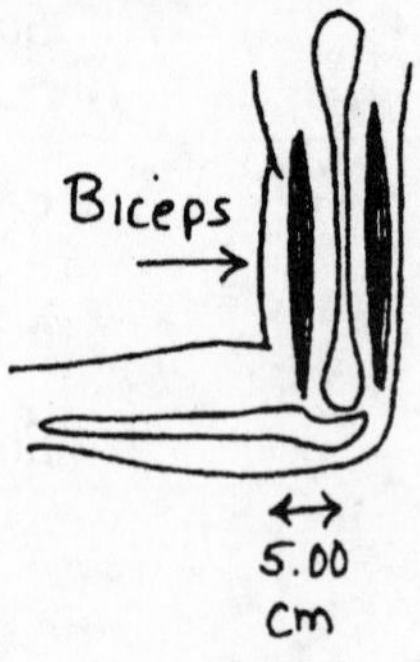

Answer: _____

Exercise 14: When building the pyramids, the ancient Egyptians were able to raise large stones to very great heights by using inclines. If an incline has an ideal mechanical advantage of 4.00 and the pyramid is 15.0 m tall, how much of an angle would the incline need in order for the Egyptian builder to reach the top?

Answer: _____

Exercise 15: The Ramseys are moving to a new town, so they have called in the ACME moving company to take care of their furniture. Debbie, one of the movers, slides the Ramseys' 2200-N china cabinet up a 6.0-m-long ramp to the moving van, which stands 1.0 m off the ground. a) What is the ideal mechanical advantage of the incline? b) If Debbie must exert a 500.-N force to move the china cabinet up the ramp with a constant speed, what is the actual mechanical advantage of the ramp? c) What is the efficiency of the ramp?

Answer: **a.** _____

Answer: **b.** _____

Answer: **c.** _____

Additional Exercises

A-1: On a ski weekend in Colorado, Bob, whose mass is 75.0 kg, skis down a hill that is inclined at an angle of 15.0° to the horizontal and has a vertical rise of 25.0 m. How much work is done by gravity on Bob as he goes down the hill?

A-2: A pile driver is a device used to drive stakes into the ground. While building a fence, Adam drops a pile driver of mass 3000. kg through a vertical distance of 8.0 m. The pile driver is opposed by a resisting force of 5.0×10^6 N. How far is the stake driven into the ground on the first stroke?

A-3: At Six Flags New England in Agawam, Massachusetts, a ride called the Cyclone is a giant roller coaster that ascends a 34.1-m hill and then drops 21.9 m before ascending the next hill. The train of cars has a mass of 4727 kg. a) How much work is required to get an empty train of cars from the ground to the top of the first hill? b) What power must be generated to bring the train to the top of the first hill in 30.0 s? c) How much PE is converted into KE from the top of the first hill to the bottom of the 21.9-m drop?

A-4: A flea gains 1.0×10^{-7} J of PE jumping up to a height of 0.030 m from a dog's back. What is the mass of the flea?

A-5: At target practice, Diana holds her bow and pulls the arrow back a distance of 0.30 m by exerting an average force of 40.0 N. What is the potential energy stored in the bow the moment before the arrow is released?

A-6: The coyote, whose mass is 20.0 kg, is chasing the roadrunner when the coyote accidentally runs off the edge of a cliff and plummets to the ground 30.0 m below. What force does the ground exert on the coyote as he makes a coyote-shaped dent 0.420 m deep in the ground?

A-7: A 0.080-kg robin, perched on a power line 6.0 m above the ground, swoops down to snatch a worm from the ground and then returns to an 8.0-m-high tree branch with his catch. a) By how much did the bird's PE increase in its trip from the power line to the tree branch? b) How would your answer have changed if the bird had flown around a bit before landing on the tree branch?

A-8: Blackie, a cat whose mass is 5.45 kg, is napping on top of the refrigerator when he rolls over and falls. Blackie has a KE of 85.5 J just before he lands on his feet on the floor. How tall is the refrigerator?

A-9: Calories measure energy we get from food, and one dietary Calorie is equal to 4187 J. The average food energy intake for human beings is 2000. Calories/day. Assume you have a mass of 55.0 kg and you want to burn off all the Calories you consume in one day. How high a mountain would you have to climb to do so? (Note: This calculation ignores the large amount of energy the body continually loses to heat.)

A-10: From a height of 2.15 m above the floor of Boston's Fleet Center, forward Paul Pierce tosses a shot straight up next to the basketball hoop with a KE of 5.40 J. If his regulation-size basketball has a mass of 0.600 kg, will his shot go as high as the 3.04-m hoop? Use the law of conservation of energy.

A-11: Mr. Macintosh, a computer technician, uses a screwdriver with a handle of radius 1.2 cm to remove a screw in the back of a computer. The screw moves out 0.20 cm on each complete turn. What is the ideal mechanical advantage of the screwdriver?

A-12: Tom's favorite pastime is fishing. a) How much work is required for Tom to reel in a 10.0-kg bluefish from the water's surface to the deck of a fishing boat, 5.20 m above the water, if the reel of his fishing pole is 85.0% efficient? b) If Tom applies a force of 15 N to the reel's crank handle, what is the actual mechanical advantage of the fishing pole? c) What is the ideal mechanical advantage of the fishing pole?

A-13: A nutcracker 16 cm long is used to crack open a Brazil nut that is placed 12 cm from where your hand is squeezing the nutcracker. What is the ideal mechanical advantage of the nutcracker?

Challenge Exercises for Further Study

B-1:   A 5.00-N salmon swims 20.0 m upstream against a current that provides a resistance of 1.50 N. This portion of the stream rises at an angle of 10.0° with respect to the horizontal. a) How much work is done by the salmon against the current? b) What is the gain in PE by the salmon? c) What is the total work that must be done by the salmon? d) If the salmon takes 40.0 s to swim the distance, what power does it exert in doing so?

B-2:   A 30-kg shopping cart full of groceries sitting at the top of a 2.0-m hill begins to roll until it hits a stump at the bottom of the hill. Upon impact, a 0.25-kg can of peaches flies horizontally out of the shopping cart and hits a parked car with an average force of 490 N. How deep a dent is made in the car?

B-3:   Using her snowmobile, Midge pulls a 60.0-kg skier up a ski slope inclined at an angle of 12.0° to the horizontal. The snowmobile exerts a force of 200. N parallel to the hill. If the coefficient of friction between the skis and the snow is 0.120, how fast is the skier moving after he has been pulled for 100.0 m starting from rest? (Ignore the effects of the static friction that must be overcome to initially start him in motion.) Use the law of conservation of energy.

B-4:   Jose, whose mass is 45.0 kg, is riding his 5.0-kg skateboard down the sidewalk with a constant speed of 6.0 m/s when he rolls across a 10.0-m-long patch of sand on the pavement. The sand provides a force of friction of 6.0 N. What is Jose's speed as he emerges from the sandy section?

B-5:   Eben lifts an engine out of his Volkswagen with the help of a winch that allows him to raise the engine 0.020 m for every 0.90 m he pulls on the cable. Eben expends 1000. J of energy to lift the 800.-N engine 0.50 m. a) What is the efficiency of the winch? b) What is the ideal mechanical advantage of the winch? c) What is the actual mechanical advantage of the winch? d) What force does Eben exert to lift the engine?

6 Circular Motion

6-1 Centripetal Acceleration and Force

Period, Frequency, and Speed

Vocabulary   **Period:** The time it takes for one full rotation or revolution of an object.

Vocabulary   **Frequency:** The number of rotations or revolutions per unit time.

Period and frequency are reciprocals of each other. In other words,

$$T = \frac{1}{f} \quad \text{and} \quad f = \frac{1}{T}$$

Since period is a measure of time, its SI unit is the **second**, while the unit for frequency is the reciprocal of this, or 1/second. Another way of writing 1/second is with the unit **hertz (Hz)**.

When an object spins in a circle, the distance it travels in one revolution is the circumference of the circle, $2\pi r$. The time it takes for one revolution is the period, T. Therefore,

$$\text{speed} = \frac{2\pi(\text{radius})}{\text{period}} \quad \text{or} \quad v = \frac{2\pi r}{T}$$

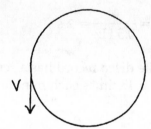

where v is called the **linear** or **tangential speed** because at any given time, the velocity is tangent to the circle as shown in the diagram. Although the velocity is constant in magnitude (speed), it is always changing direction.

Centripetal Acceleration and Centripetal Force

An object can move around in a circle with a constant speed yet still be accelerating because its direction is constantly changing. This acceleration, which is always directed in toward the center of the circle, is called **centripetal acceleration**. The magnitude of this acceleration is written as

$$\text{centripetal acceleration} = \frac{(\text{linear speed})^2}{\text{radius}} \qquad \text{or} \qquad a_c = \frac{v^2}{r}$$

If a mass is being accelerated toward the center of a circle, it must be acted upon by an unbalanced force that gives it this acceleration. This force, called the **centripetal force**, is always directed inward toward the center of the circle. The magnitude of this force is written as

$$\text{centripetal force} = (\text{mass})(\text{centripetal acceleration})$$

$$\text{or} \qquad F_c = ma_c = \frac{mv^2}{r}$$

The units for centripetal acceleration and centripetal force are m/s² and N, respectively.

Solved Examples

Example 1: After closing a deal with a client, Kent leans back in his swivel chair and spins around with a frequency of 0.5 Hz. What is Kent's period of spin?

Given: $f = 0.5$ Hz

Unknown: $T = ?$
Original equation: $T = \dfrac{1}{f}$

Solve: $T = \dfrac{1}{f} = \dfrac{1}{0.5 \text{ Hz}} = \textbf{2 s}$

Example 2: Curtis' favorite disco record has a scratch 12 cm from the center that makes the record skip 45 times each minute. What is the linear speed of the scratch as it turns?

Solution: The record makes 45 revolutions every 60. seconds, so find the period of the record first.

$$T = \frac{60. \text{ s}}{45 \text{ rev}} = 1.3 \text{ s}$$

Given: $r = 12$ cm
$T = 1.3$ s

Unknown: $v = ?$
Original equation: $v = \dfrac{2\pi r}{T}$

Solve: $v = \dfrac{2\pi r}{T} = \dfrac{2\pi(12 \text{ cm})}{1.3 \text{ s}} = \textbf{58 cm/s}$

Example 3: Missy's favorite ride at the Topsfield Fair is the rotor, which has a radius of 4.0 m. The ride takes 2.0 s to make one full revolution.
a) What is Missy's linear speed on the rotor?
b) What is Missy's centripetal acceleration on the rotor?

Solution: The ride takes 2.0 s to make one full revolution, so the period is 2.0 s.

a. *Given:* $r = 4.0$ m
$T = 2.0$ s

Unknown: $v = ?$
Original equation: $v = \dfrac{2\pi r}{T}$

Solve: $v = \dfrac{2\pi r}{T} = \dfrac{2\pi(4.0\text{ m})}{2.0\text{ s}} = $ **13 m/s**

b. *Given:* $v = 13$ m/s
$r = 4.0$ m

Unknown: $a_c = ?$
Original equation: $a_c = \dfrac{v^2}{r}$

Solve: $a_c = \dfrac{v^2}{r} = \dfrac{(13\text{ m/s})^2}{4.0\text{ m}} = $ **42 m/s^2**

Example 4: Captain Chip, the pilot of a 60 500-kg jet plane, is told that he must remain in a holding pattern over the airport until it is his turn to land. If Captain Chip flies his plane in a circle whose radius is 50.0 km once every 30.0 min, what centripetal force must the air exert against the wings to keep the plane moving in a circle?

Solution: First, convert km to m and min to s.

$$50.0\text{ km} = 5.00 \times 10^4\text{ m} \qquad 30.0\text{ min} = 1.80 \times 10^3\text{ s}$$

Before solving for the centripetal force, find the speed of the airplane.

Given: $T = 1.80 \times 10^3$ s
$r = 5.00 \times 10^4$ m

Unknown: $v = ?$
Original equation: $v = \dfrac{2\pi r}{T}$

Solve: $v = \dfrac{2\pi r}{T} = \dfrac{2\pi(5.00 \times 10^4\text{ m})}{1.80 \times 10^3\text{ s}} = $ **175 m/s**

Use this speed to solve for the centripetal force.

Given: $m = 60\ 500$ kg
$v = 175$ m/s
$r = 5.00 \times 10^4$ m

Unknown: $F_c = ?$
Original equation: $F_c = \dfrac{mv^2}{r}$

Solve: $F_c = \dfrac{mv^2}{r} = \dfrac{(60\ 500\text{ kg})(175\text{ m/s})^2}{5.00 \times 10^4\text{ m}} = $ **3.71 × 10^4 N**

Practice Exercises

Exercise 1: Marianne puts her favorite Backstreet Boys disc in her CD player. If it spins with a frequency of 1800 revolutions per minute, what is the period of spin of the compact disc?

Answer: _____

Exercise 2: Hamlet, a hamster, runs on his exercise wheel, which turns around once every 0.5 s. What is the frequency of the wheel?

Answer: _____

Exercise 3: A sock stuck to the inside of the clothes dryer spins around the drum once every 2.0 s at a distance of 0.50 m from the center of the drum. a) What is the sock's linear speed? b) If the drum were twice as wide but continued to turn with the same frequency, would the linear speed of a sock stuck to the inside be faster than, slower than, or the same speed as your answer to part a?

Answer: **a.** _____

Answer: **b.** _____

Exercise 4: What is the radius of an automobile tire that turns with a frequency of 11 Hz and has a linear speed of 20.0 m/s?

Answer: _____

Exercise 5: Luigi twirls a round piece of pizza dough overhead with a frequency of 60 revolutions per minute. a) Find the linear speed of a stray piece of pepperoni stuck on the dough 10. cm from the pizza's center. b) In what direction will the pepperoni move if it flies off while the pizza is spinning? Explain the reason for your answer.

Answer: **a.** —————————————

Answer: **b.** —————————————

Exercise 6: Earth turns on its axis approximately once every 24 hours. The radius of Earth is 6.38×10^6 m. a) If some astronomical catastrophe suddenly brought Earth to a screeching halt (a physical impossibility as far as we know), with what speed would Earth's inhabitants who live at the equator go flying off Earth's surface? b) Because Earth is solid, it must turn with the same frequency everywhere on its surface. Compare your linear speed at the equator to your linear speed while standing near one of the poles.

Answer: **a.** —————————————

Answer: **b.** —————————————

Exercise 7: Jessica is riding on a merry-go-round on an outer horse that sits at a distance of 8.0 m from the center of the ride. Jessica's sister, Julie, is on an inner horse located 6.0 m from the ride's center. The merry-go-round turns around once every 40.0 s. a) Explain which girl is moving with the greater linear speed. b) What is the centripetal acceleration of Julie and her horse?

Answer: **a.** —————————————

Answer: **b.** —————————————

Exercise 8:   A cement mixer of radius 2.5 m turns with a frequency of 0.020 Hz. What is the centripetal acceleration of a small piece of dried cement stuck to the inside wall of the mixer?

Answer: ———————————

Exercise 9:   A popular trick of many physics teachers is to swing a pail of water around in a vertical circle fast enough so that the water doesn't spill out when the pail is upside down. If Mr. Lowell's arm is 0.60 m long, what is the minimum speed with which he can swing the pail so that the water doesn't spill out at the top of the path?

Answer: ———————————

Exercise 10:   To test their stamina, astronauts are subjected to many rigorous physical tests before they fly in space. One such test involves spinning the astronauts in a device called a *centrifuge* that subjects them to accelerations far greater than gravity. With what linear speed would an astronaut have to spin in order to experience an acceleration of 3 g's at a radius of 10.0 m? (1 g = 10.0 m/s^2)

Answer: ———————————

Exercise 11: At the Fermilab particle accelerator in Batavia, Illinois, protons are accelerated by electromagnets around a circular chamber of 1.00-km radius to speeds near the speed of light before colliding with a target to produce enormous amounts of energy. If a proton is traveling at 10% the speed of light, how much centripetal force is exerted by the electromagnets? (Hint: The speed of light is 3.00×10^8 m/s, $m_p = 1.67 \times 10^{-27}$ kg)

Answer: ─────────────────

Exercise 12: Roxanne is making a strawberry milkshake in her blender. A tiny, 0.0050-kg strawberry is rapidly spun around the inside of the container with a speed of 14.0 m/s, held by a centripetal force of 10.0 N. What is the radius of the blender at this location?

Answer: ─────────────────

6-2 Torque

Vocabulary **Torque:** A measurement of the tendency of a force to produce a rotation about an axis.

$$\textbf{torque = perpendicular force} \times \textbf{lever arm} \qquad \text{or} \qquad \tau = F \times d$$

The lever arm, d, is the distance from the pivot point, or fulcrum, to the point where the component of the force perpendicular to the lever arm is being exerted. The longer the lever arm, the larger the torque. This is why it is easier to loosen a tight screw with a long wrench than with your hand or a short pair of tweezers.

If a torque causes a counterclockwise rotation of an object around the fulcrum, it is positive. If the torque causes a clockwise rotation of an object around the fulcrum, it is negative. This convention works even if the object remains balanced and the torques just *attempt* to cause a rotation.

The SI unit for torque is the **newton·meter (N·m)**. However, unlike work, which is measured in the same unit, torque is not a form of energy and is not equivalent to a joule.

In most of the exercises in this book, all the torques are balanced. For example, if two people are sitting on either side of a seesaw and they want to remain level, they can position themselves so that all the torques on one side of the seesaw equal all the torques on the other side. The total torque on a system equals the sum of all the individual torques, or

$$\tau = (F_1 \times d_1) + (F_2 \times d_2) + \ldots$$

The ... means that there may be more than only two torques acting on a system at any one time. Keep in mind that when an object is balanced, all the torques must also balance. Therefore, the total torque, τ, is zero.

Vocabulary **Center of Gravity:** The point on any object that acts like the place at which all the weight is concentrated.

The weight of an object, which acts as if it is concentrated at the center of gravity, is one of the forces that can cause it to rotate. The weight produces a torque if the object is not supported at its center of gravity.

Solved Examples

Example 5: Ned tightens a bolt in his car engine by exerting 12 N of force on his wrench at a distance of 0.40 m from the fulcrum. How much torque must Ned produce to turn the bolt?

Given: $F = 12$ N   *Unknown:* $\tau = ?$
        $d = 0.40$ m   *Original equation:* $\tau = F \times d$

Solve: $\tau = F \times d = (12 \text{ N})(0.40 \text{ m}) = \textbf{4.8 N·m}$

Example 6: Mabel and Maude are seesawing on the school playground and decide to see if they can move to the correct location to make the seesaw balance. Mabel weighs 400. N and she sits 2.00 m from the fulcrum of the seesaw. Where should 450.-N Maude sit to balance the seesaw?

Solution: It helps to draw a diagram of the situation to allow yourself to visualize what is happening.

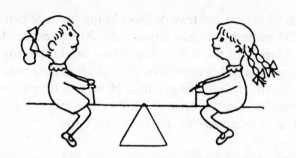

Given: $F_1 = 400.$ N
$F_2 = 450.$ N
$d_1 = 2.00$ m

Unknown: $d_2 = ?$
Original equation:
$\tau = (F_1 \times d_1) + (F_2 \times d_2)$

Solve: If 400.-N Mabel makes the seesaw turn in a counterclockwise direction, then 450.-N Maude makes the seesaw turn in a clockwise direction. Therefore, $\tau = (F_1 \times d_1) + -(F_2 \times d_2)$. If the seesaw is balanced, then $\tau = 0$ and the equation becomes $\tau = (F_1 \times d_1) + -(F_2 \times d_2) = 0$, or $(F_1 \times d_1) = (F_2 \times d_2)$. Therefore,

$$d_2 = \frac{(F_1 \times d_1)}{F_2} = \frac{(400. \text{ N})(2.00 \text{ m})}{450. \text{ N}} = \textbf{1.78 m} \text{ from the fulcrum.}$$

Practice Exercises

Exercise 13: A water faucet is turned on when a force of 2.0 N is exerted on the handle, at a distance of 0.060 m from the pivot point. How much torque must be produced to turn the handle?

Answer: _____

Exercise 14: Nancy, whose mass is 60.0 kg, is working at a construction site and she sits down for a bite to eat at noon. If Nancy sits on the very end of a 3.00-m-long plank pivoted in the middle on a saw horse, how much torque must her co-worker provide on the other end of the plank in order to keep Nancy from falling on the ground?

Answer: _____

Exercise 15: Barry carries his tray of food to his favorite cafeteria table for lunch. The 0.50-m-long tray has a mass of 0.20 kg and holds a 0.40-kg plate of food 0.20 m from the right edge. Barry holds the tray by the left edge with one hand, using his thumb as the fulcrum, and pushes up 0.10 m from the fulcrum with his finger tips. How much upward force must his finger tips exert to keep the tray level? b) How might Barry make the tray easier to carry if he still chooses to use only one hand?

Answer: **a.** _____

Answer: **b.** _____

Exercise 16: Soon-Yi is building a mobile to hang over her baby's crib. She hangs a 0.020-kg toy sailboat 0.010 m from the left end and a 0.015-kg toy truck 0.20 m from the right end of a bar 0.50 m long. If the lever arm itself has negligible mass, where must the support string be placed so that the arm balances?

Answer: _____

Exercise 17: Orin and Anita, two paramedics, rush a 60.0-kg man from the scene of an accident to a waiting ambulance, carrying him on a uniform 3.00-kg stretcher held by the ends. The stretcher is 2.60 m long and the man's center of mass is 1.00 m from Anita. How much force must Orin and Anita each exert to keep the man horizontal?

Answer: _____

6-3 Moment of Inertia and Angular Momentum

Vocabulary   **Moment of Inertia:** The resistance of an object to changes in its rotational motion.

The equation for the moment of inertia varies depending upon the shape of the rotating object. For an object rotating around an axis at a distance r,

$$\textbf{moment of inertia} = \textbf{(mass)(radius)}^2 \qquad \text{or} \qquad I = mr^2$$

The SI unit for moment of inertia is the **kilogram·meter squared (kg·m²).**

Other moments of inertia can be found in your textbook, and are summarized as follows.

> hoop rotating about its center: $I = mr^2$
>
> hoop rotating about its diameter: $I = \left(\frac{1}{2}\right)mr^2$
>
> solid cylinder: $I = \left(\frac{1}{2}\right)mr^2$
>
> stick rotating about its center of gravity: $I = \left(\frac{1}{12}\right)m\ell^2$
>
> stick rotating about its end: $I = \left(\frac{1}{3}\right)m\ell^2$
>
> solid sphere rotating about its center of gravity: $I = \left(\frac{2}{5}\right)mr^2$

Newton's first law says that inertia is the tendency of an object to stay at rest or remain in motion in a straight line with a constant speed unless acted upon by an unbalanced force. Similarly, an object that is rotating tends to continue spinning at a constant rate unless an unbalanced force acts to alter that rotation. This is called the rotational inertia.

Think of moment of inertia as being the rotational equivalent of the term "mass." Just as inertia is greater for a greater mass, rotational inertia is greater for a greater moment of inertia.

Vocabulary   **Angular Momentum:** The measure of how difficult it is to stop a rotating object.

$$\textbf{angular momentum} = \textbf{(mass)(velocity)(radius)} \qquad \text{or} \qquad L = mvr$$

The SI unit for angular momentum is the **kilogram·meter squared per second (kg·m²/s).**

Think of angular momentum as being the rotational equivalent of *linear momentum.* Just as linear momentum is the product of the mass and the velocity, angular momentum is the product of the mass and the velocity for an object rotating at a distance r from the axis.

Momentum is conserved when no outside forces are acting. Similarly, angular momentum is conserved when no outside torques are acting. A spinning ice skater has angular momentum. When the skater pulls her arms in (decreasing her radius of spin), she spins faster (increasing her velocity). Doing so conserves her angular momentum.

Solved Examples

Example 7: On the Wheel of Fortune game show, a contestant spins the 15.0-kg wheel that has a radius of 1.40 m. What is the moment of inertia of this disk-shaped wheel?

Solution: A disk is a thin cylinder, so the moment of inertia of a disk is the same as that of a cylinder.

Given: $m = 15.0$ kg   Unknown: $I = ?$
         $r = 1.40$ m   Original equation: $I = \left(\frac{1}{2}\right)mr^2$

Solve: $I = \left(\frac{1}{2}\right)(15.0 \text{ kg})(1.40 \text{ m})^2 = \mathbf{14.7 \text{ kg} \cdot m^2}$

Example 8: Trish is twirling her 0.60-m majorette's baton that has a mass of 0.40 kg. What is the moment of inertia of the baton as it spins about its center of gravity?

Given: $m = 0.40$ kg   Unknown: $I = ?$
         $\ell = 0.60$ m   Original equation: $I = \left(\frac{1}{2}\right)m\ell^2$

Solve: $I = \left(\frac{1}{2}\right)m\ell^2 = \left(\frac{1}{2}\right)(0.40 \text{ kg})(0.60 \text{ m})^2 = \mathbf{0.072 \text{ kg} \cdot m^2}$

Example 9: At Wellesley College in Massachusetts there is a favorite tradition called hoop rolling. In their caps and gowns, seniors roll wooden hoops in a race in which the winner is said to be the first in the class to marry. Hilary rolls her 0.2-kg hoop across the finish line. The moment of inertia of the hoop is 0.032 kg·m². What is the radius of the hoop?

Given: $m = 0.2$ kg   Unknown: $r = ?$
         $I = 0.032$ kg·m²   Original equation: $I = mr^2$

Solve: $r = \sqrt{\dfrac{I}{m}} = \sqrt{\dfrac{0.032 \text{ kg} \cdot m^2}{0.2 \text{ kg}}} = \sqrt{0.16 \text{ m}^2} = \mathbf{0.4 \text{ m}}$

Example 10: Jupiter orbits the sun with a speed of 2079 m/s at an average distance of 71 398 000 m. a) If Jupiter has a mass of 1.90×10^{27} kg, what is its angular momentum as it orbits?

Given: $m = 1.90 \times 10^{27}$ kg   *Unknown:* $L = ?$
$\quad\quad\;\; v = 2079$ m/s   *Original equation:* $L = mvr$
$\quad\quad\;\; r = 71\,398\,000$ m

Solve: $L = mvr = (1.90 \times 10^{27}$ kg$)(2079$ m/s$)(71\,398\,000$ m$) = \mathbf{2.82 \times 10^{38}\ kg \cdot m^2/s}$

Practice Exercises

Exercise 18: Veanna is in Las Vegas waiting for her number to be called at the roulette
wheel, a large 3.0-kg disk of radius 0.60 m. What is the moment of inertia of
the wheel?

Answer: _____

Exercise 19: Earth has a mass of 5.98×10^{24} kg and a radius of 6.38×10^6 m. What is the
moment of inertia of Earth as it turns on its axis?

Answer: _____

Exercise 20: Olga, the 50.0-kg gymnast, swings her 1.6-m-long body around a bar by her
outstretched arms. a) What is Olga's moment of inertia? b) If Olga were to
pull in her legs, thereby cutting her body length in half, how would this
change her moment of inertia? (Assume her mass is evenly distributed all
along her body.)

Answer: **a.** _____

Answer: **b.** _____

Exercise 21: Priya removes her 0.012-kg, 0.60-cm-diameter wedding band and spins it on the coffee table on its edge. What is the moment of inertia of the ring?

Answer: _____

Exercise 22: Hickory dickory dock, the 20.0-g mouse ran up the clock, and took turns riding on the 0.20-m-long second hand, the 0.20-m-long minute hand, and the 0.10-m-long hour hand. What was the angular momentum of the mouse on each of the three hands?

Answer: _____

Answer: _____

Answer: _____

Exercise 23: In a physics experiment, Ingrid, the ice skater, spins around in the rink at 1.2 m/s with each of her arms stretched out 0.70 m from the center of her body. In each hand she holds a 1.0-kg mass. If angular momentum is conserved, how fast will Ingrid begin to spin if she pulls her arms to a position 0.15 m from the center of her body?

Answer: _____

Additional Exercises

A-1: In the Biblical tale of David and Goliath, the giant is slain when David hits him with a rock that he has spun around overhead in a sling. If the rock is spun with a frequency of 100 revolutions per minute, what is the rock's period?

A-2: Ashton the ant is crawling on the still blade of a ceiling fan when the fan is turned on, causing Ashton to go for a ride. If Ashton sits on the fan blade at a distance of 0.80 m from the center of the fan and turns with a frequency of 1.2 Hz, a) how fast does Ashton spin? b) If Ashton slips off the spinning fan, describe the path he will take.

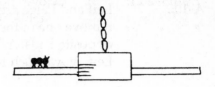

A-3: In "Rumpelstiltskin," the miller's daughter is spinning straw into gold on a spinning wheel that turns at a speed of 7.5 m/s, making one revolution every 0.50 s. How long is a strand of gold that makes one complete turn around the wheel?

A-4: A 3.20-kg hawk circles overhead in search of prey. a) If the hawk circles once every 10.0 s in a circle 12.0 m in radius, what is the linear speed of the hawk? b) What centripetal force allows him to remain in a circle? c) What is providing the centripetal force?

A-5: Sasha's favorite ride at the fair is the Ferris wheel that has a radius of 7.0 m. a) If the ride takes 20.0 s to make one full revolution, what is the linear speed of the wheel? b) What centripetal force will the ride exert on Sasha's 50.0-kg body? c) Does Sasha feel as if she is being pulled in or out by the ride? d) Explain the difference between what she feels and what is really happening at the top and bottom of the wheel.

A-6: In order for Sasha (in A-5) to feel weightless at the top of the ride, a) at what linear speed must the Ferris wheel turn? b) At this speed, how much will she appear to weigh at the bottom of the Ferris wheel?

A-7: Earth orbits the sun approximately once every 365.25 days at an average distance of about 1.5×10^{11} m. The mass of Earth is 5.98×10^{24}kg. a) What is the centripetal acceleration of Earth? b) What is the centripetal force of the sun on Earth? c) What is the centripetal force of Earth on the sun? d) If this force exists between the sun and Earth, does this mean that Earth is "falling into" the sun? Explain.

A-8: Most doorknobs are placed on the side of the door opposite the hinges instead of in the center of the door. a) Why is this so? b) If a torque of 1.2 N·m is required to open a door, how much force must be exerted on a doorknob 0.76 m from the hinges compared to a doorknob in the middle of the door, 0.38 m from the hinges?

A-9: Priscilla is working out in the gym with a 2.00-kg mass that she holds in one hand and gradually lifts up and down. a) Will Priscilla find it easier to lift the mass if she pivots her arm at the shoulder or at the elbow? b) If Priscilla's arm is 0.60 m long from her shoulder to her palm and 0.28 m long from her elbow to her palm, how much torque must she produce in each case to lift the weight?

A-10: Leif and Paige are rearranging the heights of their movable bookshelves; they remove one of the 2.00-kg, 0.60-m-long shelves by the two of them holding opposite ends. A 5.00-kg stack of books is piled up on the shelf 0.20 m from Leif. How much force must Leif and Paige each exert to hold the shelf level?

A-11: Brewster hits a 0.30-kg pool ball across the pool table and sinks it in the side pocket. If the pool ball has a radius of 3.5 cm, what is its moment of inertia as it rolls?

A-12: Rocky, a raccoon, squeezes into a 0.60-m-diameter cylindrical trash can to find a late-night snack. However, the can tips over and begins to roll. If Rocky and the can have a combined mass of 40.0 kg, what is the moment of inertia of the system?

A-13: Mieko sharpens a knife on a grinding wheel whose angular momentum is 27 kg·m^2/s. The 5.0-kg wheel has a radius of 0.30 m. What is the linear speed of the wheel?

Challenge Problems for Further Study

B-1: The "Bake-a-Lite" Cake Company truck is on its way to deliver a birthday cake for the MacKenzie party when it rounds a curve of radius 20.0 m at a speed of 12 m/s. What coefficient of friction is needed between the cake pan and the truck in order to keep the pan from slipping?

B-2: On his way home from the office, Steven's car rounds an unbanked curve that has a radius of 100 m. If the coefficient of friction between the tires and the road is 0.40, what is the fastest speed at which the car can round this curve without risking an accident?

B-3: Pretending to be Tarzan, 50.0-kg Zach swings from the end of a 5.0-m-long rope attached to a tree branch. The tree branch will break if subjected to a force greater than 750 N. What is the maximum speed with which Zach can swing in order to avoid breaking the branch?

B-4: Hanging in front of the office of Lewis Skeirik, D.D.M., is a sign that weighs 120 N and is suspended at the end of a 0.80-m-long support beam that weighs 10.0 N, as shown. What is the tension in a supporting wire that holds the sign at an angle of 20.0°?

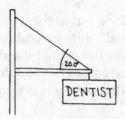

7   Law of Universal Gravitation

7-1 Gravitational Force

Vocabulary   **Law of Universal Gravitation:** Every particle attracts every other particle with a force that is proportional to the mass of the particles and inversely proportional to the square of the distance between them.

$$F \propto \frac{mM}{d^2}$$

The sign $\propto$ means "proportional to." To make an equation out of the above situation, insert a quantity called the **universal constant of gravitation, G.**

$$G = 6.67 \times 10^{-11} \text{ N} \cdot \text{m}^2/\text{kg}^2$$

Now the magnitude of this gravitational force can be represented as

$$\text{Force} = \frac{(\textbf{universal constant of gravitation})(\textbf{mass 1})(\textbf{mass 2})}{(\textbf{distance})^2}$$

$$\text{or} \quad F = \frac{GmM}{d^2}$$

Like all other forces, the gravitational force of attraction between two objects is measured in newtons.

Solved Examples

Example 1:   The gravitational force of attraction between Earth and the sun is 1.6×10^{23} N. What would this force have been if Earth were twice as massive?

Solution: The gravitational force of attraction between two bodies is proportional to the mass of each of the two bodies. As one mass increases, the gravitational force between the two bodies increases proportionally. Therefore, if Earth's mass were doubled, the gravitational force between the sun and Earth would double as well.

Therefore, $F = 2F_o = 2(1.6 \times 10^{23} \text{ N}) = \textbf{3.2} \times \textbf{10}^{\textbf{23}}$ **N**

Example 2: The gravitational force of attraction between Earth and the sun is 1.6×10^{23} N. What would this gravitational force have been if Earth had formed twice as far away from the sun?

Solution: The gravitational force of attraction between two bodies is inversely proportional to the square of the distance between them. In this case, if the distance is twice as great, the force between Earth and the sun would be 1/4 as much.

$$\text{Therefore, } F \propto \frac{1}{d^2} \quad \text{or} \quad F = \frac{F_o}{4} = \frac{(1.6 \times 10^{23}\,\text{N})}{4} = 4.0 \times 10^{22}\,\text{N}$$

Example 3: Oliver, whose mass is 65 kg, and Olivia, whose mass is 45 kg, sit 2.0 m apart in their physics classroom. a) What is the force of gravitational attraction between Oliver and Olivia? b) Why don't Oliver and Olivia drift toward each other?

a) *Given:* $m_{Oliver} = 65$ kg   *Unknown:* $F = ?$
$M_{Olivia} = 45$ kg   *Original equation:* $F = \dfrac{GmM}{d^2}$
$\phantom{Given:\ m_{Oliver} = }d = 2.0$ m
$\phantom{Given:\ m_{Oliver} = }G = 6.67 \times 10^{-11}$ Nm^2/kg^2

Solve: $F = \dfrac{GmM}{d^2} = \dfrac{(6.67 \times 10^{-11}\,\text{Nm}^2/\text{kg}^2)(65\,\text{kg})(45\,\text{kg})}{(2.0\,\text{m})^2} = 4.9 \times 10^{-8}\,\text{N}$

b) Because the gravitational force of Earth is much greater than the force Oliver and Olivia exert on each other.

Practice Exercises

Exercise 1: When Royce was 10 years old, he had a mass of 30 kg. By the time he was 16 years old, his mass increased to 60 kg. How much larger is the gravitational force between Royce and Earth at age 16 compared to age 10?

Age 10   Age 16

Answer: _____

Exercise 2: If John Glenn weighed 640 N on Earth's surface, a) how much would he have weighed if his Mercury spacecraft had (hypothetically) remained at twice the distance from the center of Earth? b) Why is it said that an astronaut is never truly "weightless?"

Answer: **a.** _____

Answer: **b.** _____

Exercise 3: Mr. Gewanter, whose mass is 60.0 kg, is doing a physics demonstration in the front of the classroom. a) How much gravitational force does he exert on 55.0-kg Martha in the front row, 1.50 m away? b) How does this compare to what he exerts on 65.0-kg Lester, 4.00 m away in the back row?

Answer: **a.** _____

Answer: **b.** _____

Exercise 4: Astrologers claim that your personality traits are determined by the positions of the planets in relation to you at birth. Scientists argue that these gravitational effects are so small that they are totally insignificant. Compare the gravitational attraction between you and Mars to the gravitational attraction between you and your 70.0-kg doctor at the moment of your birth, if the doctor stands 0.500 m away. (Note: $M_M = 6.42 \times 10^{23}$ kg, $d_{E\ to\ M} = 7.83 \times 10^{10}$ m. This is the average distance between Earth and Mars. This distance varies as the two planets orbit the sun.)

Answer: _____

Answer: _____

Exercise 5: Our galaxy, the Milky Way, contains approximately 4.0×10^{11} stars with an average mass of 2.0×10^{30} kg each. How far away is the Milky Way from our nearest neighbor, the Andromeda Galaxy, if Andromeda contains roughly the same number of stars and attracts the Milky Way with a gravitational force of 2.4×10^{30} N?

Answer: _____

Exercise 6: Tides are created by the gravitational attraction of the sun and moon on Earth. Calculate the net force pulling on Earth during a) a new moon, b) a full moon, c) a first quarter moon. The diagram is intended to help your understanding of the situation but is *not* drawn to scale. ($m_M = 7.35 \times 10^{22}$ kg, $m_E = 5.98 \times 10^{24}$ kg, $m_S = 1.99 \times 10^{30}$ kg, $d_{E-M} = 3.84 \times 10^8$ m, $d_{E-S} = 1.50 \times 10^{11}$ m)

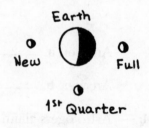

Answer: **a.** _____

Answer: **b.** _____

Answer: **c.** _____

7-2 Gravitational Acceleration

You can use the law of universal gravitation to find the gravitational acceleration, g, of any body if you know that body's mass and radius. For example, let's look at the situation on Earth. The weight of an object on Earth's surface is equal to the gravitational force between that object and Earth:

$$mg = \frac{GmM}{d^2}$$

The m on the left represents the mass of an object, such as a human being. The m on the right side of the equation stands for this same mass, so the term cancels out of the equation. The M on the right represents the mass of Earth or other celestial body on which the person is standing. The d in the denominator is equal to the radius of the celestial body. So the equation becomes

$$g = \frac{GM}{d^2}$$

In this equation, g is the acceleration due to gravity on the celestial body in question. On Earth you already know that this value is 10.0 m/s^2.

Solved Examples

Example 4: Temba is standing in the lunch line 6.38×10^6 m from the center of Earth. Earth's mass is 5.98×10^{24} kg. a) What is the acceleration due to gravity? b) When Temba eats his lunch and his mass increases, does this change the acceleration due to gravity?

a. *Given:* $M = 5.98 \times 10^{24}$ kg   *Unknown:* $g = ?$
          $d = 6.38 \times 10^6$ m   *Original equation:* $g = \dfrac{GM}{d^2}$
          $G = 6.67 \times 10^{-11} \text{ N} \cdot \text{m}^2/\text{kg}^2$

Solve: $g = \dfrac{GM}{d^2} = \dfrac{(6.67 \times 10^{-11} \text{ N} \cdot \text{m}^2/\text{kg}^2)(5.98 \times 10^{24} \text{ kg})}{(6.38 \times 10^6 \text{ m})^2} = 9.80 \text{ m/s}^2$

b. No, his acceleration due to gravity does not change because it is not dependent on his mass.

Example 5: The sun has a mass that is 333 000 times Earth's mass and a radius 109 times Earth's radius. What is the acceleration due to gravity on the sun?

Solution: One way to solve this exercise is to actually multiply the given values by the mass and radius of Earth. However, there is an easier and much neater way to come up with the correct answer. By working with ratios, you can find an answer without any information about Earth.

Given: $M_S = 333\ 000\ M_E$　　　　　*Unknown:* $g = ?$

　　　$G = 6.67 \times 10^{-11}\ \mathrm{N \cdot m^2/kg^2}$　*Original equation:* $g = \dfrac{GM}{d^2}$

　　　$d_s = 109\ d_E$

Solve: Set up the above equation as a ratio of sun to Earth before substituting numbers.

$$\frac{g_S}{g_E} = \frac{\dfrac{GM_S}{d_S^2}}{\dfrac{GM_E}{d_E^2}}$$

Simplifying gives　　$\dfrac{g_S}{g_E} = \dfrac{M_S d_E^2}{M_E d_S^2} = \dfrac{(333\ 000\ M_E)(d_E^2)}{(M_E)(109 d_E)^2} = \dfrac{(333\ 000)}{(109)^2} = 28.0$

Therefore, $g_S = 28.0\ g_E$ so the acceleration due to gravity on the sun is 28.0 times what it is on Earth. In other words, it is 28.0 times 10.0 m/s², or **280. m/s²**.

Practice Exercises

Exercise 7:　In *The Little Prince*, the Prince visits a small asteroid called B612. If asteroid B612 has a radius of only 20.0 m and a mass of 1.00×10^4 kg, what is the acceleration due to gravity on asteroid B612?

Answer: _____

Exercise 8:　In Exercise 5 in the previous section, what is the Andromeda Galaxy's acceleration rate toward the Milky Way?

Answer: _____

Exercise 9: Black holes are suspected when a visible star is being noticeably pulled by an invisible partner that is more than 3 times as massive as the sun. a) If a red giant (a dying star) is gravitationally accelerated at 0.075 m/s^2 toward an object that is 9.4×10^{10} m away, how large a mass must the unseen body possess? b) How many times more massive is the object than the sun? ($M_s = 1.99 \times 10^{30}$ kg)

Answer: **a.** ——————————

Answer: **b.** ——————————

Exercise 10: The planet Saturn has a mass that is 95 times Earth's mass and a radius that is 9.4 times Earth's radius. What is the acceleration due to gravity on Saturn?

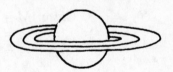

Answer: ——————————

7-3 Escape Speed

Vocabulary   **Escape Speed:** The minimum speed an object must possess in order to escape from the gravitational pull of a body.

In Chapter 5, you worked with gravitational potential energy and kinetic energy. When an object moves away from Earth, its gravitational potential energy increases. Since its total energy is conserved, its kinetic energy decreases. When the object is close to Earth, the gravitational force on it is a fairly constant mg. However, as you know, the gravitational force drops rapidly as you get farther from Earth. If an object moves upward from Earth with enough speed, it will never run out of kinetic energy and will escape from Earth.

The escape speed for an object leaving the surface of any celestial body of mass M and radius d is

$$v = \sqrt{\frac{2GM}{d}}$$

Notice that the mass of the escaping object does not affect the escape speed.

Solved Examples

Example 6:   Earth has a mass of 5.98×10^{24} kg and a radius of 6.38×10^6 km. What is the escape speed of a rocket launched on Earth?

Given: $M = 5.98 \times 10^{24}$ kg $\qquad$ *Unknown:* $v = ?$
$\qquad\quad d = 6.38 \times 10^6$ m $\qquad\qquad$ *Original equation:* $v = \sqrt{\frac{2GM}{d}}$
$\qquad\quad G = 6.67 \times 10^{-11}$ N·m²/kg²

Solve: $v = \sqrt{\frac{2GM}{d}} = \sqrt{\dfrac{2(6.67 \times 10^{-11} \text{ N·m}^2/\text{kg}^2)(5.98 \times 10^{24} \text{ kg})}{6.38 \times 10^6 \text{ m}}}$

$\qquad = \textbf{11 200 m/s}$

Any rocket trying to escape Earth's gravitational pull must be going at least 11 200 m/s before engine cut-off, in order to get away.

Example 7:   Compare Example 6 with the escape speed of a rocket launched from the moon. The mass of the moon is 7.35×10^{22} kg and the radius is 1.74×10^6 m.

Given: $M = 7.35 \times 10^{22}$ kg $\qquad$ *Unknown:* $v = ?$
$\qquad\quad d = 1.74 \times 10^6$ m $\qquad\qquad$ *Original equation:* $v = \sqrt{\frac{2GM}{d}}$
$\qquad\quad G = 6.67 \times 10^{-11}$ N·m²/kg²

$$\text{Solve: } v = \sqrt{\frac{2GM}{d}} = \sqrt{\frac{2(6.67 \times 10^{-11} \text{ N} \cdot \text{m}^2/\text{kg}^2)(7.35 \times 10^{22} \text{ kg})}{1.74 \times 10^6 \text{ m}}} = \textbf{2370 m/s}$$

Notice that you can escape from the moon by traveling much more slowly than you must travel to escape the gravitational pull of Earth. This is why launching a Lunar Module from the moon's surface was so much easier than launching an *Apollo* spacecraft from Earth.

Practice Exercise

Exercise 11:   How fast would you need to travel a) to escape the gravitational pull of the sun? ($M_S = 1.99 \times 10^{30}$ kg, $d_S = 6.96 \times 10^8$ m) b) As the sun begins to die, it will become a red giant. This means that its mass will remain the same but its diameter will increase substantially (perhaps even out as far as Earth's orbit!). When the sun becomes a red giant, will its escape speed be greater than, less than, or the same as, it is now?

Answer: **a.** ———————————

Answer: **b.** ———————————

Exercise 12:   How fast would the moon need to travel in order to escape the gravitational pull of Earth, if Earth has a mass of 5.98×10^{24} kg and the distance from Earth to the moon is 3.84×10^8 m?

Answer: ———————————

Exercise 13: What is the escape speed needed a) to escape the gravitational pull of Asteroid B612 (see Exercise 7)? b) What would happen if you jumped up on Asteroid B612?

Answer: a. _____

Answer: b. _____

Exercise 14: Scotty finds it difficult to play catch on planet Apgar because the planet's escape speed is only 5.00 m/s, and if Scotty throws the ball too hard, it flies away. If planet Apgar has a mass of 1.56×10^{15} kg, what is its radius?

Answer: _____

Additional Exercises

A-1: Halley's Comet orbits the sun about every 75 years due to the gravitational force the sun provides. Compare the gravitational force between Halley's Comet and the sun when the comet is at aphelion (its greatest distance from the sun) and d is about 4.5×10^{12} m to the force at perihelion (or closest approach), where d is about 5.0×10^{10} m.

A-2: In Exercise A-1, what is the comet's acceleration a) at aphelion? b) at perihelion? ($M_S = 1.99 \times 10^{30}$ kg)

A-3: An early planetary model of the hydrogen atom consisted of a 1.67×10^{-27}-kg proton in the nucleus and a 9.11×10^{-31}-kg electron in orbit around it at a distance of 5.0×10^{-11} m. In this model, what is the gravitational force between a proton and an electron?

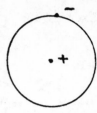

A-4: At what height above Earth would a 400.0-kg weather satellite have to orbit in order to experience a gravitational force half as strong as that on the surface of Earth?

A-5: It is said that people often behave in unusual ways during a full moon. a) Calculate the gravitational force that the moon would exert on a 50.0-kg student in your physics class. The moon is 3.84×10^8 m from Earth and has a mass of 7.35×10^{22} kg. b) Does the moon attract the student with a force that is greater than, less than, or the same as the force with which the student attracts the moon?

A-6: The tiny planet Mercury has a radius of 2400 km and a mass of 3.3×10^{23} kg. a) What would be the gravitational acceleration of an astronaut standing on the surface of Mercury? b) Compare the motion of a ball dropped on the surface of Mercury to that of a ball dropped on Earth.

A-7: The acceleration due to gravity on Venus is 0.89 that of Earth. a) If the radius of Venus is 6.05×10^6 m, what is Venus' mass? b) How does this compare to Earth's mass? c) If you were on a diet and had to "weigh in," would you rather stand on a scale on Venus or on Earth in order to appear as if you had lost the most weight?

A-8: The planet Mars has a mass that is 0.11 times Earth's mass and a radius that is 0.54 times Earth's radius. a) How much would a 60.0-kg astronaut weigh if she were to stand on the surface of Mars? b) Although Mercury is much smaller than Mars, it has almost the same gravitational acceleration. Describe how you might explain this phenomenon.

A-9: On October 26, 2000, the NEAR Shoemaker spacecraft swooped within 3 miles of the asteroid Eros, taking images and collecting data from a distance closer than any spacecraft has ever come to an asteroid. Eros has a mass of 6.69×10^{15} kg. The strange potato-like shape of Eros makes its diameter difficult to determine. If the NEAR spacecraft is orbiting a distance of 18 300 m from Eros' center of mass, what gravitational acceleration does Eros provide on NEAR?

A-10: Find the NEAR spacecraft's escape speed from Eros, using the information given in A-9.

A-11: NASA has announced that a mission to Mars to return rock samples to Earth could come as early as 2011. If NASA landed a 360.-kg spacecraft on the surface of Mars a) what would be the weight of the spacecraft on the planet's surface b) what escape speed would be needed for the craft to leave the planet and head back to Earth with its rock samples. ($M_m = 6.42 \times 10^{23}$ kg, $d_M = 3.39 \times 10^6$ m)

Challenge Exercises for Further Study

B-1: At what distance from Earth's center must a spacecraft be in order to experience the same gravitational attraction from both Earth and the moon when directly between the two? ($M_E = 5.98 \times 10^{24}$ kg, $M_M = 7.35 \times 10^{22}$ kg $d_{E-M} = 3.84 \times 10^8$ m)

B-2: Jupiter's innermost Galilean satellite, Io, is covered with active volcanoes, which exist because of the immense gravitational tugging on the satellite by Jupiter and the other moons near Io. Io orbits 4.2×10^8 m from the center of Jupiter. The other Galilean satellites are located as follows from Jupiter's center. Europa: 6.7×10^8 m, Ganymede: 1.0×10^9 m, and Callisto: 1.9×10^9 m. If Jupiter and its satellites are lined up as shown, what gravitational force does the satellite Io experience? ($M_I = 8.9 \times 10^{22}$ kg, $M_E = 4.9 \times 10^{22}$ kg, $M_G = 1.5 \times 10^{24}$ kg, $M_C = 1.1 \times 10^{23}$ kg, $M_J = 1.9 \times 10^{27}$ kg)

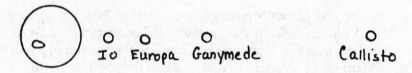

B-3: Saturn's satellite, Titan, orbits the planet in a little less than 16 days. Titan orbits Saturn at an average distance of 1.216×10^9 m from the center of the planet. Use this information to find the mass of Saturn.

8 Special Relativity

8-1 Time Dilation

Relative Speed

The speed of an object depends upon what frame of reference you use to measure that speed. If a ball is thrown forward out of a stationary car at 4 m/s, the ball will continue to travel horizontally at 4 m/s until it hits the ground. However, if the car is in motion, a number of different things can happen.

For example, according to a stationary observer, if the car is moving forward at 10 m/s, the ball is also traveling 10 m/s in addition to the 4 m/s given to the ball when it is thrown. Therefore, it has a speed relative to the observer of 14 m/s.

Now, if the ball is thrown at 4 m/s in a direction opposite to the car's motion, the initial 4 m/s with which the ball is thrown is subtracted from the 10 m/s speed of the forward-moving car. The ball has a speed of 6 m/s relative to a stationary observer. It is still moving in the same direction as the car but at a reduced speed with respect to the ground.

Time Dilation

When an object (such as a spaceship) is traveling near the speed of light, the time interval between two events that occur at the same place on the moving object seems longer from the perspective of a stationary observer than it does from the perspective of the moving observer. In other words, time appears to be **dilated,** or stretched out. The stationary observer thinks that the traveler's clock has slowed down. This dilation is written as

$$\Delta t = \frac{\Delta t_o}{\sqrt{1 - (v^2/c^2)}}$$

where Δt is the time interval between two events, as measured by an observer who is in motion with respect to the events;
Δt_o is the time interval between two events, as measured by an observer who is at rest with respect to the events (also called the proper time);
v is the speed of the moving object;
c is the speed of light.

Therefore, when a spaceship is traveling close to the speed of light, its inhabitants will appear to age more slowly and, in fact, all events will occur more slowly from the perspective of an Earth-based observer.

In physics, astronomical distances are often written with the unit **light-years,** (**ly**). A light-year is the distance light travels in 1 year. It is equivalent to 9.46×10^{15} m.

Solved Examples

Example 1: Farmer MacGregor is throwing bales of hay off the back of his hay wagon with a speed of 3 m/s relative to the wagon, which is pulled by a tractor moving forward with a speed of 7 m/s. With what horizontal velocity do the bales of hay hit the ground?

Solution: First, consider the direction of each of the velocities and treat them as vectors. Relative to the truck, the bales of hay are traveling at 3 m/s. However, relative to the ground, the speed is somewhat different, as shown.

$$7 \text{ m/s}$$

$$4 \text{ m/s} \qquad 3 \text{ m/s}$$

$v = 7$ m/s $- 3$ m/s $= 4$ **m/s (in the direction of the tractor's motion)**

Example 2: Monty is being pulled in his wagon with a speed of 2 m/s when he tosses in front of the wagon a Frisbee whose speed is 5 m/s relative to the ground. Neglecting air resistance, how fast is the Frisbee moving when his dog, Snoopy, catches it in his mouth?

Solution: The wagon is moving at 2 m/s while the Frisbee travels an additional 5 m/s in the same direction. Therefore,

$$2 \text{ m/s} \qquad 5 \text{ m/s}$$

$$7 \text{ m/s}$$

$v = 2$ m/s $+ 5$ m/s $= 7$ **m/s forward,** relative to the ground.

Example 3: A light beam takes 3.0×10^{-8} s to bounce back and forth vertically between two mirrors inside a moving spaceship, according to an observer on board the spaceship. How long would the beam take according to Gerard, a stationary observer on Earth, if the spacecraft were moving directly overhead in a direction perpendicular to the line of sight with a speed of $0.60c$?

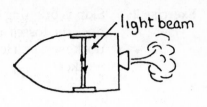

Solution: The number $0.60c$ in the exercise means that the speed of the spacecraft is $6/10$ the speed of light. The speed of light is represented with the letter c.

Given: $\Delta t_o = 3.0 \times 10^{-8}$ s

$v = 0.60c$

Unknown: $\Delta t = ?$

Original equation: $\Delta t = \dfrac{\Delta t_o}{\sqrt{1 - (v^2/c^2)}}$

Solve: $\Delta t = \dfrac{\Delta t_o}{\sqrt{1 - (v^2/c^2)}} = \dfrac{3.0 \times 10^{-8}\,\text{s}}{\sqrt{1 - [(0.60c)^2/c^2]}} = \dfrac{3.0 \times 10^{-8}\,\text{s}}{\sqrt{1 - 0.36}} = \dfrac{3.0 \times 10^{-8}\,\text{s}}{\sqrt{0.64}}$

$= \mathbf{4.7 \times 10^{-8}\ s}$

Therefore, if the spacecraft is traveling at $0.60c$, a time interval of 3.0×10^{-8} s according to the clocks on the spacecraft actually takes 4.7×10^{-8} s according to the clocks on Earth.

Practice Exercises

Exercise 1: Fiona is on her way home from France but she must leave her new-found love, Pierre, behind. As Fiona's train pulls out of the station at 4 m/s, Pierre tosses Fiona a bouquet of flowers with a speed of 6 m/s. According to Fiona, how fast are the flowers moving when she catches them?

Answer: _____

Exercise 2: Skip is bringing his boat into port with a speed of 7 m/s and as he nears the dock, he tosses a tow rope from the bow with a speed of 3 m/s to a waiting dock worker. How fast is the rope moving when it is caught by the dock worker?

Answer: _____

Exercise 3: Superman leaves Lois in Metropolis to rescue a malfunctioning space probe sent up from Earth. Flying at a speed of 0.70c, Superman reaches the probe in 20. hours according to his wristwatch. How long would the trip take according to Lois's clock on Earth?

Answer: _____

Exercise 4: An elementary particle called a pion has a lifetime of 2.6×10^{-8} s when at rest. a) Will its lifetime be longer or shorter, as viewed from the stationary frame of reference, if it is made to travel at 0.80c? b) What will its lifetime be according to a stationary observer?

Answer: **a.** _____

Answer: **b.** _____

Exercise 5: It is the year 3539 and, on his 30th birthday, Albert leaves for a new job opening on the planet Zil. After saying good-bye to his twin brother Henry, Albert jumps in his spacecraft and takes off for Zil traveling at a speed of 0.95c. The total trip takes 3.0 years according to the clocks on board Albert's spaceship. How old are Henry and Albert when the three-year journey is complete?

Answer: _____

Exercise 6: The brightest star visible from the northern hemisphere is the star Sirius, which is 8.7 light-years from Earth in the constellation of Canis Major. It takes a spaceship 4.9 y to travel from Earth to Sirius, according to the spaceship's on-board clocks. According to Earth clocks, the trip takes 10.0 years. At what fraction of the speed of light did the spacecraft travel?

Answer: _____

8-2 Relativistic Length and Energy

Length Contraction

When an object is traveling close to the speed of light, the length of that object along the direction of motion appears to shrink as seen by a stationary observer. In other words, length appears to **contract.** This contraction is written as

$$L = L_0 \sqrt{1 - (v^2/c^2)}$$

where L is the length (or distance) between two points as measured by an observer who is in motion with respect to the points;
L_o is the length (or distance) between two points as measured by an observer who is at rest with respect to the two points (also called the proper length);
v is the speed of the moving object;
c is the speed of light.

Therefore, when a spaceship is traveling close to the speed of light, the spaceship itself will seem shorter, from the perspective of an Earth-based observer.

Energy

Einstein proposed the idea that anything that has mass has energy. This energy is called the **rest energy**, E_o. It is measured in joules.

$$\text{rest energy} = \text{(rest mass)}\text{(speed of light)}^2 \quad \text{or} \quad E_o = m_o c^2$$

If the object is moving at a speed v, the total energy of the object is greater, as measured by a stationary observer.

$$E = mc^2 = \frac{E_o}{\sqrt{1 - (v^2/c^2)}} = \frac{m_o c^2}{\sqrt{1 - (v^2/c^2)}}$$

where E is the total energy of an object as measured by an observer who is in motion with respect to the object;
E_o is the total energy of an object as measured by an observer who is at rest with respect to the object;
m is the mass of the object as measured by an observer who is in motion with respect to the object;
m_o is the mass of the object as measured by an observer who is at rest with respect to the object;
v is the speed of the moving object;
c is the speed of light.

Solved Examples

Example 4: The star Betelgeuse in the constellation of Orion is 520 light-years away as perceived by an observer on Earth. If a space traveler journeyed to Betelgeuse at 99% the speed of light (0.99c), how long would this distance be according to the traveler?

Given: $L_o = 520$ ly   *Unknown:* $L = ?$
       $v = 0.99c$ *Original equation:* $L = L_o \sqrt{1 - (v^2/c^2)}$

Solve: $L = L_o\sqrt{1 - (v^2/c^2)} = (520 \text{ ly})\sqrt{1 - [(0.99c)^2/c^2]} = (520 \text{ ly})\sqrt{0.14}$
       $= \textbf{73 ly}$

So the distance to the star would appear considerably shorter to the space traveler.

Example 5: An electron and a positron meet, each with a rest mass of 9.11×10^{-31} kg, and are converted to energy (gamma rays). How much energy is converted from the rest energy into gamma rays in the collision?

Solution: Because the mass in this exercise is actually the combination of the electron's mass and the positron's mass, add these two masses together to obtain 1.82×10^{-30} kg.

Given: $m_o = 1.82 \times 10^{-30}$ kg   *Unknown:* $E = ?$
       $c = 3.00 \times 10^8$ m/s   *Original equation:* $E = m_oc^2$

Solve: $E = m_oc^2 = (1.82 \times 10^{-30} \text{ kg})(3.00 \times 10^8 \text{ m/s})^2 = \textbf{1.64} \times \textbf{10}^{-13}$ **J**

Example 6: A 10 000.-kg meteor falls to Earth from space. a) What is the rest energy of the meteor? b) When it is traveling at a speed of 0.0400c, what is the meteor's energy according to an observer on Earth?

a. *Given:* $m_o = 10\ 000.$ kg   *Unknown:* $E_o = ?$
         $c = 3.00 \times 10^8$ m/s   *Original equation:* $E_o = m_oc^2$

Solve: $E_o = m_oc^2 = (10\ 000. \text{ kg})(3.00 \times 10^8 \text{ m/s})^2 = \textbf{9.00} \times \textbf{10}^{21}$ **J**

b. *Given:* $E_o = 9.00 \times 10^{21}$ J   *Unknown:* $E = ?$
         $v = 0.0400c$ *Original equation:* $E = \dfrac{E_o}{\sqrt{1 - (v^2/c^2)}}$

Solve: $E = \dfrac{E_o}{\sqrt{1 - (v^2/c^2)}} = \dfrac{9.00 \times 10^{21} \text{ J}}{\sqrt{1 - [(0.0400c)^2/c^2]}} = \textbf{9.01} \times \textbf{10}^{21}$ **J**

Practice Exercises

Exercise 7: The year is 2100, and a sports car company claims to have invented a new car that can travel at 0.500c. You take one of these cars for a test drive past your house, which is 15.0 m wide. How wide does your house appear to be when the car is up to full speed?

Answer: _____

Exercise 8: A stretch limo of the future is 8.0 m long but appears to be only 6.0 m long when driven at speeds near the speed of light. How fast must Linda the limo driver be going to make the limo appear 6.0 m long to an outside observer?

Answer: _____

Exercise 9: The starship *Enterprise* is traveling past Jupiter at a speed of 0.7500c. a) If Jupiter has a diameter of 142 796 km, how wide is Jupiter according to the crew of the *Enterprise*? b) What shape will Jupiter appear to have?

Answer: **a.** _____

Answer: **b.** _____

Exercise 10: The net result of a hydrogen fusion reaction is that four hydrogen atoms combine to form one helium atom. The mass lost when rest energy is converted into radiation energy in the reaction is 4.59×10^{-29} kg. a) How much radiation energy does this reaction produce? b) In what form can this energy be observed here on Earth?

Answer: **a.** _____

Answer: **b.** _____

Exercise 11: A nuclear reactor releases 9.1×10^{13} J of energy during fission. How much mass is needed to create this amount of energy?

Answer: _____

Exercise 12: In particle accelerators such as the CERN accelerator in Geneva, Switzerland, particles are accelerated to speeds near that of light. If a proton of rest mass 1.67×10^{-27} kg travels at a speed of $0.95c$, what is the total energy of the proton according to a stationary observer?

Answer: _____

Additional Exercises

A-1: Juan gets on the school bus in the morning and, as the driver starts to pull away, Juan's mother runs toward the bus with Juan's lunch bag in her hand. When the bus is traveling at a speed of 12 m/s, Mom tosses the lunch bag to Juan and he reaches out the open window to catch it. If the bag is moving 3 m/s according to Juan, with what speed did Mom throw the lunch bag?

A-2: Ming and Wong are playing a game of table tennis in the recreation car of a train. Each boy hits the ball with a speed of 20 m/s. a) If the train is traveling at 30 m/s, describe the speed of the ball as seen by an observer standing on the ground behind the railroad crossing guardrail. b) How would Ming and Wong describe the ball's speed?

A-3: The year is 2092 and the beings of the planet Quigg have captured an alien whom they are transporting home to show to the Quiggians. The trip takes 5.0 years, traveling at a speed of $0.80c$ according to the alien's on-board clock. How long will the trip take according to the inhabitants of planet Quigg?

A-4: SpaceTours, Inc. is booking passage on a ship that will travel through space at a speed of $0.70c$. The journey will last 5.0 years according to a stationary observer on Earth. How long will Margie, one of the passengers, be gone according to the on-board clock?

A-5: As the Rebel Forces fly by the *Death Star* at a speed of 0.980c, what is the apparent diameter of the *Death Star* if its actual diameter is 7000. m?

A-6: Every time Pinocchio tells a lie, his nose grows 1.0 cm. In the past few weeks Pinocchio has told many lies and his nose is now 10.0 cm long. How fast must Pinocchio travel to make his nose appear to be 2.0 cm long to a stationary observer?

A-7: Assume that all of the radiation energy in the Big Bang was converted into the rest energy of the matter that is now the known universe. If the universe has a rest mass of 10^{51} kg, how much radiation energy will be released if the universe eventually undergoes a "Big Crunch"?

A-8: At the Bates Linear Accelerator in Middleton, Massachusetts, electrons are accelerated to near-light speeds inside a giant underground tunnel. If a 9.11×10^{-31}-kg electron is traveling at 0.89c, what is its total energy?

Challenge Exercises for Further Study

B-1: You are riding in a station wagon on a two-lane highway at 30 m/s, and you pass a sedan going in the other direction at 25 m/s.
a) Why does the sedan appear to be moving so much faster than you are?
b) How fast does the sedan appear to be moving from your perspective?
c) How fast does your station wagon appear to be moving relative to the sedan?
d) How would your answers to (b) and (c) change if the sedan were moving in the same direction as your car?
e) How fast does each car appear to be moving to an observer standing by the side of the road?

B-2: Leon observes that his heart beats 60.0 times per minute from his own frame of reference.
a) If Leon gets into a rocket on his 15th birthday and flies away from Earth fast enough so that his heartbeat appears to occur half as frequently as observed from Earth, how fast is the rocket traveling?
b) How old is Leon if he returns to Earth after Earth-based clocks said that he had been gone for 12.0 years?

9 Solids, Liquids, and Gases

9-1 Density

Vocabulary **Density:** A measure of how much mass occupies a given space.

$$\textbf{density} = \frac{\textbf{mass}}{\textbf{volume}} \quad \text{or} \quad D = \frac{m}{V}$$

The SI unit for density is the **kilogram per cubic meter (kg/m³)**.

Density is a characteristic property of a material. The density of an object does not change if the object is broken into smaller pieces. Although each piece now has less mass than the original object, it has less volume as well. Therefore, the density remains the same.

Think of density as describing how "compact" an object is. Remember, the density of a material can change with temperature because atoms and molecules move faster when they are heated, and thus usually occupy more space.

Solved Examples

Example 1: While doing dishes, Zvi drops his 3.00×10^{-3}-kg platinum wedding band into the dishwater, displacing a volume of 1.40×10^{-7} m³ of water. What is the density of the plantinum band?

Given: $m = 3.00 \times 10^{-3}$ kg   *Unknown:* $D = ?$
        $V = 1.40 \times 10^{-7}$ m³   *Original equation:* $D = \dfrac{m}{V}$

Solve: $D = \dfrac{m}{V} = \dfrac{3.00 \times 10^{-3} \text{ kg}}{1.40 \times 10^{-7} \text{ m}^3} = \textbf{2.14} \times \textbf{10}^\textbf{4} \textbf{ kg/m}^\textbf{3}$

Example 2: At a temperature of 4 °C, 5000. kg of water will fill a volume of 5.000 m³. What is the density of water at 4 °C?

Given: $m = 5000.$ kg   *Unknown:* $D = ?$
        $V = 5.000$ m³   *Original equation:* $D = \dfrac{m}{V}$

Solve: $D = \dfrac{m}{V} = \dfrac{5000. \text{ kg}}{5.000 \text{ m}^3} = \textbf{1000. kg/m}^\textbf{3}$

Practice Exercises

Exercise 1: The planet Saturn has a mass of 5.69×10^{26} kg and a volume of 8.01×10^{23} m^3. a) What is the density of Saturn? b) Would Saturn sink or float if you could place it in a gigantic bathtub filled with water?

Answer: **a.** _____

Answer: **b.** _____

Exercise 2: You are handed a 5.00×10^{-3}-kg coin and told that it is gold. You discover that the coin has a volume of 5.90×10^{-7} m^3. You know that the density of gold is 19 300 kg/m^3. Have you really been handed a gold coin, or simply a good imitation?

Answer: _____

Exercise 3: Diamond has a density of 3520 kg/m^3. During a physics lab, a diamond drops out of Virginia's necklace and falls into her graduated cylinder filled with 5.00×10^{-5} m^3 of water. This causes the water level to rise to the 5.05×10^{-5}−m^3 mark. What is the mass of Virginia's diamond?

Answer: _____

Exercise 4: You are given three different liquids—water, oil and glycerin—and asked to predict which will occupy the top, middle, and bottom layers when all three are poured into the same beaker. You take down the following data:

	mass (in kg)	volume (in m³)
water	0.1000	1.00×10^{-4}
oil	0.0500	5.39×10^{-5}
glycerin	0.0400	3.17×10^{-5}

By finding the densities, determine how these liquids will layer themselves in the beaker from top to bottom.

Answer: _____

9-2 Solids

Compression and Stretching

Vocabulary   **Elasticity:** A property of a body that causes it to deform when a force is exerted and return to its original shape when the deforming force is removed, within certain limits.

Vocabulary   **Stress:** The force exerted on an area divided by the area.

$$\text{stress} = \frac{\text{force}}{\text{area}} = \frac{F}{A}$$

The SI unit of stress is the **newton per square meter (N/m²)**.

Vocabulary   **Strain:** The ratio of change in dimension to original dimension.

Most often strain is used in describing the change in length of an object when a force is exerted.

$$\text{strain} = \frac{\text{change in length}}{\text{original length}} = \frac{\Delta L}{L}$$

Because strain is a ratio of lengths, it has no units.

Stress and strain are proportional to each other, and their ratio is equal to the elasticity of the material. The elasticity of a material is called the stretch modulus or **Young's modulus, Y**.

$$\text{Young's modulus} = \frac{\text{stress}}{\text{strain}} \quad \text{or} \quad Y = \frac{F/A}{\Delta L/L} = \frac{FL}{A\Delta L}$$

The SI unit for Young's modulus is the **newton per square meter (N/m^2)**.

Shearing

Shearing is another way of applying stress to an object to cause a distortion. However, this type of distortion is not one of dimension, but one of shape. For example, the book in Figure A will look like the one in Figure B when it is sheared.

Figure A   Figure B

In this case, the shearing stress is the force exerted on the area of one of the pages and the strain is the ratio of the horizontal distance the book moves, ΔL, to the original width of the book, L. The ratio of stress to strain is equal to the elastic modulus or the **shearing modulus, S**.

$$\text{shearing modulus} = \frac{\text{shearing stress}}{\text{shearing strain}} \quad \text{or} \quad S = \frac{F/A}{\Delta L/L} = \frac{FL}{A\Delta L}$$

Solved Examples

Example 3: Jason, the piano tuner, is tuning a 0.50-m-long steel piano wire of cross-sectional area 0.18 cm^2 by stretching it with a force of 1200 N. By how much does this lengthen the wire? ($Y_{\text{steel}} = 2.0 \times 10^{11}$ N/m^2)

Solution: First, convert cm^2 to m^2.   0.18 cm$^2 = 1.8 \times 10^{-5}$ m^2

Given: $L = 0.50$ m   *Unknown:* $\Delta L = ?$
$\quad\quad\quad F = 1200$ N   *Original equation:* $Y = \dfrac{FL}{A\Delta L}$
$\quad\quad\quad A = 1.8 \times 10^{-5}$ m^2
$\quad\quad\quad Y = 2.0 \times 10^{11}$ N/m^2

Solve: $\Delta L = \dfrac{FL}{YA} = \dfrac{(1200 \text{ N})(0.50 \text{ m})}{(2.0 \times 10^{11} \text{ N/m}^2)(1.8 \times 10^{-5} \text{ m}^2)} = \mathbf{1.7 \times 10^{-4} \text{ m}}$

Example 4: While writing his history research paper, Brent reaches across the library table for his dictionary and pulls it toward himself by the edge of the top cover with a force of 16 N, displacing the cover by 0.02 m. The top of the 0.05-m-thick dictionary measures 0.05 m². What is the shear modulus of the dictionary?

Given: $F = 16 \text{ N}$

$A = 0.05 \text{ m}^2$

$L = 0.05 \text{ m}$

$\Delta L = 0.02 \text{ m}$

Unknown: $S = ?$

Original equation: $S = \dfrac{FL}{A\Delta L}$

Solve: $S = \dfrac{FL}{A\Delta L} = \dfrac{(16 \text{ N})(0.05 \text{ m})}{(0.05 \text{ m}^2)(0.02 \text{ m})} = \mathbf{800 \text{ N/m}^2}$

Practice Exercises

Exercise 5: Two leopards are fighting over a piece of meat they caught while hunting. The leopards pull on the meat muscle with a force of 100. N, stretching the 0.10-m-long tendon by 0.0080 m. If the cross-sectional area of the tendon is $1.0 \times 10^{-5} \text{ m}^2$, what is its stretch modulus?

Answer: _____

Exercise 6: Before heading out on her big date, Ling stands in front of the bathroom mirror brushing her 0.25-m-long hair with a force of 2.0 N. If the cross-sectional area of a piece of hair is $1.0 \times 10^{-7} \text{ m}^2$, by how much does the hair stretch when it is brushed? ($Y_{hair} = 2.0 \times 10^9 \text{ N}$)

Answer: _____

Exercise 7: When a piece of wood is distorted by a karate chop, the top of the board is compressed while the bottom is stretched as shown. Therefore, you must first consider the change in length of the bottom of the board where the break begins. Chantal is a black belt in karate and she breaks a 30.0-cm piece of wood with a force of 70.0 N, changing it in length by 4.0×10^{-4} cm. What is the cross-sectional area of the piece of wood? ($Y_{wood} = 1.0 \times 10^9$ N/m^2)

Answer: _____

Exercise 8: While Miss Levesque is erasing the blackboard with her 9.0×10^{-3}-m^2 eraser, the eraser is subjected to a great amount of shearing force. If a 2.0-cm-thick eraser is pushed with a horizontal force of 1.5 N, displacing the top of the eraser by 5.0 mm, what is the shear modulus of the eraser?

Answer: _____

Exercise 9: Jorge is running down the newly-waxed school hallway and tries to slide across the floor in his sneakers. The 2.0-cm thick rubber soles each have a cross-sectional area of 0.020 m^2 and are sheared with a force of 15 000 N.
a) How much are the shoes displaced horizontally? b) Why does Jorge fall forward? ($S_{rubber} = 5.0 \times 10^9$ N/m^2)

Answer: a. _____

Answer: b. _____

9-3 Liquids

Vocabulary   **Hydrostatic Pressure:** The pressure exerted on an object by a column of fluid.

The hydrostatic pressure depends upon the original atmospheric pressure pushing on the surface of the fluid, and upon the fluid's density and height.

The farther an object is located below the surface of the fluid, the greater the pressure acting on it.

hydrostatic pressure =
atmospheric pressure + (density)(acceleration due to gravity)(height)

$$P_h = P_a + Dgh$$

For these exercises, assume that normal atmospheric pressure is 1.01×10^5 Pa.

Recall from Chapter 3 that a pascal (Pa) is equivalent to a newton per square meter (N/m^2).

Archimedes' Principle

According to **Archimedes' principle**, an object completely or partially immersed in a fluid is pushed up by a force that is equal to the weight of the displaced fluid.

buoyant force = (density)(acceleration due to gravity)(volume)

$$F_b = DgV$$

Here the density and volume are those of the displaced fluid. This equation can be used whether the object sinks or floats. However, if the object is only partially submerged, the volume used in the calculation is that of the submerged portion. Therefore, for a floating object, the buoyant force is equal to the weight of the object itself.

Pascal's Principle

According to **Pascal's principle**, the change in pressure on one part of a confined fluid is equal to the change in pressure on any other part of the confined fluid.

$$\Delta P = \frac{F_1}{A_1} = \frac{F_2}{A_2}$$

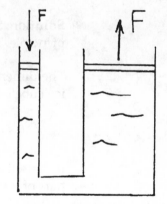

Therefore, a small force exerted over a small area will result in a large force exerted over a large area. An application of Pascal's principle is found in hydraulic lifts, which are used to raise automobiles off the ground. In a hydraulic lift, the force exerted on a smaller piston provides a pressure that is applied, undiminished, to the larger piston, enabling it to lift the car.

Solved Examples

Example 5: Wanda watches the fish in her fish tank and notices that the angel fish like to feed at the water's surface, while the catfish feed 0.300 m below at the bottom of the tank. If the average density of the water in the tank is 1000. kg/m^3, what is the pressure on the catfish?

Solution: Solve this exercise using the equation for hydrostatic pressure.

Given: $P_a = 1.01 \times 10^5$ Pa   Unknown: $P_h = ?$
$\quad\quad D = 1000.$ kg/m^3 Original equation: $P_h = P_a + Dgh$
$\quad\quad g = 10.0$ m/s^2
$\quad\quad h = 0.300$ m

Solve: $P_h = P_a + Dgh = (1.01 \times 10^5$ Pa$) + (1000.$ kg/m$^3)(10.0$ m/s$^2)(0.300$ m$)$
$\quad\quad = 1.01 \times 10^5$ Pa $+ 3.00 \times 10^3$ Pa $= \mathbf{1.04 \times 10^5}$ **Pa**

Example 6: Phyllis is being fed intravenously in her hospital bed from a bottle 0.400 m above her arm that contains a nutrient solution whose density is 1025 kg/m^3. What is the pressure of the fluid that is going into Phyllis' arm?

Given: $D = 1025$ kg/m^3 Unknown: $P_a = ?$
$\quad\quad h = 0.400$ m   Original equation: $P_h + P_a + Dgh$
$\quad\quad g = 10.0$ m/s^2
$\quad\quad P_a = 1.01 \times 10^5$ Pa

Solve: $P_h = P_a + Dgh = (1.01 \times 10^5$ Pa$) + (1025$ kg/m$^3)(10.0$ m/s$^2)(0.400$ m$)$
$\quad\quad = 1.01 \times 10^5$ Pa $+ 4.10 \times 10^3$ Pa $= \mathbf{1.05 \times 10^5}$ **Pa**

Example 7: Palmer drops an ice cube into his glass of water. The ice, whose density is 917 kg/m^3, has dimensions of 0.030 m $\times$ 0.020 m $\times$ 0.020 m, as shown in the diagram. What is the buoyant force acting on the ice?

Solution: Solve this exercise using Archimedes' principle.

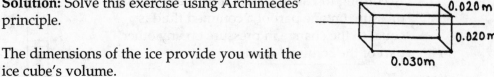

The dimensions of the ice provide you with the ice cube's volume.

$$0.030 \text{ m} \times 0.020 \text{ m} \times 0.020 \text{ m} = 1.2 \times 10^{-5} \text{ m}^3$$

Because the density of the water is less than the ice, the ice will float so that part of it is above the surface. Therefore,

buoyant force = weight of water displaced = weight of ice

Given: D_{ice} = 917 kg/m^3 *Unknown:* F_b = ?
     g = 10.0 m/^{2} *Original equation:* $F_b = DgV$
     V = 1.2 × 10^{-5} m^3

Solve: $F_b = D_{ice}gV$ = (917 kg/m^3)(10.0 m/s^2)(1.2 × 10^{-5} m^3) = **0.11 N**

Therefore, the water pushes the ice cube up with a force of 0.11 N.

Example 8:   Every Sunday morning, Dad takes the family trash to the trash compactor in the basement. When he presses the button on the front of the compactor, a force of 350 N pushes down on the 1.3-cm^2 input piston, causing a force of 22 076 N to crush the trash. What is the area of the output piston that crushes the trash?

Solution: Solve this exercise using Pascal's principle.

Given: F_1 = 350 N   *Unknown:* A_2 = ? $\dfrac{F_1}{A_1} = \dfrac{F_2}{A_2}$
     A_1 = 1.3 cm^2 *Original equation:*
     F_2 = 22 076 N

Solve: $A_2 = \dfrac{F_2 A_1}{F_1} = \dfrac{(22\ 076\ \text{N})(1.3\ \text{cm}^2)}{350\ \text{N}}$ = **82 cm^2**

Practice Exercises

Exercise 10:   The head of a giraffe is 2.0 m above its heart and the density of the blood is 1.05 × 10^3 kg/m^3. What is the difference in pressure between the giraffe's heart and head? (Fortunately, a giraffe's neck has a special circulatory system to adapt to this neck length, producing an even flow of blood to the head.)

Answer: _____

Exercise 11:   How much pressure is needed in ground-based water pipes to pump water up to the restaurant on the top floor of the World Trade Center, 410 m above the ground?

Answer: _____

Exercise 12: The difference in pressure between the atmosphere and the human lungs is 1.05×10^5 Pa. What is the longest straw you could use to draw up milk whose density is 1030 kg/m³?

Answer: _____

Exercise 13: Cadir is basting a roast turkey with a meat baster that creates a pressure of 9.980×10^4 Pa when the plastic bulb is squeezed and released. If turkey juice rises 0.0900 m up the tube of the baster, what is the density of the juice?

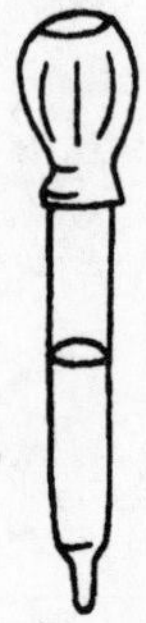

Answer: _____

Exercise 14: A 5450-m³ blimp circles Fenway Park during the World Series, suspended in Earth's 1.21-kg/m³ atmosphere. The density of the helium in the blimp is 0.178 kg/m³. a) What is the buoyant force that suspends the blimp in the air? b) How does this buoyant force compare to the blimp's weight? c) How much weight, in addition to the helium, can the blimp carry and still continue to maintain a constant altitude?

Answer: **a.** _____

Answer: **b.** _____

Answer: **c.** _____

Exercise 15: Ivory soap will float when placed in water so that most of the soap is suspended below the surface, and only a small fraction sticks up above the water line. A bar of soap has dimensions of 9.00 cm × 6.00 cm × 3.00 cm, as shown, and a density of 994 kg/m³. What is the buoyant force acting on the soap?

Answer: _____

Exercise 16: Eliza, the auto mechanic, is raising a 1200.-kg car on her hydraulic lift so that she can work underneath. If the area of the input piston is 12.0 cm², while the output piston has an area of 700. cm², what force must be exerted on the input piston to lift the car?

Answer: _____

Exercise 17: Allegra's favorite ride at the Barrel-O-Fun Amusement Park is the Flying Umbrella, which is lifted by a hydraulic jack. The operator activates the ride by applying a force of 72 N to a 3.0-cm-wide cylindrical piston, which holds the 20 000.-N ride off the ground. What is the diameter of the piston that holds the ride?

Answer: _____

9-4 Gases

The **ideal gas law** expresses the relationship between the pressure, volume, and temperature of a gas.

In the exercises in this chapter, the mass of the gas remains constant. You will be examining relationships between changes in pressure, volume, or temperature, using a combined form of the law that reads:

$$\frac{(\text{Pressure}_1)(\text{Volume}_1)}{\text{Temperature }_1} = \frac{(\text{Pressure}_2)(\text{Volume}_2)}{\text{Temperature }_2} \qquad \text{or} \qquad \frac{P_1 V_1}{T_1} = \frac{P_2 V_2}{T_2}$$

where the subscript "1" signifies the initial conditions and the subscript "2" signifies the final conditions.

When you do calculations with the ideal gas law, use the correct SI units. Temperature is measured in **kelvins (K)**, pressure is measured in **pascals (Pa)**, and volume is measured in **cubic meters (m^3)**. See Chapter 10 for an explanation of the Kelvin temperature scale.

If the temperature remains constant, the relationship between changes in pressure and volume is known as **Boyle's law.** Boyle's law says that volume decreases as the pressure increases. If the pressure remains constant, the relationship between changes in volume and temperature is known as **Charles' law.** Charles' law says that volume increases as the temperature increases.

Solved Examples

Example 9: To capture its prey, a whale will create a cylindrical wall of bubbles beneath the surface of the water, trapping confused fish inside. If an air bubble has a volume of 5.0 cm^3 at a depth where the water pressure is 2.00×10^5 Pa, what is the volume of the bubble just before it breaks the surface of the water?

Solution: In this exercise, the temperature remains the same. Remove it from both sides of the equation.

Given: $P_1 = 2.00 \times 10^5$ Pa   *Unknown:* $V_2 = ?$
   $V_1 = 5.00$ cm^3 *Original equation:* $P_1 V_1 = P_2 V_2$
   $P_2 = 1.01 \times 10^5$ Pa

Solve: $V_2 = \dfrac{P_1 V_1}{P_2} = \dfrac{(2.00 \times 10^5 \text{ Pa})(5.00 \text{ cm}^3)}{1.01 \times 10^5 \text{ Pa}} = \textbf{9.90 cm}^3$

Example 10: Tootie, a clown, carries a 2.00×10^{-3}-m^3 helium-filled mylar balloon from the 295-K heated circus tent to the cold outdoors, where the temperature is 273 K. How much does the volume of the balloon decrease?

Solution: In this exercise the pressure remains constant. Therefore, remove it from both sides of the equation.

Given: $V_1 = 2.00 \times 10^{-3} \text{ m}^3$ Unknown: $V_2 = ?$ $\dfrac{V_1}{T_1} = \dfrac{V_2}{T_2}$
       $T_1 = 295 \text{ K}$ Original equation:
       $T_2 = 273 \text{ K}$

Solve: $V_2 = \dfrac{V_1 T_2}{T_1} = \dfrac{(2.00 \times 10^{-3} \text{ m}^3)(273 \text{ K})}{295 \text{ K}} = 1.85 \times 10^{-3} \text{ m}^3$

$V_1 - V_2 = (2.00 \times 10^{-3} \text{ m}^3) - (1.85 \times 10^{-3} \text{ m}^3) = \mathbf{0.15 \times 10^{-3} \text{ m}^3}$

Example 11: Taylor is cooking a pot roast for dinner in a pressure cooker. Water will normally boil at a temperature of 373 K and an atmospheric pressure of 1.01×10^5 Pa. What is the boiling temperature inside the pot, when the pressure is increased to 1.28×10^5 Pa? The pot maintains a constant volume.

Solution: In this example the volume remains constant. Therefore, remove it from both sides of the equation.

Given: $P_1 = 1.01 \times 10^5 \text{ Pa}$ Unknown: $T_2 = ?$ $\dfrac{P_1}{T_1} = \dfrac{P_2}{T_2}$
       $T_1 = 373 \text{ K}$ Original equation:
       $P_2 = 1.28 \times 10^5 \text{ Pa}$

Solve: $T_2 = \dfrac{P_2 T_1}{P_1} = \dfrac{(1.28 \times 10^5 \text{ Pa})(373 \text{ K})}{1.01 \times 10^5 \text{ Pa}} = \mathbf{473 \text{ K}}$

Practice Exercises

Exercise 18: The Caloric value of food is measured with a device called a bomb calorimeter. Oxygen is forced into this sealed container and kept at a constant volume. Once the internal pressure is increased to 1.50×10^5 Pa, a small piece of food inside the calorimeter is ignited with a spark. As the food burns, the temperature inside the sealed vessel rapidly increases from 293 K to 523 K. What is the new pressure of the gas inside the chamber when the temperature rises?

Answer: ─────────────

Exercise 19: Brandon takes Yvonne on a surprise hot-air balloon ride for her birthday. However, once the pair is airborne, Yvonne announces that she is afraid of heights. The 2200.-m³ balloon is filled to capacity with 350.0 K air at a height where the surrounding air presure is 1.01×10^5 Pa. When Brandon turns off the heating unit, the air in the balloon begins to cool and the balloon descends. a) Why do both the pressure and volume of the air in the balloon remain constant, even though the balloon's air cools to a temperature of 300.0 K? b) Hot-air balloons are always made so that the bottom remains open throughout the flight. By how much would the balloon's volume change if the balloon could be manually closed as the temperature dropped to 300.0 K? (Assume atmospheric pressure remains constant.)

Answer: **a.** _____

Answer: **b.** _____

Exercise 20: During Annette's first airplane ride, her plane ascends from sea level, where cabin pressure is 1.01×10^5 Pa, to flying altitude, where the cabin pressure drops slightly to 1.00×10^5 Pa despite pressurized conditions. Annette feels a sensation in her middle ear, whose volume is 6.0×10^{-7} m³. a) What is the new volume of air inside Annette's middle ear? b) What could Annette do to compensate for this change in volume?

Answer: **a.** _____

Answer: **b.** _____

Exercise 21: Theo has won a a new car on a game show, and when his shiny new vehicle arrives on a warm 301-K (28°C) fall day, the 0.016-m³ tires have an air pressure of 2.02×10^5 Pa. However, two weeks later, when the temperature drops to 273 K (0°C), Theo's pressure gauge reads only 1.90×10^5 Pa. What is the new volume of the car tires?

Answer: _____

Additional Exercises

A-1: A 1.9–kg piece of wood from a sunken pirate ship has a volume of 2.16×10^{-3} m^3. Will this piece of wood float to the surface of the water or remain submerged with the ship?

A-2: Ursula drops a 0.0330-kg ice cube into her glass of soda water. The ice cube has dimensions of 3.0 cm $\times$ 3.0 cm $\times$ 4.0 cm. Does the ice cube float or sink in Ursula's drink?

A-3: Which is more dense, a 20.0-g silver bullet that occupies a volume of 1.9 cm^3, or the 5.98×10^{24}-kg Earth, that occupies a volume of 1.08×10^{21} m^3?

A-4: In her gymnastics routine, Regina dismounts from the uneven–parallel bars and lands straight-legged on the ground, compressing her 0.250–m–long femur by 2.10×10^{-5} m. If the femur has a cross-sectional area of 3.00×10^{-4} m^2 and the stress modulus of bone is 2.00×10^{10} N/m^2, with how much force does Regina hit the ground?

A-5: When they go swimming in their favorite water hole, Jeb and Dixie like to swing over the water on an old tire attached to a tree branch with a 3.0-m nylon rope. If the diameter of the rope is 2.00 cm, by how much does the rope stretch when 60.0-kg Dixie swings from it? ($Y_{nylon} = 3.7 \times 10^9$ N/m^2)

A-6: Lucy is going skin diving to see coral off the coast of Mexico in sea water with a density of 1025 kg/m^3. a) How great is the pressure pushing on Lucy at a depth of 20.0 m? b) How will the pressure change if Lucy swims deeper?

A-7: A water tower sits on the top of a hill and supplies water to the citizens below. The difference in pressure between the water tower and the Daileys' house is 1.1×10^5 Pa, while the difference in pressure between the tower and the Stearns' house is 3.2×10^5 Pa. a) Which house sits at a higher elevation, the Daileys' or the Stearns'? b) What is the difference in elevation between the two houses?

A-8: Eileen is floating on her back in the beautiful blue Caribbean during her spring vacation. If Eileen's density is 980 kg/m^3 and she has a volume of 0.060 m^3, what is the buoyant force that supports her in the sea water of density 1025 kg/m^3?

A-9: While swimming in her backyard pool, Nicole attempts to hold a 0.9000-m^3 inner tube completely submerged under the water. a) What buoyant force will be exerted on the inner tube as Nicole attempts to force it under the water? b) When Nicole lets go of the inner tube, it pops up to the surface with a force of 8990. N. What is the weight of the inner tube?

A-10: Irene is testing the strength of her model balsa wood bridge with a hydraulic press before the National Contest in Denver. Irene exerts a force of 3.0 N on a 1-cm-radius input piston, and a force is exerted on the 10.0-cm-radius output piston. If the bridge can withstand a force of 350 N before breaking, will the bridge survive the test and make it into the contest?

A-11: In exercise A-6, if Lucy were to foolishly hold her breath as she ascends to the water's surface, a) by how many times would the volume of her lungs change (assuming the water temperature remains constant)? b) Would her lungs be crushed or would they blow up like a balloon? c) What is the best way to ascend after diving?

A-12: Dong-Jae is bottling his own root beer in his basement where the air temperature is 315 K. The pressure inside each root beer bottle is 1.20×10^5 Pa, but the caps will pop off the bottles if the pressure inside exceeds 1.35×10^5 Pa. After the bottles are sealed and labeled, Dong-Jae stores them in his attic, which heats up to 364 K on a hot summer day. What happens to the pressure inside the bottles?

Challenge Exercises for Further Study

B-1: A 40.0-m-long steel elevator cable has a cross-sectional area of 4.0×10^{-4} m^2 and is able to stretch 1.0 cm before breaking. If the elevator itself has a mass of 1000. kg, how many 70.0-kg people can safely ride in the elevator? ($Y_{steel} = 2.0 \times 10^{11}$ N/m^2)

B-2: A can of soda displaces 3.79×10^{-4} m^3 of water when completely submerged. Each 0.018-kg can contains 3.54×10^{-4} m^3 of soda. a) Compare the buoyant force on a can of diet soda of density 1001 kg/m^3 to the force on a can of regular soda of density 1060. kg/m^3. b) If many cans of diet and regular soda are in a large tub of water and ice, how can you easily pick out the diet soda?

B-3: Saul ascends from the city of Tucson, Arizona, to the top of Kitt Peak, 2900 m above sea level. Usually Saul will feel his ears "pop" as the pressure inside his ears attempts to maintain equilibrium with the surrounding air. However, on this day Saul has a cold and his Eustachian tube is clogged, causing a tremendous pressure behind his 4.0×10^{-5}-m^2 ear drum. a) What force does Saul feel pushing on his ears? b) Is this pressure pushing in or out of his ear as he ascends? ($D_{air} = 1.20$ kg/m^3)

B-4: Hannah and her friends go fishing in her 1.20-m^3 rowboat, which has a mass of 100. kg. How many 60.0-kg people can get into the boat before the boat sinks?

10 Temperature and Heat

10-1 Temperature and Expansion

Vocabulary **Temperature:** A quantity that you can measure with a thermometer.

There are many different scales for measuring the temperature of an object. The SI unit for temperature is the **kelvin (K)**. The Kelvin scale is based on absolute zero, a point at which the internal movement of an object's atoms or molecules is a minimum and no heat can be removed. An increase of one kelvin on the Kelvin scale is equal to an increase of one degree Celsius on the Celsius scale. Respectively, the freezing and boiling temperatures of water on these two scales are 0°C = 273 K and 100°C = 373 K.

Notice that the Kelvin scale does not use the degree symbol, °. We say, "Zero degrees Celsius equals two hundred seventy-three kelvins."

However, the Fahrenheit scale is most common on household thermometers. Degrees Fahrenheit can be changed to degrees Celsius by writing.

$$T_C = \frac{5}{9}(T_F - 32.0)$$

Degrees Celsius can be changed to degrees Fahrenheit by writing

$$T_F = \left(\frac{9}{5}T_C\right) + 32.0$$

Heating an object will generally make its atoms or molecules move faster and cause the object to increase in size.

Linear Expansion

When a solid object experiences a temperature change, its length will increase by a certain amount depending upon the nature of the material.

> **change in length =**
> **(original length)(coefficient of expansion)(change in temperature)**
> or $\quad \Delta L = L_0 \alpha \Delta T$

where α, the **coefficient of linear expansion**, is a characteristic property of the material. The SI unit for the coefficient of linear expansion is $°C^{-1}$ (which is the same as $1/°C$).

Area Expansion

An object may also expand in area when heated. The equation for area expansion is

change in area =

2(original area)(coefficient of linear expansion)(change in temperature)

or $\quad \Delta A = 2A_o\alpha\Delta T$

Volume Expansion

If the volume of a solid or liquid expands, the equation is written as

change in volume =

(original volume)(coefficient of volume expansion)(change in temperature)

or $\quad \Delta V = V_o\beta\Delta T$

where β is the coefficient of volume expansion.

Solved Examples

Example 1: Justin is trying to convince his mother that he has a fever and should stay home from school. However, he has a thermometer that will measure his temperature in degrees Celsius. If Justin's temperature is 39.0°C and "normal" is 98.6°F, is Justin's temperature high enough to keep him home?

Given: $T_C = 39.0°C$ $\qquad$ *Unknown:* $T_F = ?$
$\qquad\qquad\qquad\qquad\qquad\qquad$ *Original equation:* $T_F = \left(\dfrac{9}{5}T_C\right) + 32.0$

Solve: $T_F = \left(\dfrac{9}{5}T_C\right) + 32.0 = \dfrac{9}{5}(39.0°C) + 32.0 = \mathbf{102°F}$

Yes. He should stay home.

Example 2: The layer of the sun that we see is called the photosphere. It has a temperature of 5600 K. What is the sun's temperature a) in degrees Celsius? b) in degrees Fahrenheit?

a. *Given:* $T_K = 5600\ K$ $\qquad$ *Unknown:* $T_C = ?$
$\qquad\qquad\qquad\qquad\qquad\qquad$ *Original equation:* $T_C = T_K - 273$

Solve: $T_C = T_K - 273 = 5600 - 273 = \mathbf{5327°C}$

b. *Given:* $T_C = 5327°C$

Unknown: $T_F = ?$

Original equation: $T_F = \left(\dfrac{9}{5}T_C\right) + 32.0$

Solve: $T_F = \left(\dfrac{9}{5}T_C\right) + 32.0 = \dfrac{9}{5}(5327°C) + 32.0 = \textbf{9621°F}$ Pretty hot!

Example 3: Ernesto is knitting his wife a sweater in his 18°C air-conditioned living room with 0.30-m-long aluminum knitting needles, when he decides to knit outside in the 27°C air. How much will the knitting needles expand when Ernesto takes them outside? ($\alpha_{aluminum} = 24 \times 10^{-6}°C^{-1}$)

Given: $L_o = 0.30$ m
$\alpha = 24 \times 10^{-6}°C^{-1}$
$T_o = 18°C$
$T_f = 27°C$

Unknown: $\Delta L = ?$
Original equation: $\Delta L = L_o\alpha\Delta T$

Solve: $\Delta L = L_o\alpha\Delta T = L_o\alpha(T_f - T_o) = (0.30 \text{ m})(24 \times 10^{-6}°C^{-1})(27°C - 18°C)$

$= \textbf{6.5} \times \textbf{10}^{-5}$ **m**

Example 4: Jacques, the French chef, is kneading the dough for French bread in his 21°C kitchen. He places the dough on a 0.40-m $\times$ 0.60-m aluminum cookie sheet. If the oven temperature is 177°C, how much does the cookie sheet expand in area while it is in the oven? ($\alpha_{aluminum} = 24 \times 10^{-6}°C^{-1}$)

Solution: Because the cookie sheet will expand in two directions, it is necessary to use the equation for area expansion. The area of the cookie sheet is 0.40 m $\times$ 0.60 m = 0.24 m².

Given: $A_o = 0.24$ m²
$\alpha = 24 \times 10^{-6}°C^{-1}$
$T_o = 21°C$
$T_f = 177°C$

Unknown: $\Delta A = ?$
Original equation: $\Delta A = 2A_o\alpha\Delta T$

Solve: $\Delta A = 2A_o\alpha\Delta T = 2(0.24 \text{ m}^2)(24 \times 10^{-6}°C^{-1})(177°C - 21°C)$

$= \textbf{0.0018 m}^2$

Example 5: A thermometer contains 0.50 cm³ of mercury at room temperature (21°C) when Pilar takes it into the physics lab for an experiment. By how much does the volume of mercury in the thermometer change after it sits in an 80.°C beaker of water? ($\beta_{mercury} = 18 \times 10^{-5}°C^{-1}$)

Given: $V = 0.50$ cm³
$\beta_{mercury} = 18 \times 10^{-5}°C^{-1}$
$T_o = 21°C$
$T_f = 80.°C$

Unknown: $\Delta V = ?$
Original equation: $\Delta V = V_o\beta\Delta T$

Solve: $\Delta V = V_o\beta\Delta T = V_o\beta(T_f - T_o) = (0.50 \text{ cm}^3)(18 \times 10^{-5}°C^{-1})(80.°C - 21°C)$

$= \textbf{0.0053 cm}^3$

Practice Exercises

Exercise 1: On a summer day at the equator on Mars, the temperature never rises higher than 50.0°C. Find this temperature in degrees Fahrenheit in order to determine if this would be a comfortable temperature for a human visiting Mars.

Answer: ——————————

Exercise 2: The highest temperature ever recorded on Earth was 136.4°F at Al' Aziziyah, Libya, on September 13, 1922. The lowest temperature ever recorded was −128.6°F at Vostok, Antarctica, on July 22, 1983. Calculate both of these temperatures in degrees Celsius.

Answer: ——————————

——————————

Exercise 3: The barium-yttrium ceramic compound used to demonstrate superconductivity will work only if supercooled to a temperature of 125 K. What is the equivalent temperature a) in °C? b) in °F?

Answer: ——————————

Exercise 4: Most bridges contain interlocking grates that allow the bridge to expand and contract with the change in temperature. The Golden Gate Bridge in San Francisco is about 1350 m long. a) The seasonal temperature variation in San Francisco ranges from about 0°C to 30.°C. How much will the bridge expand between these extremes? ($\alpha_{steel} = 12 \times 10^{-6}$°C^{-1}) b) Approximately how wide is this gap compared to the length of an automobile?

Answer: **a.** _____

Answer: **b.** _____

Exercise 5: Selena has a fire in the fireplace to warm her 20.°C apartment. She realizes that she has left the iron poker in the fire. How hot is the fire if the 0.60-m poker lengthens 0.30 cm? ($\alpha_{iron} = 12 \times 10^{-6}$°C^{-1})

Answer: _____

Exercise 6: Leila is building an aluminum-roofed shed in her backyard to store her garden tools. The flat roof will measure 2.0 m × 3.0 m in area during the coldest winter months when the temperature is −10°C, but temperatures in Leila's neighborhood can reach as high as 38°C in the summer. What is the area of the roof that should stick out from the shed in the summer so that the roof just fits the structure during cold winter nights?
($\alpha_{aluminum} = 24 \times 10^{-6}$°C^{-1})

Answer: _____

Exercise 7: Just before midnight, when the air temperature is 10.0°C, Karl stops and fills the 0.0600-m^3 gas tank of his car. At noon the next day, when the temperature has risen to 32.0°C, Karl finds a puddle of gasoline beneath his car. a) What do you think happened? b) How much gasoline spilled out of Karl's car (assuming no change in the volume of the tank)? ($\beta_{gasoline} = 3.00 \times 10^{-4}$°C^{-1})

Answer: **a.** _____

Answer: **b.** _____

10-2 Heat

Vocabulary   **Heat:** The transfer of energy between two objects that differ in temperature.

Vocabulary   **Specific heat:** A measure of the amount of heat needed to raise the temperature of 1 kg of a substance by 1°C.

The common unit for specific heat is the **joule per kilogram degree celsius (J/kg°C).**

The transfer of heat from an object depends upon the object's mass, the specific heat, and the difference in temperature between the object and its surroundings.

> **change in heat = (mass)(specific heat)(change in temperature)**
>
> or $\Delta Q = mc\Delta T$

The SI unit for heat is the **joule (J).** This is the same unit used for mechanical energy in Chapter 5.

The heat lost by one object equals the heat gained by another object.

> **Heat lost = Heat gained**   or $(mc\Delta T)_{lost} = (mc\Delta T)_{gained}$

For each object in the system, an $mc\Delta T$ term is needed.

Water has a very high specific heat. It makes a good cooling agent because it takes a long time for water to absorb enough heat to greatly increase its temperature. In the following exercises, you will need to know the specific heat of water and of ice.

$$c_{\text{water}} = 4187 \text{ J/kg°C} \qquad c_{\text{ice}} = 2090 \text{ J/kg°C}$$

All other values for specific heat will be given in the exercises.

Heat of Fusion

Vocabulary   **Heat of Fusion:** The quantity of heat needed per kilogram to melt a solid (or solidify a liquid) at a constant temperature and atmospheric pressure.

The amount of heat needed to melt a solid is

change in heat = (mass)(heat of fusion)   or $\Delta Q = mh_f$

The SI unit for the heat of fusion is the **joule per kilogram (J/kg).**

For water, which will be used most frequently in the exercises, the heat of fusion is **3.35×10^5 J/kg.** This means that 3.35×10^5 J of heat is required to turn 1 kg of ice into water. The same amount of heat is given off when 1 kg of water turns into ice.

Heat of Vaporization

Vocabulary   **Heat of Vaporization:** The quantity of heat needed per kilogram to vaporize a liquid (or liquify a gas) at a constant temperature and atmospheric pressure.

The amount of heat needed to vaporize a liquid is

change in heat = (mass)(heat of vaporization)   or $\Delta Q = mh_v$

The SI unit for the heat of vaporization is the **joule per kilogram (J/kg).**

For water, the heat of vaporization is **2.26×10^6 J/kg.** This is more than six times the heat of fusion for water.

Note that "steam" is not the same thing as water vapor. Water vapor is an invisible gas that results when water boils or evaporates. Steam is what you see when water vapor is cooled and condenses back into water droplets.

Solved Examples

Example 6: Hypothermia can occur if the body temperature drops to 35.0°C, although people have been known to survive much lower temperatures. On January 19, 1985, 2-year-old Michael Trode was found in the snow near his Milwaukee home with a body temperature of 16.0°C. If Michael's mass was 10.0 kg, how much heat did his body lose, assuming his normal body temperature was 37.0°C? ($c_{\text{human body}}$ = 3470 J/kg°C)

Given: m = 10.0 kg
$\qquad\ c$ = 3470 J/kg°C
$\qquad\ T_f$ = 16.0°C
$\qquad\ T_o$ = 37.0°C

Unknown: ΔQ = ?
Original equation: $\Delta Q = mc\Delta T$

Solve: $\Delta Q = mc\Delta T = mc(T_f - T_o) = (10.0 \text{ kg})(3470 \text{ J/kg°C})(16.0°C - 37.0°C)$
$\qquad\quad$ = **−729 000 J**

The negative answer implies that there was a heat loss. The encouraging (and amazing) end to this example is that Michael survived!

Example 7: Gwyn's bowl is filled with 0.175 kg of 60.0°C soup (mostly water) that she stirs with a 20.0°C silver spoon of mass 0.0400 kg. The spoon slips out of her hand and slides into the soup. What equilibrium temperature will be reached if the spoon is allowed to remain in the soup and no heat is lost to the outside air? (c_{spoon} = 240. J/kg°C) Assume that the temperature of the bowl does not change.

Given: m_{water} = 0.175 kg
$\qquad\ c_{\text{water}}$ = 4187 J/kg°C
$\qquad\ T_{\text{water}}$ = 60.0°C
$\qquad\ m_{\text{spoon}}$ = 0.0400 kg
$\qquad\ c_{\text{spoon}}$ = 240. J/kg°C
$\qquad\ T_{\text{spoon}}$ = 20.0°C

Unknown: T_f = ?
Original equation: Heat lost = Heat gained

Solve: $mc\Delta T_{\text{water}} = mc\Delta T_{\text{spoon}}$

$(0.175 \text{ kg})(4187 \text{ J/kg°C})(60.0°C - T_f) = (0.0400 \text{ kg})(240. \text{ J/kg°C})(T_f - 20.0°C)$
$43\ 963 \text{ J} - (732.7\ T_f)\text{J/°C} = (9.6\ T_f)\text{J/°C} - 192 \text{ J}$
$44\ 155 \text{ J} = (742.3\ T_f)\text{J/°C}$
$$T_f = \frac{44\ 155 \text{ J}}{742.3 \text{ J/°C}} = \textbf{59.5°C}$$

Therefore, the temperature of the spoon and soup both reach equilibrium at 59.5°C, so the spoon has become much hotter but the soup has only cooled by 0.5°C.

Example 8: An igloo is made of 224 blocks of ice at 0°C, each with a mass of 12.0 kg. How much heat must be gained by the ice to melt the entire igloo?

Solution: The total mass of the ice is 224 (12.0 kg) = 2690 kg

Given: $m = 2690$ kg

$\quad\quad h_f = 3.35 \times 10^5$ J/kg

Unknown: $\Delta Q = ?$

Original equation: $\Delta Q = mh_f$

Solve: $\Delta Q = mh_f = (2690 \text{ kg})(3.35 \times 10^5 \text{ J/kg}) = \mathbf{9.01 \times 10^8}$ **J**

Example 9: Gus is cooking soup in his hot pot and finds that he has added too much water. If Gus needs to boil off 0.200 kg of water in order for his soup to have the correct consistency, how much additional heat must Gus add once the soup is boiling?

Given: $m = 0.200$ kg

$\quad\quad h_v = 2.26 \times 10^6$ J/kg

Unknown: $\Delta Q = ?$

Original equation: $\Delta Q = mh_v$

Solve: $\Delta Q = mh_v = (0.200 \text{ kg})(2.26 \times 10^6 \text{ J/kg}) = \mathbf{4.52 \times 10^6}$ **J**

Example 10: To cool her 0.200-kg cup of 75.0°C hot chocolate (mostly water), Heidi drops a 0.0300-kg ice cube at 0°C into her insulated foam cup. What is the temperature of the hot chocolate after all the ice is melted?

Solution: The relationship "Heat lost = Heat gained" can take on many forms depending upon what is happening in the exercise. In this exercise, heat is lost from the hot chocolate ($mc\Delta T_{water}$) and gained by the ice cube, first melting it (mh_f) and then raising its temperature ($mc\Delta T_{water}$).

Given: $\quad m_{ice} = 0.0300$ kg

$\quad\quad m_{water} = 0.200$ kg

$\quad\quad\quad h_f = 3.35 \times 10^5$ J/kg

$\quad\quad c_{water} = 4187$ J/kg°C

$\quad\quad T_{water} = 75.0$°C

$\quad\quad\quad T_{ice} = 0$°C

Unknown: $T_f = ?$

Original equation: Heat lost = Heat gained

Solve: $mc\Delta T_{water} = mh_{f(ice)} + mc\Delta T_{water} = (0.200 \text{ kg})(4187 \text{ J/kg°C})(75.0°C - T_f)$

$= (0.0300 \text{ kg})(3.35 \times 10^5 \text{ J/kg}) + (0.0300 \text{ kg})(4187 \text{ J/kg°C})(T_f - 0°C)$

$= 62\,805 \text{ J} - (837.4 \ T_f)\text{J/°C} = 10\,050 \text{ J} + 125.6 \ T_f(\text{J/°C})$

$= 52\,755 \text{ J} = (963.0 \ T_f)\text{J/°C} \quad$ so $\quad T_f = \dfrac{52\,755 \text{ J}}{963.0 \text{ J/°C}} = \mathbf{54.8°C}$

Practice Exercises

Exercise 8: Peter is heating water on the stove to boil eggs for a picnic. How much heat is required to raise the temperature of his 10.0-kg vat of water from 20.0°C to 100.0°C?

Answer: _____

Exercise 9: Nova, whose mass is 50.0 kg, stays out skiing for too long and her body temperature drops by 2.00°C. What is the amount of heat lost from Nova's body? ($c_{human\ body}$ = 3470 J/kg°C)

Answer: _____

Exercise 10: Phoebe's insulated foam cup is filled with 0.150 kg of the coffee (mostly water) that is too hot to drink, so she adds 0.010 kg of milk at 5.0°C. If the coffee has an initial temperature of 70.0°C and the specific heat of milk is 3800 J/kg°C, how hot is the coffee after the milk is added? (Assume that no heat leaks out through the cup.)

Answer: _____

Exercise 11: Emily is testing her baby's bath water and finds that it is too cold, so she adds some hot water from a kettle on the stove. If Emily adds 2.00 kg of water at 80.0°C to 20.0 kg of bath water at 27.0°C, what is the final temperature of the bath water?

Answer: _____

Exercise 12: Finishing his ginger ale, Ramesh stands at a party holding his insulated foam cup that has nothing in it but 0.100 kg of ice at 0°C. How much heat must be gained by the ice in order for all of it to melt?

Answer: _____

Exercise 13: In Exercise 12, how much more heat must be gained to raise the temperature of the melted ice to room temperature of 23.0°C?

Answer: _____

Exercise 14: Under the spreading chestnut tree the village blacksmith dunks a red-hot horseshoe into a large bucket of 22.0°C water. How much heat was lost by the horseshoe in vaporizing 0.0100 kg of water?

Answer: _____

Exercise 15: While Laurie is boiling water to cook spaghetti, the phone rings, and all 1.5 kg of water boils away during her conversation. If the water was initially at 15°C, how much heat must have been gained for all of it to turn into water vapor?

Answer: _____

Exercise 16: By January, the 3.0 kg of water in the birdbath in Robyn's backyard has frozen to a temperature of $-7.0°C$. As the season changes, how much heat must be added to the water to make it a comfortable 25°C for the birds?

Answer: _____

Additional Exercises

A-1: The hottest temperature on a planet was 864°F recorded on Venus by the Soviet *Venera* probe and the U.S. *Pioneer* probe. The coldest place in the solar system is Pluto where the temperature is estimated at $-360.0°F$. Calculate each of these temperatures in degrees Celsius.

A-2: The temperature of background radiation left over from the Big Bang during the creation of the universe is 3 K. What is the temperature of the universe a) in °C? b) in °F?

A-3: As he rides the train to work on a $-4.0°C$ winter day, Mr. Trump notices that he can hear the click of the train going over spaces between the rails. Six months later, on a 30.0-°C summer day, the rails are pushed tightly together and he hears no click. If the rails are 5.00 m long, how large a gap is left between the rails on the cold winter day? ($\alpha_{steel} = 12 \times 10^{-6}°C^{-1}$)

A-4: Bradley, working in his 23°C kitchen, is cooking himself a crepe in an iron skillet that has a circular bottom with a diameter of 30.00 cm. How hot must the skillet be in order for Bradley to make a 710.3-cm^2 crepe that just fills the bottom of the pan? ($\alpha_{iron} = 12 \times 10^{-6}°C^{-1}$)

A-5: A popular winter activity of many college students is "traying," or sliding down a snow-covered hill on a tray borrowed from the dining hall. If Joanne removes a 0.35-m $\times$ 0.65-m aluminum tray from the 20.°C dining hall to go traying in the brisk $-8°C$ winter air, how much will the tray shrink when taken outside? ($\alpha_{aluminum} = 24 \times 10^{-6}°C^{-1}$)

A-6: A 0.50-m³ brass treasure chest is pulled out of the cold 15°C ocean and onto the deck of a ship, where the air temperature is 40°C. How much does the volume of the treasure chest expand? ($\beta_{brass} = 56 \times 10^{-6}°C^{-1}$)

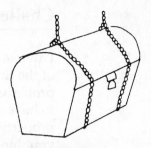

A-7: Leslie takes a full bottle of benzene from the 25.0°C chemistry lab into the 10.0°C refrigerated storage locker. Later, Leslie enters the storage locker and finds that 37.0 cm³ of benzene is missing from the bottle. What was the original volume of benzene in the bottle? ($\beta_{benzene} = 1240 \times 10^{-6}°C^{-1}$)

A-8: Sidney is home from school with a cold, so Mom has made him a bowl of chicken soup (mostly water), which she ladles from a pot into a glass bowl. If 0.600 kg of soup at 90.0°C is placed in a 0.200-kg bowl that is initially at 20.0°C, what will be the temperature of the soup when the bowl and soup have reached equilibrium? ($c_{glass} = 840.$ J/kg°C)

A-9: In A-8 above, when the soup and bowl are at 80.0°C, a chilled dumpling with a mass of 0.100 kg and a temperature of 10.0°C is added. What will be the temperature of the dumpling, soup, and bowl when the three have reached equilibrium? ($c_{dumpling} = 110.$ J/kg°C)

A-10: Nils is emptying the dishwasher. He removes a 0.200-kg glass that has a temperature of 30.0°C. Into it he pours 0.100 kg of diet soda (mostly water), which comes out of the refrigerator with a temperature of 5.00°C. Assuming no external heat loss, what will be the final equilibrium temperature of the glass of diet soda? ($c_{glass} = 840.$ J/kg°C)

A-11: In Exercise A-10, Nils doesn't feel that his drink is cold enough, so he throws in an ice cube whose temperature is −3.0°C. What is the mass of the ice cube if his drink (and glass) are now cooled to 1.0°C?

A-12: A puddle filled with 20. kg of water is completely frozen to −6.0°C in the middle of the winter. How much heat must be absorbed by the puddle to melt the ice and warm the water up to 20.°C during the spring thaw?

A-13: Before ironing his shirt for work, Nathaniel drops some water on his iron to test whether it is hot enough to iron his clothes. How much heat is needed to vaporize a 5.0×10^{-4}-kg drop of 20.°C water?

Challenge Exercises for Further Study

B-1: Lawrence, a civil engineer, uses a steel tape measure to figure the dimensions of the Emersons' property. When the temperature is 37°C, he determines the property line to be 152.000 m long. However, the length of the property seems to have changed when Lawrence returns on a 5.0°C winter day. a) Does the property appear to be longer in the warm weather or the cold? Explain why you think this is so. b) How long is the property when measured by his steel tape in the winter? ($\alpha_{steel} = 12 \times 10^{-6}$°C^{-1})

B-2: One cool 5.0°C spring morning, Mason lays a brick sidewalk up to his house, placing the 25.0-cm-long bricks end to end against each other. However, Mason forgets to leave a space for expansion and when the temperature reaches 36.0°C, the bricks buckle. How high will the bricks rise? ($\alpha_{brick} = 10.0 \times 10^{-6}$°C^{-1})

$\vdash$ 25.0 cm $\dashv\vdash$ 25.0 cm $\dashv$

B-3: Phil is making a sandwich and he is having trouble getting the lid off the jar of mayonnaise. a) If the steel lid and the glass jar each have a diameter of 10. cm at a room temperature of 21°C, should Phil run the lid under water that is 20.°C warmer or 20.°C cooler to remove the lid? b) When he completes the correct procedure to free the lid, what is the size of the space between the lid and the jar? ($\alpha_{aluminum} = 24 \times 10^{-6}$°C^{-1} and $\alpha_{glass} = 8.5 \times 10^{-6}$°C^{-1})

B-4: Pablo brings a 6000.-cm^3 aluminum can filled all the way to the top with turpentine up from the 20.0°C basement and sets it outside where he is painting. The noonday sun heats the turpentine and the aluminum container to 45.0°C. Will the turpentine overflow the container? If so, how much will spill out? If not, how much more could be added to the empty space created? ($\beta_{aluminum} = 77 \times 10^{-6}$°C^{-1} and $\beta_{turpentine} = 900. \times 10^{-6}$°C^{-1})

B-5: In a physics experiment, a 0.100-kg aluminum calorimeter cup holding 0.200 kg of ice is removed from a freezer, where both ice and cup have been cooled to −5.00°C. Next, 0.0500 kg of steam at 100.°C is added to the ice in the cup. What will be the equilibrium temperature of the system after the ice has melted? ($c_{aluminum} = 920.$ J/kg°C)

11 Simple Harmonic Motion

11-1 Springs

Vocabulary **Period:** The time it takes for a vibrating object to repeat its motion.

Vocabulary **Frequency:** The number of vibrations made per unit time.

Period and frequency are the reciprocals of each other. In other words,

$$T = \frac{1}{f} \quad \text{and} \quad f = \frac{1}{T}$$

Since period is a measure of time, its SI unit is the **second,** while the unit for frequency is the reciprocal of this, or **1/second.** Another way of writing 1/s is with the unit **hertz (Hz).**

You may recognize this as being similar to the explanation of period and frequency in Chapter 6 on circular motion.

Hooke's Law

Whenever a spring is stretched from its equilibrium position and released, it will move back and forth on either side of the equilibrium position. The force that pulls it back and attempts to restore the spring to equilibrium is called the **restoring force.** Its magnitude can be written as

restoring force = (force constant)(displacement from equilibrium)
or $F = kx$

This relationship is known as **Hooke's law.** The force constant is a measure of the stiffness of the spring. The SI unit for the force constant is the **newton per meter (N/m).**

Keep in mind that this is the force required to restore the spring back to its original position. The force that acts to move the spring *away* from the equilibrium position is equal in magnitude to the restoring force, but opposite in direction.

Simple harmonic motion is motion that occurs when the restoring force acting on an object is proportional to the object's displacement from its rest position. Objects at the end of springs move in simple harmonic motion when they are displaced from their rest position and bounce up and down on the spring, or oscillate.

149

Period of a Mass on a Spring in Simple Harmonic Motion

The only two things that affect the period of an object hanging on a bouncing spring are the object's mass and the force constant of the spring on which the object is oscillating.

$$\text{Period} = 2\pi\sqrt{\frac{\text{mass}}{\text{force constant}}} \quad \text{or} \quad T = 2\pi\sqrt{\frac{m}{k}}$$

To prove that this equation does indeed give the period in seconds, simplify the units for $\sqrt{m/k}$ by writing

$$\sqrt{\frac{\text{kg}}{\text{N/m}}} = \sqrt{\frac{\text{kg}}{\frac{\text{kg}\cdot\text{m/s}^2}{\text{m}}}} = \sqrt{\text{s}^2} = \text{s}$$

Solved Examples

Example 1: A hummingbird beats its wings up and down with a frequency of 80.0 Hz. What is the period of the hummingbird's flaps?

Given: $f = 80.0$ Hz

Unknown: $T = ?$
Original equation: $T = \dfrac{1}{f}$

Solve: $T = \dfrac{1}{f} = \dfrac{1}{80.0 \text{ Hz}} = \textbf{0.0125 s}$

Example 2: In anticipation of her first game, Alesia pulls back the handle of a pinball machine a distance of 5.0 cm. The force constant of the spring in the handle is 200 N/m. How much force must Alesia exert?

Solution: First, convert cm to m.   5.0 cm = 0.050 m

Given: $k = 200$ N/m
$x = 0.050$ m

Unknown: $F = ?$
Original equation: $F = kx$

Solve: $F = kx = (200 \text{ N/m})(0.050 \text{ m}) = \textbf{10 N}$

Example 3: As Bianca stands on a bathroom scale, whose force constant is 220 N/m, the needle on the scale vibrates from side to side. a) If Bianca has a mass of 180 kg, what is the period of vibration of the needle as it comes to rest? b) If Bianca goes on a diet, how will this change the period of vibration?

a. *Given:* $m = 180$ kg

$k = 220$ N/m

Unknown: $T = ?$

Original equation: $T = 2\pi\sqrt{\dfrac{m}{k}}$

Solve: $T = 2\pi\sqrt{\dfrac{m}{k}} = 2\pi\sqrt{\dfrac{180 \text{ kg}}{220 \text{ N/m}}} = \textbf{5.7 s}$

In other words, this is the amount of time for one complete oscillation.

b. Because the mass will be smaller, the period of vibration will be smaller. In other words, it will take less time for the needle on the scale to bounce from side to side as it comes to rest.

Practice Exercises

Exercise 1:   Terry jumps up and down on a trampoline with a frequency of 1.5 Hz. What is the period of Terry's jumping?

Answer: _____

Exercise 2:   Gary Stewart of Reading, Ohio set a pogo stick record in 1990 by jumping 177 737 times. a) If the pogo stick he used had a force constant of 6000. N/m and was compressed 0.12 m on each jump, what force must Gary have exerted on the pogo stick upon each jump? b) What force would be exerted back up on Gary each time he went up?

Answer: **a.** _____

Answer: **b.** _____

Exercise 3: At the post office, Cliff, a postal worker, places a 0.60-kg package on a scale, compressing the scale by 0.03 m. a) What is the force constant of the spring in the postal scale? b) What happens to the force constant if Cliff weighs a heavier package?

Answer: **a.** _____

Answer: **b.** _____

Exercise 4: A jack-in-the-box lid will pop open when a crank is turned on the outside of the box. If Jack pushes against the inside of the box with a force of 3.00 N when the lid is closed, and the spring is compressed 10.0 cm from equilibrium, what is the force constant of the spring?

Answer: _____

Exercise 5: Sam, a butcher, puts 3.0 kg of chopped beef on the 1.0-kg pan of his scale, which has a spring whose force constant is 400. N/m. What is the period of vibration of the pan as it comes to rest? b) If Sam adds more beef to the scale, what will this do to the period of vibration?

Answer: **a.** _____

Answer: **b.** _____

Exercise 6: A toy bobs up and down over Campbell's crib with a period of 1.0 s. The toy hangs from the end of a spring whose force constant is 20.0 N/m. What is the mass of the toy?

Answer: _____

11-2 Pendulums

The period of a pendulum depends only upon the pendulum's length (if the angle of swing is not too large). A long pendulum has a longer period than a short pendulum. The relationship between period and length can be shown with the following equation.

$$\text{Period} = 2\pi\sqrt{\frac{\text{length}}{\text{acceleration due to gravity}}} \quad \text{or} \quad T = 2\pi\sqrt{\frac{L}{g}}$$

It should be noted that this equation works only for a pendulum whose mass is considerably larger than the mass of the string from which it swings. To simplify calculations, in the following exercises you will be working with pendulums swinging from strings of negligible mass.

Solved Examples

Example 4: A tall, thin tree sways back and forth in the breeze with a frequency of 2 Hz. What is the period of the tree?

Given: $f = 2 \text{ Hz}$ 　　　　　　*Unknown:* $T = ?$
　　　　　　　　　　　　　　　　　Original equation: $T = \dfrac{1}{f}$

Solve: $T = \dfrac{1}{f} = \dfrac{1}{2 \text{ Hz}} = \textbf{0.5 s}$

Example 5: World-reknowned hypnotist Paulbar the Great swings his watch from a 20.0-cm chain in front of a subject's eyes. What is the period of swing of the watch?

Solution: First, convert cm to m.   20.0 cm = 0.20 m

Given: $L = 0.20$ m   *Unknown:* $T = ?$
           $g = 10.0$ m/s^2 *Original equation:* $T = 2\pi\sqrt{\dfrac{L}{g}}$

Solve: $T = 2\pi\sqrt{\dfrac{L}{g}} = 2\pi\sqrt{\dfrac{0.20 \text{ m}}{10.0 \text{ m/s}^2}} = $ **0.89 s**

Therefore, it takes 0.89 s for the watch to swing in one direction and back again, through one full cycle.

Example 6: A spider swings in the breeze from a silk thread with a period of 0.6 s. How long is the spider's strand of silk?

Solution: The answer is determined using the pendulum equation, but now it must be set up in terms of the unknown, L. First, square all of the terms to get rid of the radical. The equation becomes

$T^2 = 4\pi^2 \dfrac{L}{g}$. Then rearrange the equation as shown.

Given: $T = 0.60$ s   *Unknown:* $L = ?$
           $g = 10.0$ m/s^2 *Original equation:* $T = 2\pi\sqrt{\dfrac{L}{g}}$

Solve: $L = \dfrac{gT^2}{4\pi^2} = \dfrac{(10.0 \text{ m/s}^2)(0.6 \text{ s})^2}{4\pi^2} = $ **0.09 m**

Practice Exercises

Exercise 7: A metronome is a device used by many musicians to get the desired rhythm for a musical piece. If a metronome is clicking back and forth with a frequency of 0.5 Hz, what is the period of the metronome?

Answer: _____

Exercise 8: Many amusement parks feature a ride in which a giant ship swings back and forth. If the period of the ship is 8.00 s, what is the frequency of the swinging ship?

Answer: ─────────────

Exercise 9: Tegan, a trapeze artist, swings from a 2.5-m-long trapeze, high above the three-ring circus. a) What is Tegan's period of swing? b) Would Tegan's period of swing change if she were more massive? If so, how?

Answer: **a.** ─────────────

Answer: **b.** ─────────────

Exercise 10: Danielle is pushing her twin Daniel on a swing that hangs from a tree branch by 2.0-m-long ropes. With what frequency will Danielle have to push Daniel as he swings?

Answer: ─────────────

Exercise 11: Marla, a maid, is standing on the Vanderbilt's dining room table dusting the chandelier. While Marla is reaching up, she slips and grabs hold of the chandelier to catch her balance. When she lets go, the chandelier begins to swing with a period of 1.6 s. How long is the cable connecting the chandelier to the ceiling?

Answer: _____

Exercise 12: You have been commissioned by NASA to travel to Jupiter's innermost Galilean satellite, Io, to learn more about this volcanic moon. As you board the spacecraft, you are handed a rock tied to a 10.0-cm string, and a stopwatch, and are asked to derive an experiment that would allow you to determine the acceleration due to gravity on Io. You must use both pieces of equipment and nothing more. a) Describe how you would calculate Io's gravitational acceleration. b) If the pendulum swings with a period of 1.48 s, what is the gravitational acceleration on Io?

Answer: **a.** _____

Answer: **b.** _____

Additional Exercises

A-1: Mr. Knote, a piano tuner, taps his 440-Hz tuning fork with a mallet. What is the period of the vibrating tuning fork?

A-2: Denny jumps up and down on his bed, taking 0.75 s for each jump. What is the frequency of Denny's jumping?

A-3: Inside most ball-point pens is a small spring that compresses as the pen is pressed against the paper. If a force of 0.1 N compresses the pen's spring a distance of 0.005 m, what is the force constant of the tiny spring?

A-4: Maureen is trying to predict the period of a mass hung on a spring. She has a spring of negligible mass and four weights to hang on the end. Maureen collects the following data as she observes the stretch of the spring:

force (N)	displacement (m)
2.5	0.050
5.0	0.102
7.5	0.149
10.0	0.199

a) Plot a graph of force (on the y-axis) vs. displacement (on the x-axis). b) Find the slope of the graph. What does this slope represent? c) Use the information you have obtained to find the period of the spring when a 3.0 kg mass is hung on the end.

A-5: Kim drives her empty dump truck over a berm (also called a speed bump) at the construction site. The truck has a mass of 3000. kg and the force constant for one of the truck's springs is 100 000. N/m. (Remember, the truck has 4 wheels.) a) What is the resulting period of the bouncing truck as it goes over the bump? b) If Kim leaves the construction site with a load of dirt in her truck, what will this do to the period of her dump truck as it crosses the berm?

A-6: A monkey swings from a jungle vine by his 0.30-m-long tail. a) What is the period of swing of the monkey? b) With what frequency does the monkey swing?

A-7: A wrecking ball used to demolish buildings swings from a 10.0-m-long cable. What is the period of the wrecking ball as it swings?

A-8: A crow attempts to land on a small bird feeder, causing it to swing back and forth with a frequency of 0.350 Hz. How long is the wire from which the feeder hangs?

A-9: The acceleration due to gravity on the moon is 1/6 that on Earth. a) If you wanted a pendulum clock to tell time on the moon the same as it does on Earth (i.e., have the same period), would you need to lengthen or shorten the pendulum? b) If the pendulum was originally 24.0 cm long on Earth, how long should it be on the moon?

Challenge Exercises for Further Study

B-1: Ezra, a 60.0-kg high school student, is sleeping on his waterbed when his 2.0-kg cat, Muffin, jumps onto his back, causing Ezra to sink 2.0 cm deeper into the waterbed. a) If Muffin then jumps off Ezra from this new equilibrium position, what will be the period of Ezra's bobbing motion on the waterbed? b) Will this period slow down, speed up, or remain the same as the amplitude of the bounces gets smaller and smaller? Explain your answer.

B-2: Andy (mass 80.0 kg), Randy (mass 60.0 kg), and twins Candy and Mandy (each with a mass of 70.0 kg) climb into a 1000.-kg car, causing each of the four springs to compress 4.00 cm. Find the period of vibration of the car as it comes to rest after the four get in.

B-3: Tanja talks long distance with her boyfriend every night from her dormitory pay phone, and her phone bills are getting rather high. She has decided that she must limit each of her calls to 10 minutes. Since Tanja doesn't have a watch, she devises a unique way to time her calls. Tanja notices that the pay phones each have a cord that is 0.800 m long. Therefore, as she talks on one phone, she can swing the receiver of the adjacent phone to time her call. How many complete swings will the nearby phone receiver make before Tanja must hang up?

B-4: On a 0°C-winter day, a 10.000-m-long brass Foucault pendulum hanging in the covered entrance to the science museum swings back and forth with the rotation of Earth. The outdoor temperature variations range from 0°C in the winter to 30.0°C in the summer. How does the period of the pendulum change throughout the year? ($\alpha_{brass} = 19 \times 10^{-6}°C^{-1}$)

B-5: Gillian buys a pendulum clock at a discount store and discovers when she gets it home that it loses 6.00 minutes each day. a) Should she lengthen or shorten the pendulum in order for it to keep accurate time? b) If the pendulum has a period of 2.00 s, by how much must the length be changed so that the clock keeps accurate time?

12 Waves and Sound

12-1 Wave Motion

Vocabulary   **Wave:** A disturbance in a medium.

In this chapter you will be working with waves that are periodic or that repeat in a regular, rhythmic pattern.

$$\textbf{wave speed} = (\textbf{wavelength})(\textbf{frequency}) \quad \text{or} \quad v = \lambda f$$

The SI unit for wave speed is the **meter per second (m/s).** The speed of sound in air increases with air temperature. For the following exercises, the speed of sound will be written as 340.0 m/s. All electromagnetic radiation including radio waves and light waves travel at the speed of light, 3.00×10^8 m/s.

The wavelength of a wave is the distance from one point on a wave to the next identical point on the same wave, for example, from crest to crest, trough to trough, or condensation to condensation. The symbol for wavelength is the Greek letter "lambda," λ.

The SI unit for wavelength is the **meter (m),** which is the same unit used for length in earlier chapters.

The SI unit for frequency is the **hertz (Hz).** When talking about the broadcast frequency of a radio station, frequencies of FM radio stations are given in megahertz, or MHz, and frequencies of AM radio stations are given in kilohertz, or kHz.

$$1 \text{ MHz} = 1 \times 10^6 \text{ Hz} \quad \text{and} \quad 1 \text{ kHz} = 1 \times 10^3 \text{ Hz}$$

Solved Examples

Example 1:   Radio station WKLB in Boston broadcasts at a frequency of 99.5 MHz. What is the wavelength of the radio waves emitted by WKLB?

Given: $v = 3.00 \times 10^8$ m/s   *Unknown:* $\lambda = ?$
$ f = 99.5 \times 10^6$ Hz   *Original equation:* $v = \lambda f$

Solve: $\lambda = \dfrac{v}{f} = \dfrac{3.00 \times 10^8 \text{ m/s}}{99.5 \times 10^6 \text{ Hz}} = $ **3.02 m**

Therefore, the distance from one point on the wave to the next identical point on the same wave is 3.02 m.

Example 2:   In California, Clay is surfing on a wave that propels him toward the beach with a speed of 5.0 m/s. The wave crests are each 20. m apart. a) What is the frequency of the water wave? b) What is the period?

a. *Given:* $v = 5.0$ m/s   *Unknown:* $f = ?$
     $\lambda = 20.$ m   *Original equation:* $v = \lambda f$

Solve: $f = \dfrac{v}{\lambda} = \dfrac{5.0 \text{ m/s}}{20. \text{ m}} = $ **0.25 Hz**

b. *Given:* $f = 0.25$ Hz   *Unknown:* $T = ?$
                              Original equation: $T = \dfrac{1}{f}$

Solve: $T = \dfrac{1}{f} = \dfrac{1}{0.25 \text{ Hz}} = $ **4.0 s**

One crest comes along every 4.0 s.

Practice Exercises

Exercise 1:   Harriet is told by her doctor that her heart rate is 70.0 beats per minute. If Harriet's average blood flow in the aorta during systole is 1.5×10^{-2} m/s, what is the wavelength of the waves of blood in Harriet's aorta, created by her beating heart?

Answer: _____

Exercise 2:   Dogs are able to hear much higher frequencies than humans are capable of detecting. For this reason, dog whistles that are inaudible to the human ear can be heard easily by a dog. If a dog whistle has a frequency of 3.0×10^4 Hz, what is the wavelength of the sound emitted?

Answer: _____

Exercise 3: While flying to Tucson, Connie's plane experiences turbulence that causes the coffee in her cup to oscillate back and forth 4 times each second. If the waves of coffee have a wavelength of 0.1 m, what is the speed of a wave moving through the coffee?

Answer: _____

Exercise 4: At a country music festival in New Hampshire, the Oak Ridge Boys are playing at the end of a crowded 184-m field when Ronny Fairchild hits a note on the keyboard that has a frequency of 400. Hz. a) How many full wavelengths are there between the stage and the last row of the crowd? b) How much delay is there between the time a note is played and the time it is heard in the last row?

Answer: **a.** _____

Answer: **b.** _____

12-2 Doppler Effect

Vocabulary   **Doppler Effect:** A change in the apparent frequency of sound due to the motion of the source of the receiver.

You probably associate the Doppler effect with the change in pitch (frequency) of a loud car or siren just as it passes you. The pitch suddenly drops just as the object moves by. Light can also be Doppler shifted but the Doppler shift of light will not be discussed in this chapter.

The equation that describes this effect can be used whether the source is approaching or receding from the observer. It also works if either the source or observer is at rest, or if there is a chase situation in which both are moving in the same direction.

$$\text{perceived frequency} = \text{actual frequency} \frac{(\text{speed of sound} + \text{speed of observer})}{(\text{speed of sound} - \text{speed of source})}$$

or $\quad f = f_0 \dfrac{(v + v_o)}{(v - v_s)}$

Here, f_0 refers to the actual frequency being emitted by an object, while f is the frequency heard by the observer as the source approaches or recedes. If a source approaches, the perceived frequency will be higher than the actual frequency. If a source recedes, the perceived frequency is lower than the actual frequency.

In order for this equation to work properly, there is a standard convention to which you must adhere whenever solving Doppler exercises.

v_o is $(+)$ if the observer moves toward the source.
v_o is $(-)$ if the observer moves away from the source.
v_s is $(+)$ if the source moves toward the observer.
v_s is $(-)$ if the source moves away from the observer.

Remember, it is not necessary to always have both the observer and the source in motion. Often one will be moving and the other will be at rest.

Solved Examples

Example 3: Sitting on the beach at Coney Island one afternoon, Sunny finds herself beneath the flight path of the airplanes leaving Kennedy Airport. What frequency will Sunny hear as a jet, whose engines emit sound at a frequency of 1000. Hz, flies toward her at a speed of 100.0 m/s?

Solution: First draw a diagram of the situation. Notice in the calculation below that Sunny is sitting at rest and the plane is approaching. Therefore, the source is moving toward the observer. The observer remains stationary.

Given: $f_0 = 1000.$ Hz   *Unknown:* $f = ?$
$\quad\quad\quad v_o = 0$ m/s   *Original equation:* $f = f_0 \dfrac{(v + v_o)}{(v - v_s)}$
$\quad\quad\quad\quad v = 340.\,0$ m/s
$\quad\quad\quad v_s = 100.0$ m/s

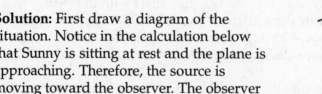

Solve: $f = f_0 \dfrac{(v + v_o)}{(v - v_s)} = 1000.$ Hz $\dfrac{(340.0 \text{ m/s} + 0 \text{ m/s})}{(340.0 \text{ m/s} - 100.0 \text{ m/s})} = \mathbf{1417\ Hz}$

Example 4: In the previous example, what frequency will Sunny observe as the jet travels away from her at the same speed?

Solution: Again, draw a diagram of the situation. This time, the source is moving away from the observer, so the value for v_s must be negative.

Given: $f_o = 1000.$ Hz Unknown: $f = ?$
$v_o = 0$ m/s   Original equation: $f = f_o \dfrac{v + v_o}{v - v_s}$
$v = 340.0$ m/s
$v_s = -100.0$ m/s

Solve: $f = f_o \dfrac{(v + v_o)}{(v - v_s)} = 1000.$ Hz $\dfrac{(340.0 \text{ m/s} + 0 \text{ m/s})}{(340.0 \text{ m/s} - [-100.0 \text{ m/s}])} = \textbf{772.7 Hz}$

Example 5: A sparrow chases a crow with a speed of 4.0 m/s, while chirping at a frequency of 850.0 Hz. What frequency of sound does the crow hear as he flies away from the sparrow with a speed of 3.0 m/s?

Given: $f_o = 850.0$ Hz Unknown: $f = ?$
$v_o = -3.0$ m/s   Original equation: $f = f_o \dfrac{(v + v_o)}{(v - v_s)}$
$v = 340.0$ m/s
$v_s = 4.0$ m/s

Solve: $f = f_o \dfrac{(v + v_o)}{(v - v_s)} = 850.0$ Hz $\dfrac{(340.0 \text{ m/s} + [-3.0 \text{ m/s}])}{(340.0 \text{ m/s} - 4.0 \text{ m/s})} = \textbf{852.5 Hz}$

Therefore, since the sparrow is approaching the crow, the crow hears a frequency that is higher than the original.

Practice Exercises

Example 5: One foggy morning, Kenny is driving his speed boat toward the Brant Point lighthouse at a speed of 15.0 m/s as the fog horn blows with a frequency of 180.0 Hz. What frequency does Kenny hear as he moves?

Answer: ─────────────

Example 6: Dad is driving the family station wagon to Grandma's house when he gets tired and pulls over in a roadside rest stop to take a nap. Junior, who is sitting in the back seat, watches the trucks go by on the highway and notices that they make a different sound when they are coming toward him than they do when they are moving away. a) If a truck with a frequency of 85.0 Hz is traveling toward Junior with a speed of 27.0 m/s, what frequency does Junior hear as the truck approaches? b) After the truck passes, what frequency does Junior hear as the truck moves away?

Answer: **a.** _____

Answer: **b.** _____

Exercise 7: One way to tell if a mosquito is about to sting is to listen for the Doppler shift as the mosquito is flying. The buzzing sound of a mosquito's wings is emitted at a frequency of 1050 Hz. a) If you hear a frequency of 1034 Hz, does this mean that the mosquito is coming in for a landing or that it has just bitten you and is flying away? b) At what velocity is the mosquito flying?

Answer: **a.** _____

Answer: **b.** _____

Exercise 8:   Barney, a bumblebee flying at 6.00 m/s, is being chased by Betsy, a bumblebee who is flying at 4.00 m/s. Barney's wings beat with a frequency of 90.0 Hz. What frequency does Betsy hear as she flies after Barney?

Answer: _____

Exercise 9:   Mrs. Gonzalez is about to give birth and Mr. Gonzalez is rushing her to the hospital at a speed of 30.0 m/s. Witnessing the speeding car, Officer O'Malley jumps in his police car and turns on the siren, whose frequency is 800. Hz. If the officer chases after the Gonzalez' car with a speed of 35.0 m/s, what frequency do the Gonzalezes hear as the officer approaches?

Answer: _____

12-3 Standing Waves

Waves in Strings

When a string is plucked, a wave will reflect back and forth from one end of the string to the other, creating **nodes** (points of minimum movement) and **antinodes** (points of maximum movement). This is called a **standing wave** because it appears to stand still.

The frequency with which a string vibrates depends upon the number of antinodes, the wave speed, and the length of the string, as shown in the following relationship.

$$\textbf{frequency} = \frac{(\textbf{number of antinodes})(\textbf{wave speed})}{2(\textbf{length})} \quad \text{or} \quad f = \frac{nv}{2L}$$

If $n = 1$, as shown in the diagram, the frequency is called the **fundamental frequency.** It is the lowest frequency of a vibrating string that is fixed at both ends. Multiples of the fundamental frequency are called **overtones.**

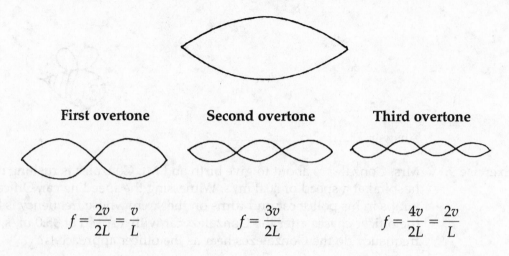

and so on.

Waves in Pipes

Waves in pipes that are open at both ends behave much like waves in strings. It is important to remember that antinodes always form at open ends of a pipe while nodes form at closed ends. If a pipe is open at both ends, the possible frequencies are

$$f = \frac{nv}{2L} \quad \text{(where } n = 1, 2, 3 \ldots \text{ for other overtones)}$$

In a pipe that is closed at one end, the possible frequencies are

$$f = \frac{nv}{4L} \quad \text{(where } n = 1, 3, 5, 7 \ldots \text{ for other overtones)}$$

Beats

If two different frequencies sound simultaneously, the wavelengths will differ, and the crests and troughs of each wave will overlap in a way that causes variations in loudness. There will be moments of reinforcement and moments of cancellation as the wave patterns interact. The resulting sound is a series of **beats,** which occur when the wave sum reaches its greatest amplitude.

The beat frequency can be found by taking the absolute value of the difference between the two frequencies of the interacting waves.

$$f_{\text{beat}} = |f_1 - f_2|$$

Solved Examples

Example 6: An orchestra tunes up for the big concert by playing an A, which resounds with a fundamental frequency of 440. Hz. Find the first and second overtones of this note.

The first overtone is 2 times the fundamental frequency:

$$f_2 = 2f_0 \quad \text{so} \quad f_2 = 2(440.\ \text{Hz}) = \textbf{880. Hz}$$

The second overtone is 3 times the fundamental frequency:

$$f_3 = 3f_0 \quad \text{so} \quad f_3 = 3(440.\ \text{Hz}) = \textbf{1320 Hz}$$

Example 7: Zeke plucks a C on his guitar string, which vibrates with a fundamental frequency of 261 Hz. The wave travels down the string with a speed of 400. m/s. What is the length of the guitar string? b) Would Zeke need longer or shorter strings to play the fundamental frequency for higher notes?

a. *Given:* $n = 1$ *Unknown:* $L = ?$
$\qquad\qquad\quad v = 400.\ \text{m/s} \qquad$ *Original equation:* $f = \dfrac{nv}{2L}$
$\qquad\qquad\quad f = 261\ \text{Hz}$

Solve: $L = \dfrac{nv}{2f} = \dfrac{(1)(400.\ \text{m/s})}{2(261\ \text{Hz})} = \textbf{0.766 m}$

b. If the wave speed remains the same for each string, as f gets larger, L gets smaller. Therefore, the higher the note, the shorter the string required to hear the fundamental frequency.

Example 8: In his physics lab, Sanjiv finds that he can take a long glass tube and fill it with water, using the air space at the top to simulate a pipe closed at one end. If Sanjiv holds a tuning fork, which vibrates with a fundamental frequency of 440 Hz, over the mouth of the pipe, how long is the air column if it vibrates at the same frequency?

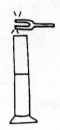

Given: $f = 440\ \text{Hz} \qquad\qquad$ *Unknown:* $L = ?$
$\qquad\quad v = 340.0\ \text{m/s} \qquad\quad$ *Original equation:* $f = \dfrac{nv}{4L}$
$\qquad\quad n = 1$

Solve: $L = \dfrac{nv}{4f} = \dfrac{(1)(340.0\ \text{m/s})}{4(440\ \text{Hz})} = \textbf{0.19 m}$

Practice Exercises

Exercise 10: Melody puts a fret on her guitar string, causing it to vibrate with a fundamental frequency of 250 Hz as a wave travels through at 350 m/s.
a) How long is the guitar string from the lower fixed end to the fret? b) How far and in which direction must the fret be moved in order to produce a fundamental frequency that is twice as high (i.e., one octave higher)?

Answer: **a.** _____

Answer: **b.** _____

Exercise 11: The fundamental frequency of a bass violin string is 1045 Hz and occurs when the string is 0.900 m long. How far from the lower fixed end of the bass violin should you place your fingers to allow the string to vibrate at a fundamental frequency 3 times as great?

Answer: _____

Exercise 12: Aaron blows across the opening of a partially filled 20.0-cm-high soft drink bottle and finds that the air vibrates with a fundamental frequency of 472 Hz. How high is the liquid in the bottle?

Answer: _____

Exercise 13: A red-headed piano tuner from Chicago is tuning the Bentz' piano when he discovers that the G above middle C is vibrating with a higher frequency than his G tuning fork, which vibrates at 392.0 Hz. He plays the piano key and tuning fork at the same time and hears a beat frequency of 2.0 Hz. What is the frequency of the G on the Bentz' piano?

Answer: _____

Additional Exercises

A-1: Find the wavelength of the ultrasonic wave emitted by a bat if it has a frequency of 4.0×10^4 Hz.

A-2: Radio station KSON in San Diego broadcasts at both 1240 kHz (AM) and 97.3 MHz (FM). a) Which of these signals, AM or FM, has the longer wavelength? b) How long is each?

A-3: What is the wavelength of a B note (frequency 494 Hz) played a) by a flute? b) If the flute and a sax play the same note, which of the following will be different: quality, pitch, or loudness?

A-4: As an anchor is being hoisted out of the water, it hits the hull of the ship, causing the anchor to vibrate with a frequency of 150. Hz. If the speed of sound in sea water is 1520 m/s, how many wavelengths of sound will fit between the boat and the ocean bottom 395 m below?

A-5: A popular pastime at sporting events is "the wave," a phenomenon where individuals in the crowd stand up and sit down in sequence, causing a giant ripple of people. If a continuous "wave" passes through a stadium of people with a speed of 20 m/s and a frequency of 0.5 Hz, what is the distance from "crest" to "crest" (in other words, the wavelength of the wave)?

A-6: From his bedroom, Garth can hear the distant sound of a train horn as the train travels through the mountains on its way from Chattanooga to Nashville. The horn has a frequency of 800.0 Hz as the train rolls along at 20.00 m/s. What frequency does Garth hear as the train travels away?

A-7: Erin is late to physics class and is coming down the hall as the bells are ringing. There are two bells in the hall, one at the far end, and one in front of the classroom she is approaching. Each rings with a frequency of 500.0 Hz. As Erin comes down the hallway with a speed of 1.000 m/s toward the classroom a) what frequency does she hear for each bell? b) What beat frequency does she hear?

A-8: Karen flies a motorized toy airplane with a frequency of 200. Hz in a circle at a speed of 18.0 m/s. Caroline stands nearby and hears a Doppler shift as the plane approaches and recedes from her. What are the a) highest and b) lowest frequencies Caroline hears?

A-9: Sonar detectors work by bouncing high-frequency sound waves of about 0.100 MHz off oncoming ships and detecting the frequency of the return signal. If a sonar detector receives a return signal of 0.101 MHz from a sub, how fast is the sub going? (Hint: Sonar travels in sea water at 1520 m/s).

A-10: A fly traveling at 3.000 m/s is pursued by a bat traveling at 6.000 m/s who emits sound at an ultrasonic frequency of 50 000. Hz. If the fly could detect such a high frequency emission, what frequency would the fly hear as it is being pursued?

A-11: Lars is jogging beside the railroad tracks at a speed of 2.00 m/s when he hears a train whistle behind him at a frequency of 2115 Hz. If the actual frequency of the train whistle is 2000. Hz, how fast is the train moving?

A-12: Walter is a bass and can hit a low E that has a frequency of 82.4 Hz. Millie is a soprano and can sing as high as the third overtone of this note. What is the highest frequency that Millie can sing?

A-13: Joyce, the church organist, is practicing on the organ and she finds that the first two overtones for the 370-Hz pipe are 1110 Hz and 1850 Hz. Is the organ pipe closed at one end or open at both ends?

A-14: A train passes through a tunnel that is 550 m long. What is the fundamental frequency of vibrating air in the tunnel?

A-15: Harvey, a harpist, plucks a 0.600-m-long string on his harp. The string has a first overtone of 1046.6 Hz. How fast does the vibration travel through the string?

A-16: Reed arrives late to practice and finds that the orchestra has already tuned up and begun to play. As one oboist hits a D with a frequency of 293.7 Hz, Reed plays a note with a frequency of 291.2 Hz. What beat frequency is heard as the two instruments are playing side by side?

Challenge Exercises for Further Study

B-1: As a train approaches a ringing crossing gate, Stacey, a passenger on the train, hears a frequency of 440 Hz from the bell. As the train recedes, she hears a frequency of 410 Hz. How fast is the train traveling?

B-2: Richard stands on the flatbed car of a moving train playing an A on his horn. The note has a fundamental frequency of 220 Hz. Calculate whether or not the train could move fast enough for a stationary observer on the ground to hear the first overtone of the horn as the train passes.

13 Reflection and Refraction

13-1 The Speed of Light

An important physical constant is the **speed of light**, c. In a vacuum, this speed is 3.00×10^8 m/s. All calculations in this book will use this value for the speed of light unless otherwise specified in the exercise.

Light has both wave and particle properties. The exercises in this chapter deal with the wave nature of light. For a wave of wavelength λ and frequency f traveling at the speed of light, c, $c = \lambda f$. The distance that light travels in a given amount of time can be represented by the equation $\Delta d = c\Delta t$.

Note that these two equations are both special cases of the more general equations, $v = \lambda f$ and $\Delta d = v\Delta t$.

Solved Examples

Example 1: How long does it take for light from the sun to reach Earth if the sun is 1.50×10^{11} m away?

Given: $\Delta d = 1.50 \times 10^{11}$ m $\qquad$ *Unknown:* $\Delta t = ?$
$\qquad\quad c = 3.00 \times 10^8$ m/s $\qquad$ *Original equation:* $\Delta d = c\Delta t$

Solve: $\Delta t = \dfrac{\Delta d}{c} = \dfrac{1.50 \times 10^{11} \text{ m}}{3.00 \times 10^8 \text{ m/s}} =$ **500. s**

This is a little more than 8 min.

Example 2: Microwave ovens emit waves of about 2450 MHz. What is the wavelength of this light?

Solution: The term MHz stands for Megahertz or 10^6 Hz. Therefore, the microwaves have a frequency of 2450×10^6 Hz.

Given: $c = 3.00 \times 10^8$ m/s $\qquad$ *Unknown:* $\lambda = ?$
$\qquad\quad f = 2450 \times 10^6$ Hz $\qquad$ *Original equation:* $c = \lambda f$

Solve: $\lambda = \dfrac{c}{f} = \dfrac{3.00 \times 10^8 \text{ m/s}}{2450 \times 10^6 \text{ Hz}} =$ **0.122 m**

Practice Exercises

Exercise 1: When you look at a distant star or planet, you are looking back in time. How far back in time are you looking when you observe Pluto through the telescope from a distance of 5.91×10^{12} m?

Answer: _____

Exercise 2: If a person could travel at the speed of light, it would still take 4.3 years to reach the nearest star, Proxima Centauri. How far away, in meters, is Proxima Centauri? (Ignore any relativistic effects.)

Answer: _____

Exercise 3: When you go out in the sun, it is the ultraviolet light that gives you your tan. The pigment in your skin called *melanin* is activated by the enzyme *tyrosinase*, which has been stimulated by ultraviolet light. What is the wavelength of this light if it has a frequency of 7.89×10^{14} Hz?

Answer: _____

Exercise 4: IRAS, the Infrared Astronomy Satellite launched by NASA in 1983, had a detector that was supercooled to enable it to measure infrared or heat radiation from different regions of space. What is the frequency of infrared light that has a wavelength of 1.00×10^{-6} m?

Answer: _____

13-2 Reflection

Vocabulary **Reflection:** The bouncing of light.

The angle a beam of light makes when it strikes a surface is described with respect to the **normal,** an imaginary line drawn perpendicular to the surface. When light shines onto a mirror, the angle at which the light enters the mirror (angle of incidence) is exactly equal to the angle at which the light leaves the mirror (angle of reflection). This is called the **law of reflection** and is easily observed in a plane (flat) mirror.

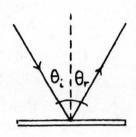

Due to the curvature of a spherical mirror, light reflected from its surface behaves somewhat differently than it does when reflected from a plane mirror. There are two types of spherical mirrors, **converging** (or concave) and **diverging** (or convex).

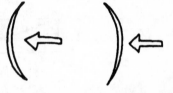

Converging   Diverging

The following terminology is used when describing how light is reflected from converging and diverging mirrors.

Vocabulary **Object distance:** The distance from the mirror to the object. This value is always a positive number.

Vocabulary **Image distance:** The distance from the mirror to the image. An image can be **real** (inverted and able to be projected on a screen), or **virtual** (right-side-up and not able to be projected on a screen).

Vocabulary **Focal point:** The point where parallel rays meet (or appear to meet) after reflecting from a mirror. The distance from this focal point to the mirror is called the **focal length**. The focal length of a converging mirror always has a positive value while the focal length of a diverging mirror always has a negative value.

Vocabulary **Mirror Equation:** $\dfrac{1}{\text{focal length}} = \dfrac{1}{\text{object distance}} + \dfrac{1}{\text{image distance}}$

$$\frac{1}{f} = \frac{1}{d_o} + \frac{1}{d_i}$$

Note: Many situations involving mirrors can also be solved using ray diagrams.

Converging (Concave) Mirror

If an object is located more than one focal length from a converging mirror as shown in Figure A, the image it forms is real, inverted, and in front of the mirror. You can actually project this image onto a piece of paper. Both d_o and d_i have positive values.

If the object is at the focal point as in figure B, no image is formed because the reflected rays are parallel.

If an object is located less than one focal length from a converging mirror as in figure C, the image it forms is virtual, upright, enlarged, and behind the mirror. In other words, you must look into the mirror to see the image. Here, d_o has a positive value and d_i has a negative value.

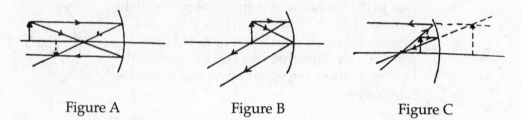

| Figure A | Figure B | Figure C |

Diverging (Convex) Mirror

The image formed by a diverging mirror is always virtual, upright, smaller, and behind the mirror. The image can be seen only by looking into the mirror. Here d_o has a positive value while d_i has a negative value.

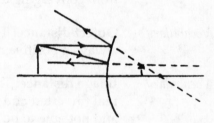

Solved Examples

Example 3: Sitting in her parlor one night, Gerty sees the reflection of her cat, Whiskers, in the living room window. If the image of Whiskers makes an angle of 40° with the normal, at what angle does Gerty see him reflected?

Solution: Because the angle of incidence equals the angle of reflection, Gerty must see her cat reflected at an angle of 40°.

Example 4: Wendy the witch is polishing her crystal ball. It is so shiny that she can see her reflection when she gazes into the ball from a distance of 15 cm. a) What is the focal length of Wendy's crystal ball if she can see her reflection 4.0 cm behind the surface? b) Is this image real or virtual?

a. *Given:* $d_o = 15$ cm

$\qquad\qquad d_i = -4.0$ cm

Unknown: $f = ?$

Original equation: $\dfrac{1}{f} = \dfrac{1}{d_o} + \dfrac{1}{d_i}$

Solve: $\dfrac{1}{f} = \dfrac{1}{d_o} + \dfrac{1}{d_i} = \dfrac{1}{15\text{ cm}} + \dfrac{1}{-4.0\text{ cm}}$

Getting a common denominator of 60 cm gives $\dfrac{1}{f} = \dfrac{4}{60\text{ cm}} - \dfrac{15}{60\text{ cm}} = \dfrac{-11}{60\text{ cm}}$

To find f, take the reciprocal of this sum. $f = \dfrac{-60\text{ cm}}{11} = \mathbf{-5.5\text{ cm}}$

The minus sign before the answer means that this is the focal length of a diverging mirror.

b. The image seen *behind* a curved surface is always a **virtual image**.

Example 5:   With his face 6.0 cm from his empty water bowl, Spot sees his reflection 12 cm behind the bowl and jumps back. a) What is the focal length of the bowl? b) What was surprising about Spot's reflection that may have caused him to jump?

a. *Given:* $d_o = 6.0$ cm

$\qquad\qquad d_i = -12$ cm

Unknown: $f = ?$

Original equation: $\dfrac{1}{f} = \dfrac{1}{d_o} + \dfrac{1}{d_i}$

Solve: $\dfrac{1}{f} = \dfrac{1}{d_o} + \dfrac{1}{d_i} = \dfrac{1}{6.0\text{ cm}} + \dfrac{1}{-12\text{ cm}}$

Getting a common denominator of 12 cm gives $\dfrac{1}{f} = \dfrac{2}{12\text{ cm}} - \dfrac{1}{12\text{ cm}} = \dfrac{1}{12\text{ cm}}$

$$f = \mathbf{12\text{ cm}}$$

The positive answer means that the bowl was acting as a converging mirror.

b. The surprising thing Spot noticed about his reflection was that it appeared larger than life!

Practice Exercises

Exercise 5:   Manish is in a house of mirrors with one of his friends when he comes to two mirrors situated at an angle of 90°. Manish stands so that light shining on his face is incident on one mirror at an angle of 50°, as shown. At what angle will this light reflect from the second mirror?

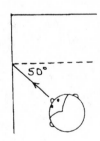

Answer: ——————————————

Exercise 6: A popular lawn ornament in the 1960s was a colored reflecting sphere that sat in the yard as a decoration. a) If a bird is 10.0 cm from a blue reflecting sphere and sees its image reflected 5.0 cm behind the sphere, what is the focal length of the spherical reflector? b) Would the bird's image appear larger or smaller than the bird itself?

Answer: **a.** _____

Answer: **b.** _____

Exercise 7: Polly applies her mascara while looking in a concave mirror whose focal length is 18 cm. She looks into it from a distance of 12 cm. a) How far is Polly's image from the mirror? b) Does it matter whether or not Polly's face is closer or farther than one focal length? Explain.

Answer: **a.** _____

Answer: **b.** _____

Exercise 8: A friend is wearing a pair of mirrored sunglasses whose convex surface has a focal length of 20.0 cm. If your face is 40.0 cm from the sunglasses, how far behind the sunglasses is your image?

Answer: _____

13-3 Refraction

Vocabulary

Refraction: The change in direction of light due to a change in speed as it passes from one medium to another.

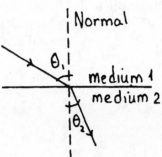

The path of light is described with respect to the normal. If light is slowed down as it enters a new medium, it bends toward the normal. If it speeds up, it bends away from the normal.

The amount of bending is represented with the letter n, which stands for the **index of refraction**. The index of refraction for a particular medium is a ratio of the speed of light in a vacuum to the speed of light in the medium.

$$\text{index of refraction} = \frac{\textbf{speed of light in a vacuum}}{\textbf{speed of light in another medium}} \quad \text{or} \quad n = \frac{c}{v}$$

Because light travels fastest in a vacuum, the index of refraction for any other medium is always greater than 1. Although the index of refraction for air is 1.0003, in this chapter the value will be written simply as 1.00.

The angle to which light will bend upon passing from one medium to another depends upon the index of refraction of each of the two media, n_1 and n_2, and the light's angle of incidence.

$$n_1 \sin \theta_1 = n_2 \sin \theta_2$$

The symbols θ_1 and θ_2 stand for the angle of incidence and the angle of refraction, respectively.

A special case of this equation is used when light travels from a more-dense medium to a less-dense medium and the refracted ray makes an angle of 90.0° with the normal as it skims along the boundary of the two media. When this happens, the incident angle θ_1 is called the **critical angle**, θ_c.

$$n_1 \sin \theta_c = n_2 \sin 90.0°$$

If the incident angle is any bigger than the critical angle, there is no refraction. Instead, all the light is reflected back inside the object. This is called **total internal reflection**.

Solved Examples

Example 6: Hickory, a watchmaker, is interested in an old timepiece that's been brought in for a cleaning. If light travels at 1.90×10^8 m/s in the crystal, what is the crystal's index of refraction?

Given: $c = 3.00 \times 10^8$ m/s $\qquad$ *Unknown:* $n = ?$
$\qquad\quad v = 1.90 \times 10^8$ m $\qquad\qquad$ *Original equation:* $n = \dfrac{c}{v}$

Solve: $n = \dfrac{c}{v} = \dfrac{3.00 \times 10^8 \text{ m/s}}{1.90 \times 10^8 \text{ m/s}} = \mathbf{1.58}$

Remember, the index of refraction has no units. It is just a ratio of the speed of light in two different media.

Example 7: While fishing out on the lake one summer afternoon, Amy spots a large trout just below the surface of the water at an angle of $60.0°$ to the vertical, and she tries to scoop it out of the water with her net. a) Draw the fish where Amy sees it. b) At what angle should Amy aim for the fish? ($n_{water} = 1.33$).

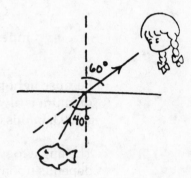

Solution: a. The fish will appear to be straight ahead according to Amy. However, because light travels slower in water than in air, the fish is closer to Amy than she thinks.

b. *Given:* $n_1 = 1.33$ (water) $\qquad$ *Unknown:* $\theta_2 = ?$
$\qquad\qquad n_2 = 1.00$ (air) $\qquad\qquad$ *Original equation:* $n_1 \sin \theta_1 = n_2 \sin \theta_2$
$\qquad\qquad \theta_2 = 60.0°$

Solve: $\sin \theta_1 = \dfrac{n_2 \sin \theta_2}{n_1} = \dfrac{(1.00) \sin 60.0°}{1.33} = 0.651 \qquad \theta_1 = \sin^{-1} 0.651 = \mathbf{40.6°}$

Example 8: Binoculars contain prisms inside that reflect light entering at an angle larger than the critical angle. If the index of refraction of a glass prism is 1.58, what is the critical angle for light entering the prism?

Given: $n_1 = 1.58$ (glass) $\qquad$ *Unknown:* $\theta_c = ?$
$\qquad\quad n_2 = 1.00$ (air) $\qquad\qquad$ *Original equation:* $n_1 \sin \theta_c = n_2 \sin 90.0°$

Solve: $\sin \theta_c = \dfrac{n_2 \sin \theta_2}{n_1} = \dfrac{(1.00) \sin 90.0°}{1.58} = 0.633 \qquad \theta_c = \sin^{-1} 0.633 = \mathbf{39.3°}$

Practice Exercises

Exercise 9: Alison sees a coin at the bottom of her swimming pool at an angle of 40.0° to the normal and she dives in to retrieve it. However, Alison doesn't like to open her eyes in the water so she must rely on her initial observation of the coin made in the air. At what angle does the light from the coin travel as it moves toward the surface? (n_{water} = 1.33)

Answer: _____

Exercise 10: Here's an interesting trick to try. Place a penny in the bottom of a cup and stand so that the penny is just out of sight, as shown. Then pour water into the cup. Without moving, you will suddenly see the penny magically appear. If you look into the cup at an angle of 70.0° to the normal, at what angle to the normal must the penny be located in order for it to just appear in the bottom of the cup when the cup is filled with water? (n_{water} = 1.33)

Answer: _____

Exercise 11: Rohit makes his girlfriend a romantic candlelight dinner and tops it off with a dessert of gelatin filled with blueberries. If a blueberry that appears at an angle of 44.0° to the normal in air is really located at 30.0° to the normal in the gelatin, what is the index of refraction of the gelatin?

Answer: _____

√ **Exercise 12:** A jeweler must decide whether the stone in Mrs. Smigelski's ring is a real diamond or a less-precious zircon. He measures the critical angle of the gem and finds that it is 31.3°. Is the stone really a diamond or just a good imitation? ($n_{diamond} = 2.41$, $n_{zircon} = 1.92$)

Answer: _____

Additional Exercises

A-1: Radio waves travel at the speed of light. How long would it take the Russians to send a message to a spacecraft orbiting Mars at a distance of 7.8×10^{10} m from Earth?

A-2: At the doctor's office, an X-ray of your hand is taken with electromagnetic radiation of frequency 3.00×10^{17} Hz. What is the wavelength of this radiation?

A-3: In order to see your back teeth more easily, your dentist uses a small mirrored instrument that can be easily manipulated in your mouth. If the dentist places this mirror directly under a real molar, and tilts it 20°, at what angle to the normal will the dentist need to look into the mirror in order to see the tooth?

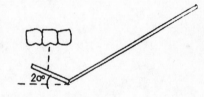

A-4: While decorating his Christmas tree, Vinnie discovers that he can see his reflection in a Christmas tree ball. a) If Vinnie looks into the ornament from a distance of 20.0 cm and focuses on his reflection 4.0 cm behind the ball, what is the focal length of the Christmas ball? b) Is Vinnie's image upright or inverted? c) Is his image larger or smaller?

A-5: Some rear-view mirrors on cars and trucks are curved to allow for a wider field of view. a) Would these mirrors be converging or diverging? b) Why might this be a little dangerous for a driver unaccustomed to this type of mirror? c) If the mirror has a focal length of 20.0 cm and the truck driver looks in the mirror from a distance of 30.0 cm, where does he see his image?

A-6: Wes stands in his hotel room in Cancun and admires his tan in a mirror that allows him to look "larger than life." a) What type of mirror is Wes using? b) Where should Wes stand in relation to the focal point of the mirror in order to appear enlarged? c) If the mirror has a focal length of 75.0 cm, and Wes stands 50.0 cm from the mirror's surface, how far behind the mirror is his image? d) Where does he see his image if he stands 200. cm from the mirror?

A-7: An automobile headlight is made by placing a filament at the focal point of a concave mirrored surface. a) If the focal length of the mirrored surface is 5.0 cm, calculate the image distance. b) Why is this the desired image distance for automobile headlights?

A-8: A blue glow from a bug light strikes the Bradford's swimming pool at an angle of 35.0°. At what angle is the light refracted into the pool? ($n_{water} = 1.33$)

A-9: The index of refraction of ethyl alcohol is 1.36, while the index of refraction of water is 1.33. a) Does light travel faster in alcohol or in water? b) What is the speed of light in each?

A-10: Heather is snorkeling in Oahu's Hanuma Bay when she looks up through the water at a palm tree on the shore. a) If the index of refraction of water is 1.33 and Heather sees the palm tree at an angle of 45°, at what angle is the palm tree really located with respect to the normal?

A-11: Spenser, a cat, enjoys watching the family goldfish from the top of the fish tank. If the goldfish, swimming in water, appears to be at an angle of 28.0° as seen by Spenser, at what true angle is the goldfish from the normal? ($n_{water} = 1.33$)

A-12: Evan has taken Eva out to dinner to propose marriage and he has hidden the engagement ring in her drink as a surprise. When Eva has finished her drink, she spots the ring beneath an ice cube. If Eva looks down into the glass at an angle of 61.0° but the ice cube refracts the ring at an angle of 42.0°, what is the index of refraction of ice?

A-13: In her bedroom, Mia has a fiber optic light that glows as hundreds of fiber optic cables are lit from below. a) If each fiber optic cable has an index of refraction of 1.48, at what critical angle must light enter the cable in order for total internal reflection to occur? b) Explain why total internal reflection is important to a fiber optic lamp.

Challenge Exercises for Further Study

B-1: Marian admires a new dress in a department store dressing room mirror. If Marian stands as shown, making an angle of 70° with the center mirror, at what angle will the light be reflected from the mirror on the right?

B-2: Your friend is stranded 10.0 m high in a tall tree with a hungry tiger beneath, while you lie on the beach a distance away. He has only a mirror, which he uses to signal you by holding it perpendicular to the horizon as shown. If the sun hits the mirror at a 30.0° angle to the normal and reflects back in your eye, how far away are you from the tree?

B-3: As you are walking toward a swimming pool on a hot summer day, you suddenly notice a glare of sunlight off the water's surface that is so bright it makes you close your eyes. If the angle of incidence of the incoming sunlight is 70.0° and you stand 1.80 m tall, how far (horizontally) are you standing from the point where the incident ray hits the water?

B-4: The deepest section of ocean in the world is the Marianas Trench, located in the Pacific Ocean. Here, the ocean floor is as low as 10 918 m below the surface. If the index of refraction of water is 1.33, how long would it take a laser beam to reach the bottom of the trench?

14 Lenses, Diffraction, and Interference

14-1 Lenses, Telescopes, and Magnifying Glasses

When light shines through a lens, it is **refracted** or bent due to the shape and material of the lens. Parallel rays of light passed through some lenses will eventually converge at the **focal point**. The terminology used for lenses is much the same as that used for mirrors in Chapter 13.

Vocabulary   **Object distance:** The distance from the center of the lens to the object.

Vocabulary   **Image distance:** The distance from the center of the lens to the image. An image can be **real** (able to be projected on a screen), or **virtual** (not able to be projected on a screen).

Vocabulary   **Focal point:** The point where parallel rays meet (or appear to meet) after passing through a lens. The distance from this focal point to the center of the lens is called the **focal length**.

$$\text{Thin Lens Equation: } \frac{1}{\text{focal length}} = \frac{1}{\text{object distance}} + \frac{1}{\text{image distance}}$$

$$\text{or} \quad \frac{1}{f} = \frac{1}{d_o} + \frac{1}{d_i}$$

NOTE: Many situations involving lenses can also be solved using ray diagrams.

The Converging (Positive) Lens

The focal length of a converging lens is always a positive number.

If an object is located outside the focal point of a converging lens, the image it forms is real, inverted, and on the opposite side of the lens. Both d_o and d_i are positive numbers.

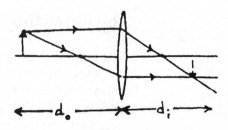

If an object is located inside the focal point of a converging lens, the image it forms is virtual, upright, enlarged, and on the same side as the object. In this instance, d_o is positive and d_i is negative.

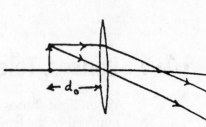

If the object is at the focal point, the rays do not converge and therefore no image is formed.

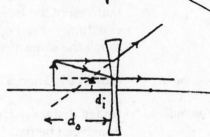

The Diverging (Negative) Lens

The focal length of a diverging lens is always a negative number.

The image formed by a diverging lens is always virtual, upright, smaller, and on the same side of the lens as the object. In this instance, d_o is positive and d_i is negative.

If an object appears taller when seen through a lens, the object is magnified. The **linear magnification** of an object can be found by comparing the image distance to the object distance, or by comparing the image height, h_i, to the object height, h_o.

$$\text{linear magnification} = \frac{\text{image distance}}{\text{object distance}} = \frac{\text{image height}}{\text{object height}}$$

$$\text{or} \quad m = \frac{d_i}{d_o} = \frac{h_i}{h_o}$$

Note that a negative magnification implies a virtual image.

Linear magnification has no units. It is simply a ratio of image to object distance or a ratio of image to object height.

The Refracting Telescope

A refracting telescope is a device that uses one lens to produce a real image, and a second lens to produce the virtual image that is seen by your eye. The amount of linear magnification you see when you look at an object through a telescope depends upon the focal length of each of the lenses. The lens that points toward the object is the objective lens and the lens you look through is the eyepiece. The focal lengths of each of these lenses are labeled f_o and f_e, respectively.

$$\text{linear magnification} = \frac{\text{focal length of objective lens}}{\text{focal length of eyepiece}} \quad \text{or} \quad m = \frac{f_o}{f_e}$$

The Magnifying Glass

When using a magnifying glass, the amount of **angular magnification** of an object depends upon how close you hold the magnifying glass to the object. It also depends upon the near point of your own eye, which is the closest point at which an unaided eye can focus on an object. A person's near point increases with age and the eyes lose some of their adaptable, elastic properties. However, for the ease of calculations, assume the near point of the eye is 25 cm unless otherwise noted.

$$\text{angular magnification} = \frac{\text{near point}}{\text{focal length}} \quad \text{or} \quad M = \frac{\text{near point}}{f}$$

Solved Examples

Example 1:   Mukluk, an Inuit, makes a converging lens out of ice that will enable him to concentrate light from the sun to start a fire. When he holds the ice lens 1.00 m from a snow-covered wall, an image of his 5.00-m-distant igloo is projected onto the snow. a) What is the focal length of the ice lens? b) Draw a ray diagram of the situation.

a. *Given:* $d_o = 5.00$ m   *Unknown:* $f = ?$
            $d_i = 1.00$ m   *Original equation:* $\frac{1}{f} = \frac{1}{d_o} + \frac{1}{d_i}$

Solve: $\dfrac{1}{f} = \dfrac{1}{d_o} + \dfrac{1}{d_i} = \dfrac{1}{5.00 \text{ m}} + \dfrac{1}{1.00 \text{ m}} = 1.20 \text{ m}^{-1}$

Taking the reciprocal gives $f = \dfrac{1}{1.20 \text{ m}^{-1}} = $ **0.833 m**

The focal length of 0.833 m is close to the image distance of 1.00 m.

b.

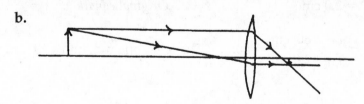

Example 2:   A diverging lens is placed 5.0 cm in front of a laser beam to spread the light for the production of a hologram. a) What is the focal length of the lens if the beam of laser light seems to come from a point 2.0 cm behind the lens? b) Draw a ray diagram of the situation.

a. *Given:* $d_o = 5.0$ cm   *Unknown:* $f = ?$
            $d_i = -2.0$ cm   *Original equation:* $\frac{1}{f} = \frac{1}{d_o} + \frac{1}{d_i}$

Solve: $\dfrac{1}{f} = \dfrac{1}{d_o} + \dfrac{1}{d_i} = \dfrac{1}{5.0 \text{ cm}} + \dfrac{1}{-2.0 \text{ cm}} = \dfrac{2}{10. \text{ cm}} - \dfrac{5}{10.0 \text{ cm}} = -\dfrac{3}{10.} \text{ cm}^{-1}$

$f = -\dfrac{10.}{3} \text{ cm} = \mathbf{-3.3 \text{ cm}}$

b.

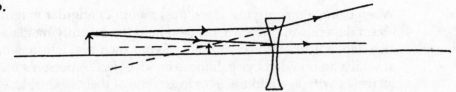

Example 3: Irwin, a coin collector, is looking at a rare coin held behind a magnifying glass whose focal length is 5.0 cm. a) If the eyes' near point is 25 cm, what is the angular magnification? b) If the coin is 2.0 cm in diameter, how large will its diameter appear to be when it is held in this position under the magnifying glass?

a. *Given:* near point = 25 cm   *Unknown:* $M = ?$
       $f = 5.0$ cm   *Original equation:* $M = \dfrac{\text{near point}}{f}$

Solve: $M = \dfrac{\text{near point}}{f} = \dfrac{25 \text{ cm}}{5.0 \text{ cm}} = \mathbf{5.0}$ The coin is magnified 5.0 times.

b. *Given:* $m = 5.0$ *Unknown:* $h_i = ?$
       $h_o = 2.0$ cm   *Original equation:* $m = \dfrac{h_i}{h_o}$

Solve: $h_i = mh_o = (5.0)(2.0 \text{ cm}) = \mathbf{10. \text{ cm}}$

Example 4: The ship *Speedwell* brought many early settlers to this country in the 1600s. Oceanus sits high above the ship's deck in the crow's nest watching through a telescope for the first sign of land. How much does the telescope magnify if the eyepiece has a 2.0-cm focal length and the objective lens has a 80.-cm focal length?

Given: $f_o = 80.$ cm   *Unknown:* $m = ?$
       $f_e = 2.0$ cm   *Original equation:* $m = \dfrac{f_o}{f_e}$

Solve: $m = \dfrac{f_o}{f_e} = \dfrac{80. \text{ cm}}{2.0 \text{ cm}} = \mathbf{40.}$ The telescope magnifies 40. times.

Practice Exercises

√ **Exercise 1:** Harold and Roland find a discarded plastic lens lying on the beach. The boys discuss what they learned in physics last semester and argue whether the lens is a converging or a diverging one. When they look through the lens, they notice that objects are inverted. a) If an object sitting 25.0 cm in front of the lens forms an image 20.0 cm behind the lens, what is the focal length of the lens? b) Is it a converging or a diverging lens?

Answer: **a.** ――――――――――

Answer: **b.** ――――――――――

Exercise 2:   Sadie looks at her friend's face through a diverging lens. a) Is the image real or virtual? b) If her friend's face is 50.0 cm from the lens that forms an image at a distance of 20.0 cm, what is the focal length of the lens? c) Draw a ray diagram of the situation.

Answer: **a.** ――――――――――

Answer: **b.** ――――――――――

Exercise 3:   Giorgio is clicking shots of the fashion model Nadine as she walks toward him across the studio. Giorgio's camera contains a lens with a focal length of 0.0500 m. a) How far back must the film be located when Nadine is 3.00 m from the camera? b) Should the lens be moved in or out as Nadine approaches closer to the photographer? c) Draw a ray diagram of the situation with Nadine at 3.00 m and 1.00 m from the camera.

Answer: **a.** ――――――――――

Answer: **b.** ――――――――――

Exercise 4:   Dr. Wasserman is showing slides to his biology class. a) If the slides are positioned 15.5 cm from the projector lens that has a focal length of 15.0 cm, where should the screen be placed to produce the clearest image of the slide? b) Draw a ray diagram of the situation.

Answer: **a.** ――――――――――

Exercise 5: Marlin is out on a safari. Looking through his telescope, he spots a giraffe in the distance. The telescope has an objective lens of 40-cm focal length and an eyepiece of 2-cm focal length. a) What is the magnification of the giraffe? b) How large is the image formed by the telescope if the giraffe appears to be 1.5 cm high to the naked eye?

Answer: **a.** _____

Answer: **b.** _____

Exercise 6: Emilio, an entomologist, studies a millepede that he holds behind a magnifying glass whose focal length is 2.00 cm. a) Assuming Emilio's near point is 25.0 cm, what is the angular magnification? b) Does Emilio have to bring the magnifying glass closer to, or farther from, the millipede in order to make it appear larger?

Answer: **a.** _____

Answer: **b.** _____

Exercise 7: Mr. Crabtree, a jeweler, looks through his jeweler's loupe (a small magnifying glass attached to his glasses) in order to read the engraving on a pewter bowl. The loupe has a focal length of 3 cm. If Mr. Crabtree's near point is 24 cm, what is the angular magnification of the engraving?

Answer: _____

14-2 Eyeglasses

When the eye is unable to focus incoming light directly on the retina (a layer of tissue in the back of the eye that is sensitive to light), eyeglasses or contact lenses are usually prescribed.

If the lens, or cornea, is curved so that light would focus behind the retina, the result is a condition called **farsightedness**, where only objects at a distance can be seen clearly. To correct this problem, glasses for a farsighted person have lenses that are thicker in the middle and thinner near the edges (converging lenses).

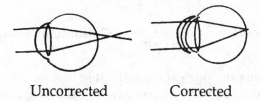

Uncorrected   Corrected

If the lens, or cornea, is curved so that light would focus in front of the retina, the result is a condition called **nearsightedness**, where only objects close up can be seen clearly. To correct this problem, glasses for a nearsighted person have lenses that are thinner in the middle and thicker near the edges (diverging lenses).

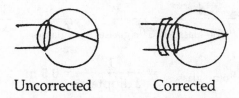

Uncorrected   Corrected

The power of a pair of prescription glasses is the reciprocal of the focal length, if the focal length is measured in meters.

$$\textbf{Power} = \frac{1}{\textbf{focal length}} \qquad \text{or} \qquad P = \frac{1}{f}$$

The SI unit for the power of eyeglasses is the **diopter**, which equals the **reciprocal of a meter (m^{-1})**.

For all the following exercises, assume that the preferred far point of the eye is infinity, ∞, and the preferred near point is 25 cm. To find the power of the lenses in a pair of glasses, take the difference between the reciprocal of how far the eye can see without glasses and how far it can see with glasses.

$$\text{power} = \frac{1}{f_{\text{glasses}}} = \frac{1}{d_{o(\text{glasses})}} - \frac{1}{d_{o(\text{no glasses})}}$$

If you wear glasses or contact lenses, ask your doctor about the power of your prescription. You may find that it can be different for each eye!

Solved Examples

Example 5: Craig is nearsighted, so he must wear glasses to see objects that are far away. If his glasses have a focal length of 0.5 m, what is their power in diopters?

Solution: The focal length must be written as a negative number because a nearsighted person will always wear glasses with diverging lenses. A diverging lens has a negative focal length.

Given: $f_{\text{glasses}} = -0.5$ m

Unknown: $P = ?$
Original equation: $P = \dfrac{1}{f}$

Solve: $P = \dfrac{1}{f} = \dfrac{1}{-0.5 \text{ m}} = \textbf{-2 diopters}$

Example 6: In the previous exercise, if Craig can see to infinity with his glasses on, what is the maximum distance he can see clearly with the glasses off?

Given: $f_{\text{glasses}} = -0.5$ m
$d_{o(\text{glasses})} = \infty$

Unknown: $d_{o(\text{no glasses})} = ?$
Original equation:
$$\dfrac{1}{f_{\text{glasses}}} = \dfrac{1}{d_{o(\text{glasses})}} - \dfrac{1}{d_{o(\text{no glasses})}}$$

Solve: $\dfrac{1}{d_{o(\text{no glasses})}} = \dfrac{1}{d_{o(\text{glasses})}} - \dfrac{1}{f_{\text{glasses}}} = \dfrac{1}{\infty} - \dfrac{1}{-0.5 \text{ m}} = 0 - (-2) = 2$ diopters

$$d_{o(\text{no glasses})} = \dfrac{1}{2 \text{ diopters}} = \textbf{0.5 m}$$

The farthest Craig can see clearly without glasses is 0.5 m.

Example 7: Dorcas must hold the phone book 0.5 m from her eyes in order to find the eye doctor's phone number. a) If Dorcas would like to read the phone book at a more comfortable distance of 0.25 m, what power glasses does she need? b) What type of lenses would these glasses contain?

a. *Given:* $d_{o(\text{no glasses})} = 0.5$ m
$d_{o(\text{glasses})} = 0.25$ m

Unknown: $P = ?$
Original equation:
$$\dfrac{1}{f_{\text{glasses}}} = \dfrac{1}{d_{o(\text{glasses})}} - \dfrac{1}{d_{o(\text{no glasses})}}$$

Solve: $\dfrac{1}{f_{\text{glasses}}} = \dfrac{1}{d_{o(\text{glasses})}} - \dfrac{1}{d_{o(\text{no glasses})}} = \dfrac{1}{0.25 \text{ m}} - \dfrac{1}{0.5 \text{ m}} = 4 - 2 = \textbf{2 diopters}$

b. Because the power of the glasses in this example is a positive number, the lenses must be converging lenses. This is supported by the fact that farsightedness must be corrected with converging lenses.

Practice Exercises

Exercise 8:   Beth is farsighted, so she must wear glasses to see objects close by. If her glasses have a focal length of 0.30 m, what is their power in diopters?

Answer: _____

Exercise 9:   Herman is able to read the newspaper at a distance of 0.75 m, but no closer. a) Is he farsighted or nearsighted? b) What power lens should he use to allow him to read the paper at 0.25 m? c) What type of lens does he need?

Answer: **a.** _____

Answer: **b.** _____

Answer: **c.** _____

Exercise 10:   At the beach, Maria can see Sandy, a surfer, clearly only when he is standing closer than 2.0 m. a) What power prescription sunglasses would Maria need in order to see Sandy when he is out on the ocean riding a wave? b) What type of lenses will her glasses contain?

Answer: **a.** _____

Answer: **b.** _____

Exercise 11: Matt is driving his "18-wheeler" while wearing his new pair of glasses whose focal length is −0.40 m. If the glasses allow Matt to see clearly at an infinite distance for normal driving, how far could Matt see clearly before he bought the glasses?

Answer: _____

Exercise 12: Moshe has gone to Bermuda for spring vacation and when he is on the beach realizes that he has picked up his father's pair of prescription sunglasses by mistake. The glasses have a power of + 3.0 diopters. a) What type of eye problem does Moshe's father have, and how do you know? b) What is the closest that Moshe's father can see clearly without his glasses? c) Will these glasses produce an image in front of, or behind, the image formed by Moshe's normal eye?

Answer: **a.** _____

Answer: **b.** _____

Answer: **c.** _____

14-3 Diffraction and Interference

Vocabulary   **Diffraction:** The spreading of a wave as it passes around an obstacle or through an opening.

Vocabulary   **Interference:** When two waves overlap to produce one new wave.

In 1801, Thomas Young attempted to prove that light was a wave by showing that it has the ability to diffract and interfere. Young passed white light through two closely-spaced slits and noticed that the light spread out as it passed through the openings (diffracted), and overlapped on a screen a few meters away (interfered), to produce alternating bands of light and dark.

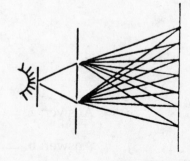

Whether light is passed through two slits or through the multiple, closely-spaced slits of a diffraction grating, the grating equation can be written as

$$\text{wavelength} = \frac{(\textbf{slit separation})(\textbf{space between bright bands})}{(\textbf{distance from slits to screen})} \quad \text{or} \quad \lambda = \frac{dx}{L}$$

This equation is a good approximation when the angular separation between the bright bands is very small. When used with a diffraction grating, however, it could produce an answer with as much as 10% error. Nevertheless, to simplify calculations and avoid the use of trigonometry, the equation will be used in this form in all exercises.

The common unit for the wavelength of light is the **nanometer (nm)**, which equals 10^{-9} m.

Solved Examples

Example 8: Miss McGillivray loses the specifications for her diffraction grating and must recalibrate it in order to determine the grating spacing. She shines a red helium-neon laser, whose wavelength is 633 nm, through the grating. Two bright spots that are each 1.40 m from the central maximum fall on the wall 4.00 m away. What is the space between the grooves on the diffraction grating?

Solution: First, convert nm to m.   633 nm = 6.33×10^{-7} m

Given: $\lambda = 6.33 \times 10^{-7}$ m   *Unknown:* $d = ?$
       $L = 4.00$ m   *Original equation:* $\lambda = \dfrac{dx}{L}$
       $x = 1.40$ m

Solve: $d = \dfrac{\lambda L}{x} = \dfrac{(6.33 \times 10^{-7}\text{ m})(4.00\text{ m})}{1.40\text{ m}} = \textbf{1.81} \times \textbf{10}^{-6}$ **m**

Example 9: In the previous exercise, Miss McGillivray uses her newly calibrated grating to determine the wavelength of a green helium-neon laser. Keeping the laser at the same distance from the wall as before, the distance from the central maximum to the first bright fringe is 1.20 m. What is the wavelength of the green HeNe laser?

Given: $d = 1.81 \times 10^{-6}$ m   *Unknown:* $\lambda = ?$
       $L = 4.00$ m   *Original equation:* $\lambda = \dfrac{dx}{L}$
       $x = 1.20$ m

Solve: $\lambda = \dfrac{dx}{L} = \dfrac{(1.81 \times 10^{-6}\text{ m})(1.20\text{ m})}{4.00\text{ m}} = 5.43 \times 10^{-7}$ m = **543 nm**

Practice Exercises

Exercise 13: Judy and Earl are sitting under the boardwalk one warm summer evening while the light of a low-pressure sodium vapor lamp whose wavelength is 589 nm passes through two small cracks in a board, producing fringes of light 0.0020 m apart on the ground. a) If the boardwalk is 3.0 m above the sand, what is the distance between the two cracks in the board? b) If the distance between the cracks were smaller, would the fringes of light on the ground be closer together or farther apart?

Answer: **a.** _____

Answer: **b.** _____

Exercise 14: Two large speakers broadcast the sound of a band tuning up before an outdoor concert. While the band plays an A whose wavelength is 0.773 m, Brenda walks to the refreshment stand along a line parallel to the speakers. If the speakers are separated by 12.0 m and Brenda is 24.0 m away, how far must she walk between the "loudspots"?

Answer: _____

Exercise 15: In an attempt to test the particle nature of matter, Claus Jönsson performed an experiment in 1961 that was very similar to Young's Double Slit experiment for light done in 1801. Jönsson sent a beam of electrons through two slits separated by 2.00×10^{-6} m onto a fluorescent screen 0.200 m away. Due to their high speed, the electrons behaved like waves with a wavelength of 2.40×10^{-11} m. How far apart were the bright lines formed on the screen?

Answer: _____

Additional Exercises

A-1: A photocopy machine is set to reduce the size of printed material by 50%. When the print is regular size, both the image and object distance are 16.0 cm. If the lens is then moved 24.0 cm from the object, how large is the new image distance?

A-2: The average normal human eye forms an image on the retina at a distance of about 0.0240 m from the lens, as shown. How much must the focal length of the lens change in order to accommodate an object moved from 10.0 m to 0.250 m? (This change in focal length is accomplished by small muscles in the eye called *cilliary muscles*. These muscles actually stretch and relax the lens.)

0.024m

A-3: Lisa is posing for her senior class picture and sits 2.00 m from the camera lens whose focal length is 17.0 cm. The camera lens is positioned 21.0 cm in front of the film. Will the photographer obtain a clear image of Lisa? If not, by how much must the camera lens be moved in our out?

A-4: Cindy is lying on the beach focusing her camera on a friend standing 5.00 m away. Her camera has a focal length of 5.00 cm. a) Where must Cindy position the camera lens relative to the film for the sharpest focus? b) What type of lens must her camera have, and why?

A-5: Sherlock Holmes discovers some telltale hairs at the scene of a crime. He views the hairs with his magnifying glass from a distance of 6.0 cm. If the hairs are magnified 4.0 times, how far is the magnified image from the lens?

A-6: Jacob attaches a solar filter to his telescope and projects an image of the sun through the objective lens that has a focal length of 2.00 m. Jacob can't decide whether to use a 40.0-mm eyepiece or a 16.0-mm eyepiece to study the solar features. a) What amount of magnification will each eyepiece provide? b) Someone may look through a telescope and ask, "What is the magnification of this instrument?" Why is it impossible to give one standard answer to the question? c) If the sun appears to be 1.00 cm across to the naked eye, how large will it appear when viewed with the 16.0-mm eyepiece?

A-7: To the naked eye, Jupiter appears to be about 0.10 cm in diameter. In a telescope whose objective lens has a focal length of 2.0 m, Jupiter appears to be 1.2 cm in diameter. What is the focal length of the eyepiece used to produce this image?

A-8: Ms. Chang is standing by the slide projector in the back of the room when she realizes that the screen is in the wrong location to get a clear image. a) If the projector has a lens with a focal length of 20.0 cm, and the slides sit 20.6 cm behind the lens, in which direction should one of the students move the screen that sits 7.00 m from the lens? b) How far away should the screen be from the projector lens?

A-9: Beverly wears bifocals. She can read close up when she looks through the bottom portion and can read far away when she looks through the top portion. a) The top of her glasses has a focal length of −0.25 m. What is the power, in diopters, of this part of the glasses? b) The bottom portion has a power of 3.5 diopters. What is the focal length of this part of the glasses?

A-10: In exercise A-9, if Beverly can see to infinity with her glasses on, a) what is the maximum distance she can see clearly with the glasses off? b) If Beverly can see an object at 25 cm with her glasses on, what is the minimum distance she can see clearly with the glasses off?

A-11: Rachel brings a note home from school. The note advises her mother that "Rachel is having a difficult time reading the words on the board and can only see the words if she is sitting closer than 2.0 m." If Rachel wants to be able to read the words from 3.0 m away, what power glasses does she need?

✓ **A-12:** Joon puts on a pair of diffraction grating glasses that he bought in a novelty shop and looks at a mercury vapor street lamp that is 5.00 m away. He sees a yellow spectral line 1.16 m on either side of the light source. If the diffraction grating glasses have a slit separation of 2.49×10^{-6} m, what is the wavelength of the light Joon is observing?

✓ **A-13:** Radio station WLLH has two transmitters that sit atop nearby hillsides broadcasting a wave that is 214 m long. As Kiesha drives down the interstate parallel to the two transmitters at a distance of 1000. m, she hears an increase in signal from the station every 30.0 m. How far apart are the two transmitters?

Challenge Exercises for Further Study

B-1: The Hale telescope at the Yerkes Observatory in Wisconsin has an objective lens with a focal length of 19 m. (For an object at infinity, the image distance equals the focal length.) If the telescope is used to observe Saturn that is 1275×10^9 m from Earth, what will be the apparent diameter of the rings if their actual diameter is 27×10^7 m?

B-2: Dr. Kirwan is preparing a slide show that he will present to the executive board at tonight's committee meeting. He places a 3.50-cm slide behind a lens of 20.0 cm focal length in the slide projector. a) How far from the lens should the slide be placed in order to shine on a screen 6.00 m away? b) How wide must the screen be to accommodate the projected image?

B-3: Madeline is working for the Eye-Spy Detective Agency and her assignment is to secretly photograph the pages of a journal. Madeline's tiny camera has the film located 2.10 cm behind the lens, and she must fill the entire piece of 1.00-cm film with the picture of the 25.0-cm-tall document. How close must Madeline be to the journal pages to get a clear image on the film?

15 Electrostatics

15-1 Electrostatic Force

Vocabulary **Electrostatics:** The study of electric charges, forces, and fields.

The symbol for electric charge is the letter "q" and the SI unit for charge is the **coulomb (C).** The coulomb is a very large unit.

$$1 \text{ C} = 6.25 \times 10^{18} \text{ electrons} \quad \text{or}$$
$$1 \text{ electron has a charge of } 1.60 \times 10^{-19} \text{ C.}$$

Electrons surrounding the nucleus of an atom carry a negative charge. Protons, found inside the nucleus of the atom, carry a positive charge of 1.60×10^{-19} C, while neutrons (which also reside in the nucleus) are neutral. It is important to remember that only electrons are free to move in a substance. Protons and neutrons usually do not move.

When two objects with like charges, positive or negative, are brought near each other, they experience a repulsive force. When objects with opposite charges, one negative and one positive, are brought side by side, they experience an attractive force. These forces can be described with Coulomb's law.

Vocabulary **Coulomb's Law:** Two charged objects attract each other with a force that is proportional to the charge on the objects and inversely proportional to the square of the distance between them.

$$F \propto \frac{q_1 q_2}{d^2}$$

This equation looks very similar to Newton's law of universal gravitation. As before, the sign $\propto$ means "proportional to." To make an equation out of this proportionality, insert a quantity called the **electrostatic constant, k.**

$$k = 9.0 \times 10^9 \text{ N} \cdot \text{m}^2/\text{C}^2$$

The magnitude of Coulomb's law can now be written as an equation.

$$\text{electrostatic force} = \frac{(\text{electrostatic constant})(\text{charge 1})(\text{charge 2})}{(\text{distance})^2} \quad \text{or} \quad F = \frac{kq_1 q_2}{d^2}$$

Like all other forces, the electrostatic force between two charged objects is measured in newtons.

Solved Examples

Example 1: Anthea rubs two latex balloons against her hair, causing the balloons to become charged negatively with 2.0×10^{-6} C. She holds them a distance of 0.70 m apart. a) What is the electric force between the two balloons? b) Is it one of attraction or repulsion?

Solution: It is not necessary to carry the sign of the charge throughout the entire exercise. However, when determining the direction of your final answer, it is important to remember the charge on each object.

Given: $q_1 = 2.0 \times 10^{-6}$ C Unknown: $F = ?$
$\quad\quad q_2 = 2.0 \times 10^{-6}$ C Original equation: $F = \dfrac{kq_1q_2}{d^2}$
$\quad\quad d = 0.70$ m
$\quad\quad k = 9.0 \times 10^9$ N $\cdot$ m^2/C^2

Solve: $F = \dfrac{kq_1q_2}{d^2} = \dfrac{(9.0 \times 10^9 \text{ N} \cdot \text{m}^2/\text{C}^2)(2.0 \times 10^{-6} \text{ C})(2.0 \times 10^{-6} \text{ C})}{(0.70 \text{ m})^2} = \textbf{0.073 N}$

b) Because both balloons are negatively charged, they will repel each other.

Example 2: Two pieces of puffed rice become equally charged as they are poured out of the box and into Kirk's cereal bowl. If the force between the puffed rice pieces is 4×10^{-23} N when the pieces are 0.03 m apart, what is the charge on each of the pieces?

Solution: Because both charges are the same, solve for both q's together. Then find the square root of that value to determine one of the charges.

Given: $F = 4 \times 10^{-23}$ N Unknown: $q = ?$
$\quad\quad d = 0.03$ m Original equation: $F = \dfrac{kq_1q_2}{d^2}$
$\quad\quad k = 9.0 \times 10^9$ N $\cdot$ m^2/C^2

Solve: $q_1q_2 = \dfrac{Fd^2}{k} = \dfrac{(4 \times 10^{-23} \text{ N})(0.03 \text{ m})^2}{9.0 \times 10^9 \text{ N} \cdot \text{m}^2/\text{C}^2} = 4 \times 10^{-36}$ C^2

This is the square of the charge on the pieces of puffed rice. To find the charge on one piece of puffed rice, take the square root of this number.

$$q = \sqrt{4 \times 10^{-36} \text{ C}^2} = \textbf{2} \times \textbf{10}^{-18} \textbf{ C}$$

Practice Exercises

Exercise 1: When sugar is poured from the box into the sugar bowl, the rubbing of sugar grains creates a static electric charge that repels the grains, and causes sugar to go flying out in all directions. If each of two sugar grains acquires a charge of 3.0×10^{-11} C at a separation of 8.0×10^{-5} m, with what force will they repel each other?

Answer: _____

Exercise 2: Boppo the clown carries two mylar balloons that rub against a circus elephant, causing the balloons to separate. Each balloon acquires 2.0×10^{-7} C of charge. How large is the electric force between them when they are separated by a distance of 0.50 m?

Answer: _____

Exercise 3: Inez uses hairspray on her hair each morning before going to school. The spray spreads out before reaching her hair partly because of the electrostatic charge on the hairspray droplets. If two drops of hairspray repel each other with a force of 9.0×10^{-9} N at a distance of 0.070 cm, what is the charge on each of the equally-charged drops of hairspray?

Answer: _____

Exercise 4: Bonnie is dusting the house and raises a cloud of dust particles as she wipes across a table. If two 4.0×10^{-14}-C pieces of dust exert an electrostatic force of 2.0×10^{-12} N on each other, how far apart are the dust particles at that time?

Answer: _____

Exercise 5: Each of two hot-air balloons acquires a charge of 3.0×10^{-5} C on its surface as it travels through the air. How far apart are the balloons if the electrostatic force between them is 8.1×10^{-2} N?

Answer: _____

15-2 Electric Field

Vocabulary

Electric Field: An area of influence around a charged object. The magnitude of the field is proportional to the amount of electrical force exerted on a positive test charge placed at a given point in the field.

$$\text{electric field} = \frac{\text{electric force}}{\text{test charge}} \quad \text{or} \quad E = \frac{F}{q_0}$$

The SI unit of electric field is the **newton per coulomb (N/C).**

The electric field around a charged object is a vector and can be represented with electric field lines that point in the direction of the force exerted on a unit of positive charge. In other words, electric field lines point away from a positive charge and toward a negative charge, as shown in the diagram.

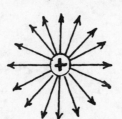 

For a point charge (or other spherical charge distribution), the magnitude of the electric field can be written as

$$E = \frac{F}{q_o} = \frac{kq_o q}{q_o d^2} = \frac{kq}{d^2}$$

where q is the charge on the surface of the object, and d is the distance between the center of the charged object and a small positive test charge, q_o, placed in the field.

Solved Examples

Example 3: Deepika pulls her wool sweater over her head, which charges her body as the sweater rubs against her cotton shirt. What is the electric field at a location where a 1.60×10^{-19} C-piece of lint experiences a force of 3.2×10^{-9} N as it floats near Deepika? b) What will happen if Deepika now touches a conductor such as a door knob?

a. *Given:* $q_o = 1.60 \times 10^{-19}$ C   *Unknown:* $E = ?$
          $F = 3.2 \times 10^{-9}$ N   *Original equation:* $F = q_o E$

Solved: $E = \dfrac{F}{q_o} = \dfrac{3.2 \times 10^{-9}\,\text{N}}{1.60 \times 10^{-19}\,\text{C}} = \mathbf{2.0 \times 10^{10}}$ **N/C**

b. She will reduce her charge in a process called **grounding,** in which excess electrons flow from her body into the ground and spread evenly over the surface of Earth.

Example 4: A fly accumulates 3.0×10^{-10} C of positive charge as it flies through the air. What is the magnitude and direction of the electric field at a location 2.0 cm away from the fly?

Solution: First, convert cm to m.   2.0 cm = 0.020 m

Given: $k = 9.0 \times 10^9$ N $\cdot$ m^2/C^2 *Unknown:* $E = ?$
          $q = 3.0 \times 10^{-10}$ C   *Original equation:* $E = \dfrac{kq}{d^2}$
          $d = 0.020$ m

Solve: $E = \dfrac{kq}{d^2} = \dfrac{(9.0 \times 10^9\,\text{N}\cdot\text{m}^2/\text{C}^2)(3.0 \times 10^{-10}\,\text{C})}{(0.020\,\text{m})^2} = \mathbf{6800}$ **N/C away from the fly**

Practice Exercises

Exercise 6: Mr. Patel is photocopying lab sheets for his first period class. A particle of toner carrying a charge of 4.0×10^{-9} C in the copying machine experiences an electric field of 1.2×10^6 N/C as it's pulled toward the paper. What is the electric force acting on the toner particle?

Answer: _____

Exercise 7: As Courtney switches on the TV set to watch her favorite cartoon, the electron beam in the TV tube is steered across the screen by the field between two charged plates. If the electron experiences a force of 3.0×10^{-6} N, how large is the field between the deflection plates?

Answer: _____

Exercise 8: Gordon the night custodian dusts off a classroom globe with a feather duster, causing the globe to acquire a charge of -8.0×10^{-9} C. What is the magnitude and direction of the electric field at a point 0.40 m from the center of the charged globe?

Answer: _____

Exercise 9: April is decorating a tree in her backyard with plastic eggs in preparation for Easter. She hangs two eggs side by side so that their centers are 0.40 m apart. April rubs the eggs to shine them up, and in doing so places a charge on each egg. The egg on the left acquires a charge of 6.0×10^{-6} C while the egg on the right is charged with 4.0×10^{-6} C. What is the electric field at a point 0.15 m to the right of the egg on the left?

Answer: _____

15-3 Electrical Potential Difference

Vocabulary **Potential Difference:** The work done to move a positive test charge from one location to another.

$$\text{potential difference} = \frac{\text{work}}{\text{test charge}} \quad \text{or} \quad V = \frac{W}{q_0}$$

The SI unit for potential difference is the **volt (V),** which equals a **joule per coulomb (J/C).**

Remember, the term "work" can be replaced with the term "energy," because to store energy in, or give energy to, an object, work must be done. Therefore, potential difference can also be defined as the electrical potential energy per unit test charge. **Voltage** is often used to mean potential difference.

The field that exists between two charged parallel plates is uniform except near the plate edges, and depends upon the potential difference between the plates and the plate separation.

$$\text{electric field} = \frac{\text{potential difference}}{\text{separation between plates}} \quad \text{or} \quad E = \frac{V}{\Delta d}$$

Here, the unit for electric field is the volt/meter. It was noted earlier that the unit for electric field is the newton/coulomb. This means that a volt/meter must equal a newton/coulomb.

$$\frac{\text{volt}}{\text{meter}} = \frac{\text{joule/coulomb}}{\text{meter}} = \frac{\text{newton} \cdot \text{meter}}{\text{coulomb} \cdot \text{meter}} = \frac{\text{newton}}{\text{coulomb}}$$

Solved Examples

Example 5: An electron in Tammie's TV is accelerated toward the screen across a potential difference of 22 000 V. How much kinetic energy does the electron lose when it strikes the TV screen?

Given: $q_0 = 1.60 \times 10^{-19}$ C $\qquad$ *Unknown:* $W = ?$
$\qquad\qquad V = 22\ 000$ V $\qquad\qquad$ *Original equation:* $V = \dfrac{W}{q_0}$

Solve: $W = q_0 V = (1.60 \times 10^{-19}$ C$)(22\ 000$ V$) = \mathbf{3.5 \times 10^{-15}}$ **J**

Example 6: Amir shuffles his feet across the living room rug, building up a charge on his body. A spark will jump when there is a potential difference of 9000 V between the door and the palm of Amir's hand. This happens when his hand is 0.3 cm from the door. At this point, what is the electric field between Amir's hand and the door?

Solution: First, convert cm to m. $\quad$ 0.3 cm = 0.003 m

Given: $\quad V = 9000$ V $\qquad\qquad$ *Unknown:* $E = ?$
$\qquad\qquad \Delta d = 0.003$ m $\qquad\qquad$ *Original equation:* $V = E\Delta d$

Solve: $E = \dfrac{V}{\Delta d} = \dfrac{9000\ \text{V}}{0.003\ \text{m}} = \mathbf{3 \times 10^6}$ **V/m**

Practice Exercises

Exercise 10: James recharges his dead 12.0-V car battery by sending 28 000 C of charge through the terminals. How much electrical potential energy must James store in the car battery to make it fully charged?

Answer: _____

Exercise 11: If an electron loses 1.4×10^{-15} J of energy in traveling from the cathode to the screen of Jeffrey's personal computer, across what potential difference must it travel?

Answer: _____

Exercise 12: A "bug zapper" kills bugs that inadvertently stray between the charged plates of the device. The bug causes sudden dielectric breakdown of the air between the plates. If two plates in a bug zapper are separated by 5.0 cm and the field between them is a uniform 2.8×10^6 V/m, what is the potential difference that kills the unsuspecting bugs?

Answer: _____

Exercise 13: While getting out of a car, Victor builds up a charge on his body as he slides across the cloth car seats. When he attempts to shut the car door, his hand discharges 12 000 V through a uniform electric field of 3.0×10^6 V/m. How far is his hand from the door at the time the spark jumps?

Answer: _____

Exercise 14: A lightning bolt from a cloud hits a tree after traveling 200 m to the ground through an electric field of 2.0×10^6 V/m. a) What is the potential difference between the cloud and the tree just before the lightning bolt strikes? b) If you are in an open field during a lightning storm and the only thing you see nearby is a tall tree, is it a good idea to stand under the tree for protection from the lightning? Why or why not?

Answer: **a.** _____

Answer: **b.** _____

Additional Exercises

A-1: A raindrop acquires a negative charge of 3.0×10^{-18} C as it falls. What is the force of attraction when the raindrop is 6.0 cm from the bulb on the end of a car antenna that holds a charge of 2.0×10^{-6} C?

A-2: In a grain elevator on Farmer Judd's farm, pieces of grain become electrically charged while falling through the elevator. If one piece of grain is charged with 5.0×10^{-16} C while another holds 2.0×10^{-16} C of charge, what is the electrostatic force between them when they are separated by 0.050 m?

A-3: Rocco, an auto body painter, applies paint to automobiles by electrically charging the car's outer surface and oppositely charging the paint particles that he sprays onto the car. This causes the paint to adhere tightly to the car's surface. If two paint particles of equal charge experience a force of 4.0×10^{-8} N between them at a separation of 0.020 cm, what is the charge on each?

A-4: After unpacking a shipment of laboratory glasswear, Mrs. Payne dumps the box of Styrofoam packing chips into a recycling bin. The chips rub together and two chips 0.015 m apart repel each other with a force of 6.0×10^{-3} N. What is the charge on each of the chips?

A-5: Wiz the cat is batting at two Ping-Pong balls hanging from insulating threads with their sides just barely touching. Each ball acquires a positive charge of 3.5×10^{-9} C from Wiz's fur and they swing apart. a) If a force of 6.0×10^{-5} N acts on one of the balls, how far apart are they from each other? b) Is the force between them one of attraction or repulsion?

A-6: A droplet of ink in an ink-jet printer carrying a charge of 8.0×10^{-13} C is deflected onto the paper by a force of 3.2×10^{-4} N. How strong is the field that causes this force?

A-7: In the human body, nerve cells work by pumping sodium ions out of a cell in order to maintain a potential difference across the cell wall. If a sodium ion carries a charge of 1.60×10^{-19} C as it is pumped with an electrical force of 2.0×10^{-12} N, what is the electric field between the inside and outside of the nerve cell?

A-8: Each of two Van de Graaff generators, whose centers are separated from one another by 0.50 m, becomes charged after they are switched on. One Van de Graaff generator holds $+3.0 \times 10^{-2}$ C while the other holds -2.0×10^{-2} C. What is the magnitude and direction of the electric field halfway between them?

A-9: Willa the witch dusts her crystal ball with her silk scarf, causing the ball to become charged with 5.0×10^{-9} C. Willa then stares into the crystal ball and the wart on the end of her nose experiences an electric field strength of 2200 N/C. How far is the tip of her nose from the center of the crystal ball?

A-10: The Millikan oil drop experiment of 1909 allowed Robert A. Millikan to determine the charge of an electron. In the experiment, an oil drop is suspended between two charged plates by an electric force that equals the gravitational force acting on the 1.1×10^{-14}-kg drop. a) What is the charge on the drop if it remains stationary in an electric field of 1.72×10^5 N/C? b) How many extra electrons are there on this particular oil drop?

A-11: In eighteenth-century Europe, it was common practice to ring the church bells in an attempt to ward off lightning. However, during one 33-year period, nearly 400 church steeples were struck while the bells were being rung. If a bolt of lightning discharges 30.0 C of charge from a cloud to a steeple across a potential difference of 15 000 V, how much energy is lost by the cloud and gained by the steeple?

A-12: In Exercise A-7, how thick is the wall of the nerve cell if there is a potential difference of 0.089 between the inside and outside of the cell?

A-13: Ulrich stands next to the Van de Graaff generator and gets a shock as he holds his knuckle 0.2 m from the machine. In order for a spark to jump, the electric field strength must be 3×10^6 V/m. At this distance, what is the potential difference between Ulrich and the generator?

Challenge Exercises for Further Study

B-1: Three glass Christmas balls become electrically charged when Noel removes them from the packaging material in their box. Noel hangs the balls on the tree as shown. If each ornament has acquired a charge of 2.0×10^{-10} C, what is the magnitude and direction of the force experienced by the ball at the top?

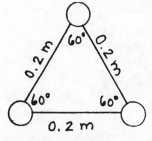

B-2: In a TV picture tube, electrons are accelerated from rest up to very high speeds through a potential difference of 22 000 V. At what speed will an electron be moving just as it strikes the TV screen? (In reality you would have to consider the effects of relativity in order to solve this exercise properly; however, ignore such relativistic effects here.)

B-3: A lightning bolt discharges into New Hampshire's Lake Winnipesaukee after passing through a potential difference of 9.00×10^7 V. What is the minimum amount of charge the lightning bolt could be carrying, if it were to vaporize 1000. kg of water in the lake that was originally at a temperature of 20.0 °C?

16 Direct Current Circuits

16-1 Current and Resistance

Vocabulary

Current: The amount of charge that passes through an area in a given amount of time.

$$\text{current} = \frac{\text{charge}}{\text{time}} \quad \text{or} \quad I = \frac{\Delta q}{\Delta t}$$

The SI unit for current is the **ampere (A),** which equals one **coulomb per second (C/s)**.

In conductors, such as metal wires, electrons are relatively free to move, and can carry energy throughout a circuit. This energy comes from a source such as a **battery** that converts chemical energy into electrical energy for use in the circuit. As energy is transformed in a battery, a potential difference, V, develops across the battery's terminals. This potential difference is called an **electromotive force,** or **EMF**. In this book, voltage between the terminals of a battery is simply referred to as potential difference.

Vocabulary

Resistance: An opposition to the flow of charge.

For a given source voltage, the resistance of a circuit determines how much charge will flow in the circuit. When charge passes through a resistance, some electrical energy is changed to other forms. This is produced by a potential difference across the resistance.

$$\text{potential difference} = (\text{current})(\text{resistance}) \quad \text{or} \quad V = IR$$

The SI unit for resistance is the **ohm (Ω),** which equals one **volt per amp (V/A)**.

Sometimes it is not desirable to use wires that have a high resistance, because considerable energy losses occur when charge flows through a resistor. However, in any device that produces heat, such as a toaster, high resistance is needed or else the toaster would not get hot. Therefore, a heating element made with superconducting wires would be useless.

The resistance of a wire depends upon the type of material that the wire is made of, its length, and its cross-sectional area. The longer the wire, the more resistant it is to the flow of charge. The larger the cross-sectional area of the wire, the less resistant it is to charge flow. Temperature also affects the resistance of a wire. The hotter the wire, the more resistant it becomes to the flow of charge. This means that more current will flow through a toaster when it is first turned on than when the coils are glowing red hot.

Solved Examples

Example 1: Household current in a circuit cannot generally exceed 15 A for safety reasons. What is the maximum amount of charge that could flow through this circuit in a house during the course of a 24.0-h day?

Solution: Because the unit ampere means coulombs per second, 24.0 h must be converted in 86 400 s.

Given: $I = 15$ A   Unknown: $\Delta q = ?$
         $\Delta t = 86\ 400$ s   Original equation: $I = \dfrac{\Delta q}{\Delta t}$

Solve: $\Delta q = I\Delta t = (15 \text{ A})(86\ 400 \text{ s}) = \mathbf{1.3 \times 10^6}$ **C**

Example 2: What is the resistance of the heating element in a car lock de-icer that contains a 1.5-V battery supplying a current of 0.5 A to the circuit?

Given: $V = 1.5$ V   Unknown: $R = ?$
       $I = 0.5$ A   Original equation: $V = IR$

Solve: $R = \dfrac{V}{I} = \dfrac{1.5 \text{ V}}{0.5 \text{ A}} = \mathbf{3\ \Omega}$

Practice Exercises

Exercise 1: Arthur is going trick-or-treating for Halloween so he puts new batteries in his flashlight before leaving the house. Until the batteries die, it draws 0.500 A of current, allowing a total of 5400. C of charge to flow through the circuit. How long will Arthur be able to use the flashlight before the batteries' energy is depleted?

Answer: _____

Exercise 2: Fabian's car radio will run from the 12-V car battery that produces a current of 0.20 A even when the car is turned off. The car battery will no longer operate when it has lost 1.2×10^6 J of energy. If Fabian gets out of the car and leaves the radio on by mistake, how long will it take for the car battery to go completely dead (that is, lose all energy)?

Answer: _____

Exercise 3: While cooking dinner, Dinah's oven uses a 220.-V line and draws 8.00 A of current when heated to its maximum temperature. What is the resistance of the oven when it is fully heated?

Answer: _____

Exercise 4: Justine's hair dryer has a resistance of 9.00 Ω when first turned on. a) How much current does the hair dryer draw from the 110.-V line in Justine's house? b) What happens to the resistance of the hair dryer as it runs for a long time?

Answer: **a.** _____

Answer: **b.** _____

Exercise 5: Camille takes her pocket calculator out of her bookbag as she gets ready to do her physics homework. In the calculator, a 0.160-C charge encounters 19.0 Ω of resistance every 2.00 seconds. What is the potential difference of the battery?

Answer: _____

16-2 Capacitance

Vocabulary **Capacitor:** A device that stores charge on conductors that are separated by an insulator.

Capacitance is a measure of the amount of charge stored on the conductors, for a given potential difference.

$$\text{capacitance} = \frac{\text{amount of charge}}{\text{potential difference}} \quad \text{or} \quad C = \frac{\Delta q}{V}$$

The SI unit for capacitance is the **farad (F),** which equals one **coulomb per volt (C/V).**

A capacitor may be used in a circuit by storing charge on two parallel plates and then periodically releasing it into the circuit, creating an intermittent flow of charge.

Solved Examples

Example 3: The first capacitor was invented by Pieter van Musschenbroek in 1745 when he and his assistant stored charge in a device called a Leyden jar. If 5×10^{-4} C of charge were stored in the jar over a potential difference of 10 000 V, what was the capacitance of the Leyden jar? (When van Musschenbroek touched the jar, he received such a large jolt that he exclaimed he would not try the experiment again for all the kingdom of France!)

Given: $\Delta q = 5 \times 10^{-4}$ C $\qquad$ *Unknown:* $C = ?$
$\qquad\quad V = 10\ 000$ V $\qquad\qquad$ *Original equation:* $C = \dfrac{\Delta q}{V}$

Solve: $C = \dfrac{\Delta q}{V} = \dfrac{5 \times 10^{-4}\,\text{C}}{10\ 000\ \text{V}} = \mathbf{5 \times 10^{-8}\ F}$

Example 4: Lydia pushes the shutter button of her camera and the flash unit releases the 4.5×10^{-3} C of charge that was stored in a 500.-μF capacitor. What is the potential difference across the plates of the capacitor inside the flash?

Solution: The term μ (micro) means 10^{-6}, so a μF means 10^{-6} farad.

Given: $\Delta q = 4.5 \times 10^{-3}$ C $\qquad$ *Unknown:* $V = ?$
$\qquad\quad C = 500. \times 10^{-6}$ F $\qquad\quad$ *Original equation:* $C = \dfrac{\Delta q}{V}$

Solve: $V = \dfrac{\Delta q}{C} = \dfrac{4.5 \times 10^{-3}\,\text{C}}{500. \times 10^{-6}\,\text{F}} = \mathbf{9.0\ V}$

Practice Exercises

Exercise 6: The nervous system of the human body contains axons whose membranes act as small capacitors. A membrane is capable of storing 1.2×10^{-9} C of charge across a potential difference of 0.070 V before discharging nerve impulses through the body. What is the capacitance of one of these axon membranes?

Answer: _____

Exercise 7: During a lightning storm, the separation between the clouds and the earth acts as a giant capacitor with a capacitance of 2500 μF. If the transmitting tower of radio station KBOZ is hit by a bolt of lightning carrying 50. C of charge, what is the potential difference between the cloud and the tower?

Answer: _____

Exercise 8: Dr. Frankenstein brings his monster to life with electroshock treatment by discharging a 50.-μF capacitor through the monster's neck across a potential difference of 24 V. How much charge flows into the monster to make him come alive?

Answer: _____

Exercise 9: On Saturday nights, Greg likes to go the Frisco Disco, where he can dance under the strobe light. The strobe contains a 200-μF capacitor that stores charge over a 1000-V potential difference. If the strobe flashes 4 times each second, what is the current flow created by the strobe's capacitor?

Answer: _____

16-3 Power

Vocabulary   **Power:** The amount of work done in a given unit of time.

As seen in the previous chapter, electrical work is done when an amount of charge, Δq, is transferred across a potential difference, V, or $W = \Delta qV$. The faster this transfer of charge occurs, the more power is generated in the circuit.

$$\textbf{Power} = \frac{\textbf{work}}{\textbf{elapsed time}} \quad \text{or} \quad P = \frac{W}{\Delta t} = \frac{\Delta qV}{\Delta t} = IV$$

Therefore, as current is drawn in a circuit to power an appliance, a potential difference occurs across the appliance.

The SI unit for electrical power is the **watt (W)**, which equals one **joule per second (J/s)**.

Solved Examples

Example 5: The lighter in Bryce's car has a resistance of 4.0 Ω. a) How much current does the lighter draw when it is run off the car's 12-V battery? b) How much power does the lighter use?

a. *Given:* $R = 4.0\ \Omega$ *Unknown:* $I = ?$
            $V = 12$ V   *Original equation:* $V = IR$

Solve: $I = \dfrac{V}{R} = \dfrac{12\ V}{4.0\ \Omega} = \textbf{3.0 A}$

b. *Given:* $I = 3.0$ A   *Unknown:* $P = ?$
            $V = 12$ V   *Original equation:* $P = IV$

Solve: $P = IV = (3.0\ A)(12\ V) = \textbf{36 W}$

Example 6: A 120.-V outlet in Carol's college dorm room is wired with a circuit breaker on a 5-A line so that students cannot overload the circuit. a) If Carol tries to iron a blouse for class with her 700-W iron, will she trip the circuit breaker? b) What is the resistance of the iron?

Solution: A circuit breaker is a switch that automatically turns a circuit off if the current is too high.

a. *Given:* $P = 700.$ W   *Unknown:* $I = ?$
            $V = 120.$ V   *Original equation:* $P = IV$

Solve: $I = \dfrac{P}{V} = \dfrac{700.\ W}{120.\ V} = \textbf{5.83 A}$ Yes, she will!

It may be difficult to see how a watt/volt equals an amp until you begin to break down the units.

$$\frac{\text{watt}}{\text{volt}} = \frac{\text{joule/second}}{\text{joule/coulomb}} = \frac{\text{coulomb}}{\text{second}} = \text{amp}$$

b. Now find the resistance using $V = IR$.

Given: $V = 120.$ V   *Unknown:* $R = ?$
          $I = 5.83$ A   *Original equation:* $V = IR$

Solve: $R = \dfrac{V}{I} = \dfrac{120.\,\text{V}}{5.83\,\text{A}} = \textbf{20.5}\ \mathbf{\Omega}$

Example 7: The Garcias like to keep their 40.0-W front porch light on at night to welcome visitors. If the light is on from 6 p.m. until 7 a.m., and the Garcias pay 8.00¢ per kWh, how much does it cost to run the light for this amount of time each week?

Solution: First, convert the power units to kilowatts, kW, because the cost of household energy is measured in kWh.   40.0 W = 0.0400 kW

Next, determine how long the light is left on each week. From 6 P.M. until 7 A.M. is 13 h. Operating 7 days a week means that the light is on for a total of 91.0 hours.

Given: $P = 0.0400$ kW   *Unknown:* $W = ?$ Cost $= ?$
          $\Delta t = 91.0$ h

Original equation: $P = \dfrac{W}{\Delta t}$

Solve: $W = P\Delta t = (0.0400\ \text{kW})(91.0\ \text{h}) = \textbf{3.64 kWh}$

$$\text{Cost} = \frac{8.00¢}{1.00\ \text{kWh}}\,(3.64\ \text{kWh}) = \textbf{29.1¢}$$

Therefore, it costs the Garcias about 29¢ to run the light all night for an entire week, or a little over $15 per year.

Practice Exercises

Exercise 10: How much power is used by a contact lens heating unit that draws 0.070 A of current from a 120-V line?

Answer: ―――――――――――――

Exercise 11: Celeste's air conditioner uses 2160 W of power as a current of 9.0 A passes through it. a) What is the voltage drop when the air conditioner is running? b) How does this compare to the usual household voltage? c) What would happen if Celeste tried connecting her air conditioner to a usual 120-V line?

Answer: **a.** _____

Answer: **b.** _____

Answer: **c.** _____

Exercise 12: Which has more resistance when plugged into a 120.-V line, a 1400.-W microwave oven or a 150.-W electric can opener?

Answer: _____

Exercise 13: Valerie's 180-W electric rollers are plugged into a 120-V line in her bedroom. a) What current do the electric rollers draw? b) What is the resistance of the rollers when they are heated? c) Combining the equations just used, derive an equation that relates power to voltage and resistance.

Answer: **a.** _____

Answer: **b.** _____

Answer: **c.** _____

Exercise 14: Mrs. Olsen leaves her 0.900-kW electric coffee maker on each day as she heads off to work at 6 A.M. because she likes to come home to a hot cup of coffee at 6 P.M. a) If the electric company charges Mrs. Olsen $0.100 per kWh, how much does running the coffee maker cost her each day? b) What is the yearly cost to run the coffee maker?

Answer: **a.** ————————————

Answer: **b.** ————————————

Exercise 15: While writing this book, the author spent about 1000 h working on her personal computer that has a power input of 60.0 W. Seventy additional hours were spent with the 60.0-W computer and the 240.-W printer running. How much did it cost for the energy use of these two devices, at a cost of $0.100 per kWh?

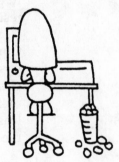

Answer: ————————————

16.4 Series and Parallel Circuits

When multiple resistors are used in a circuit, the total resistance in the circuit must be found before finding the current. Resistors can be combined in a circuit in series or in parallel.

Resistors in Series

When connected in series, the total resistance, R_T, is equal to

$$R_T = R_1 + R_2 + R_3 + \ldots$$

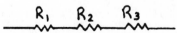

In series, the total resistance is always *larger* than any individual resistance.

Current in series resistors: In series circuits, charge has only one path through which to flow. Therefore, the current passing through each resistor in series is the same.

Potential difference across series resistors: As charge passes through each of the resistors, it loses some energy. This means that there will be a potential difference across each resistor. The sum of all the potential differences equals the potential difference across the battery, assuming negligible resistance in the connecting wires.

Resistors in Parallel

When connected in parallel, the total resistance, R_T, is equal to

$$\frac{1}{R_T} = \frac{1}{R_1} + \frac{1}{R_2} + \frac{1}{R_3} + \ldots$$

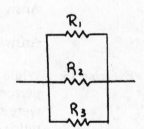

Don't forget! After finding a common denominator and determining the sum of these fractions, flip over the answer to determine R_T.

In parallel circuits, the total resistance is always *smaller* than any individual resistance.

Current in parallel resistors: In parallel circuits, there is more than one possible path and current divides itself according to the resistance of each path. Since current will take the "path of least resistance," the smallest resistor will allow the most current through, while the largest resistor will allow the least current through. The sum of the currents in each parallel resistor equals the original current entering the branches.

Potential difference in parallel resistors: The potential difference across each of the resistors in a parallel combination is the same. If there are no other resistors in the circuit, it is equal to the potential difference across the battery, assuming negligible resistance in the connecting wires.

Solved Examples

Example 8:   Find the total resistance of the three resistors connected in series.

Solve: $R_T = R_1 + R_2 + R_3 = 12\ \Omega + 4\ \Omega + 6\ \Omega = 22\ \Omega$

Example 9: Find the total resistance of the same three resistors now connected in parallel.

Solve: $\dfrac{1}{R_T} = \dfrac{1}{R_1} + \dfrac{1}{R_2} + \dfrac{1}{R_3} = \dfrac{1}{12\ \Omega} + \dfrac{1}{4\ \Omega} + \dfrac{1}{6\ \Omega}$

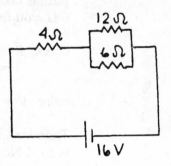

$\dfrac{1}{R_T} = \dfrac{1}{12\ \Omega} + \dfrac{3}{12\ \Omega} + \dfrac{2}{12\ \Omega} = \dfrac{6}{12\ \Omega} = \dfrac{1}{2\ \Omega} \quad R_T = \mathbf{2\ \Omega}$

Example 10: Find the total current passing through the circuit.

This circuit contains resistors in parallel that are then combined with a resistor in series. Always begin solving such a resistor combination by working from the inside out. In other words, first determine the equivalent resistance of the two resistors in parallel before combining this total resistance with the one in series.

Look first at the parallel combination.

$\dfrac{1}{R_T} = \dfrac{1}{R_1} + \dfrac{1}{R_2} = \dfrac{1}{12\ \Omega} + \dfrac{1}{6\ \Omega} = \dfrac{1}{12\ \Omega} + \dfrac{2}{12\ \Omega} = \dfrac{3}{12\ \Omega} = \dfrac{1}{4\ \Omega}$

$R_T = \mathbf{4\ \Omega}$

Now, combine this equivalent resistance with the resistor in series.

$$R_T = R_1 + R_2 = 4\ \Omega + 4\ \Omega = \mathbf{8\ \Omega}$$

To find the current flowing through the circuit, use this total resistance in combination with the potential difference from the battery.

Given: $V = 16$ V   *Unknown:* $I = ?$
         $R = 8\ \Omega$ *Original equation:* $V = IR$

Solve: $I = \dfrac{V}{R} = \dfrac{16\ \text{V}}{8\ \Omega} = \mathbf{2\ A}$

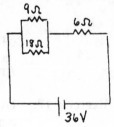

Example 11: Find the current in the 9-Ω resistor.

For the parallel branch

$\dfrac{1}{R_T} = \dfrac{1}{R_1} + \dfrac{1}{R_2} = \dfrac{1}{9\ \Omega} + \dfrac{1}{18\ \Omega} = \dfrac{2}{18\ \Omega} + \dfrac{1}{18\ \Omega} = \dfrac{3}{18\ \Omega} = \dfrac{1}{6\ \Omega}$

$R_T = \mathbf{6\ \Omega}$

Combining with the series resistor

$$R_T = R_1 + R_2 = 6\ \Omega + 6\ \Omega = \mathbf{12\ \Omega}$$

Given: $V = 36\ V$
　　　　$R = 12\ \Omega$

Unknown: $I = ?$
Original equation: $V = IR$

Solve: $I = \dfrac{V}{R} = \dfrac{36\ V}{12\ \Omega} = \mathbf{3\ A}$

This 3 A is the current through the entire circuit. Use this current to find the potential difference across the parallel combination. Remember, the potential difference across resistors wired in parallel is the same regardless of which path is taken. Because the resistors in parallel have a combined resistance of 6 Ω, you find the potential difference across the parallel branch as follows.

Given: $R = 6\ \Omega$
　　　　$I = 3\ A$

Unknown: $V = ?$
Original equation: $V = IR$

Solve: $V = IR = (3\ A)(6\ \Omega) = \mathbf{18\ V}$

Therefore, the potential difference across both the top and the bottom branches is 18 V. Now use this 18-V drop to determine the current in the 9-Ω resistor.

Given: $V = 18\ V$
　　　　$R = 9\ \Omega$

Unknown: $I = ?$
Original equation: $V = IR$

Solve: $I = \dfrac{V}{R} = \dfrac{18\ V}{9\ \Omega} = \mathbf{2\ A}$

Practice Exercises

Exercise 16: Using the diagram, a) find the total resistance in the circuit. b) Find the total current through the circuit.

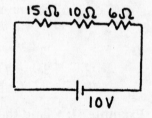

Answer: **a.** _____

Answer: **b.** _____

Exercise 17: Using the diagram, a) find the total resistance in the circuit. b) Find the total current through the circuit.

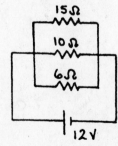

Answer: **a.** _____

Answer: **b.** _____

Exercise 18: Using the diagram, a) find the total resistance in the circuit. b) Find the total current through the circuit.

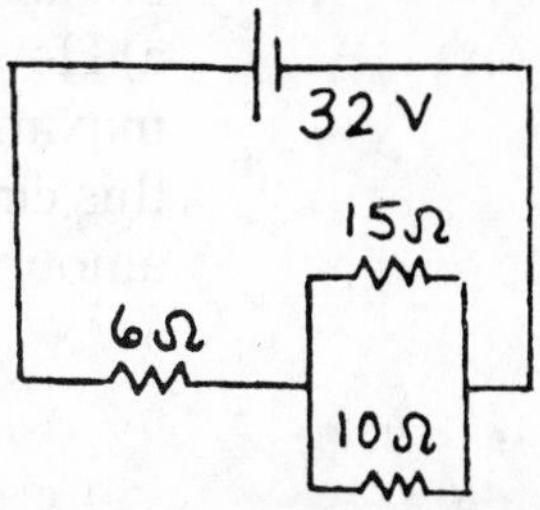

32 V

15 Ω

6 Ω

10 Ω

Answer: **a.** _____

Answer: **b.** _____

Exercise 19: Old-fashioned holiday lights were connected in series across a 120-V household line. a) If a string of these lights consists of 12 bulbs, what is the potential difference across each bulb? b) If the bulbs were connected in parallel, what would be the potential difference across each bulb?

Answer: **a.** _____

Answer: **b.** _____

Exercise 20: Before going to work each morning, Gene runs his 18-Ω toaster, 11-Ω electric frying pan, and 14-Ω electric coffee maker, all at the same time. The three are connected in parallel across a 120-V line. a) What is the current through each appliance? b) If a household circuit could carry a maximum current of 15 A, would Gene be able to run all of these appliances at the same time?

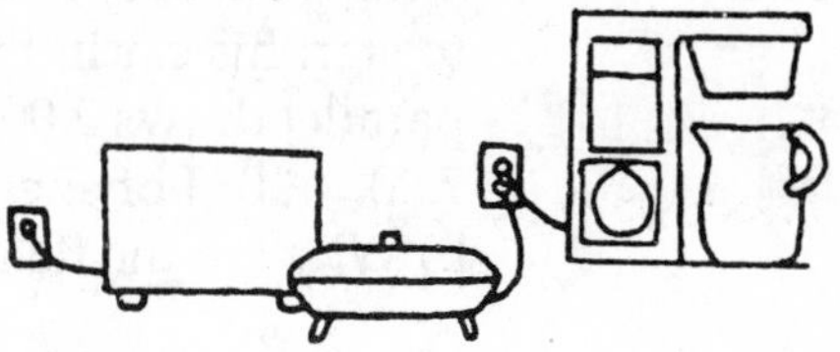

Answer: **a.** _____

Answer: **b.** _____

Exercise 21: Timmy is playing with a new electronics kit he has received for his birthday. He takes out four resistors with resistances of 15 Ω, 20 Ω, 20 Ω, and 30 Ω. a) How would Timmy have to wire the resistors so that they would allow the maximum amount of current to be drawn? Calculate the total resistance in this circuit. b) How must he wire the resistors so that they draw a minimum amount of current? Calculate the total resistance in this circuit.

Answer: **a.** _____

Answer: **b.** _____

Exercise 22: Farmer Crockett is preparing tomato seedlings for his spring planting by growing the small plants over five 46-Ω strip heaters wired in parallel. a) How much current does each heater draw from a 120-V line? b) How much current do they draw all together?

Answer: **a.** _____

Answer: **b.** _____

Additional Exercises

A-1: Otto accidently leaves his automobile headlights on overnight and is unable to start his car in the morning. Each of the two headlights connected in parallel draws 2.00 A of current from the 12.0-V battery. If the battery stores 7.50×10^5 J of energy, how long will it take for the headlights to go off? b) Why are the headlights connected in parallel?

A-2: Officer Moynihan is patrolling his beat with a 4.5-V flashlight whose lightbulb has a resistance of 12 Ω. How much current does the flashlight draw?

A-3: Each night before falling asleep, Linus turns on his electric blanket that is plugged into the 120.-V electrical outlet. A current of 1.20 A flows through the blanket. a) What is the blanket's resistance? b) Does Linus want his electric blanket to have a high resistance or a low resistance? Why?

A-4:   Herbert had just suffered a heart attack but he was revived in the hospital emergency room with a device called a defibrillator. (The paddles of a defibrillator supply a short pulse of high voltage to restart the heart.) The defibrillator contains a 20.-μF capacitor that releases 0.15 C of charge. a) What is the potential difference between the defribrillator paddles during the discharge? b) Why do you think doctors yell "Clear!" to the attendants before discharging the defibrillator?

A-5:   Sherm is typing his term paper on a computer that contains a high-speed switch, controlled with a small 100×10^{-12} F speed-up capacitor. What is the current flow created by the capacitor if it discharges every 0.1 s across a potential difference of 5 V?

A-6:   Every Sunday morning Stuart makes "breakfast in bed" for his wife. However, because the household wires can only carry a maximum current of 15 A from the 120.-V line, it is difficult to run all of the appliances simultaneously without blowing a fuse. What is the most power Stuart may use while cooking, before blowing a fuse?

A-7:   In the previous exercise, a) how much current will Stuart draw if he tries to run the 700.-W toaster and 1000.-W coffee maker at the same time? b) Will this cause him to blow the fuse?

A-8:   Xiaoyi's aquarium operates for 24.0 h a day and contains a 5.0-W heater, two 20.0-W lightbulbs, and a 35.0-W electric filter. If Xiaoyi pays $0.100 per kWh for her electricity bill, how much will it cost to maintain the aquarium for 30.0 days?

A-9:   The average power plant, running at full capacity, puts out 500. MW of power. If the power company charges its customers $0.10 per kWh, what is the revenue brought in by the power plant each day?

A-10:   Horace has invented a unique pair of reading glasses that have two small light bulbs at the bottom wired in series, so that he can see the newspaper when he is reading at night. Each of the bulbs has a resistance of 2.00 Ω, and the system runs off a 3.20-V battery. How much current is drawn by Horace's reading glasses?

A-11:   Jay has two 8-Ω stereo speakers wired in series in the front of his car connected to the 4.0-V output of the stereo. a) What is the current through each of the speakers? b) In his garage, Jay finds two more old speakers with resistances of 4 Ω and 16 Ω. He wires each in parallel with the 8-Ω combination. What is the new current through the 8-Ω speakers? c) If the loudness of each speaker is proportional to the amount of power used, how has the loudness of the two 8-Ω speakers changed?

A-12:   Find a) the total resistance in circuit A below. b) Find the total current through the circuit.

A-13:   Find a) the total resistance in circuit B below. b) Find the total current through the circuit.

A-14:   Find a) the total resistance in circuit C below. b) Find the total current through the circuit.

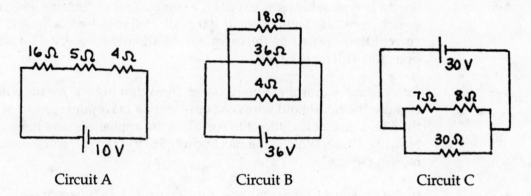

Circuit A   Circuit B   Circuit C

Challenge Exercises for Further Study

B-1:   An 800.-W submersible electric heater is put into a 20.0 °C hottub until the 50.0-kg of tub water has warmed up to 70.0 °C. How long will it take for the heater to heat the tub water? (c_{water} = 4187 J/kg°C)

B-2:   Find the total current in the circuit in the diagram.

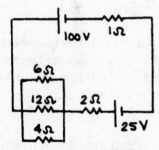

B-3:   In exercise A-10, the light bulbs are rated for 5 h of use before they burn out. If the battery can supply 5184 J to the circuit, which occurs first, energy depletion in the battery or failure of a bulb?

17 Magnetism and Electromagnetic Induction

17-1 Magnetic Forces and Fields

Vocabulary   **Magnetic Field:** An area of influence around a moving charge. The size of the field is related to the amount of magnetic force experienced by the moving charge when it is at a given location in the field.

$$\text{magnetic field} = \frac{\text{force}}{(\text{charge})(\text{speed})} \quad \text{or} \quad B = \frac{F}{qv}$$

The SI unit for magnetic field is the **tesla (T)**, which equals one **netwon per amp·meter (N/A·m)**.

When solving for the magnetic force, rewrite this equation as $F = qvB$.

The magnitude of the magnetic force can also be written in terms of the current, I, flowing through a length of wire, L.

$$\text{force} = (\text{current})(\text{length of wire})(\text{magnetic field}) \quad \text{or} \quad F = ILB$$

Unlike gravitational force or electric force, magnetic force is perpendicular to the plane formed by the field and the moving charge, and is greatest when the magnetic field and the current are perpendicular to each other.

The easiest way to detect a magnetic field is with a compass.

Solved Examples

Example 1:   A proton speeding through a synchrotron at 3.0×10^7 m/s experiences a magnetic field of 4.0 T that is produced by the steering magnets inside the synchrotron. What is the magnetic force pulling on the proton?

Solution: Remember, the charge of a proton or an electron is 1.60×10^{-19} C.

Given: $q = 1.60 \times 10^{-19}$ C   *Unknown:* $F = ?$
  $v = 3.0 \times 10^7$ m/s   *Original equation:* $F = qvB$
  $B = 4.0$ T

Solve: $F = qvB = (1.60 \times 10^{-19}$ C$)(3.0 \times 10^7$ m/s$)(4.0$ T$) = \mathbf{1.9 \times 10^{-11}}$ **N**

Example 2: A 10.0-m-long high-tension power line carries a current of 20.0 A perpendicular to Earth's magnetic field of 5.5×10^{-5} T. What is the magnetic force experienced by the power line?

> *Given:* $I = 20.0$ A   *Unknown:* $F = ?$
> $L = 10.0$ m   *Original equation:* $F = ILB$
> $B = 5.5 \times 10^{-5}$ T
>
> *Solve:* $F = ILB = (20.0 \text{ A})(10.0 \text{ m})(5.5 \times 10^{-5} \text{ T}) = \mathbf{0.011 \text{ N}}$

Practice Exercises

Exercise 1: Dean is hunting in the Northwest Territories at a location where Earth's magnetic field is 7.0×10^{-5} T. He shoots by mistake at a duck decoy, and the rubber bullet he is using acquires a charge of 2.0×10^{-12} C as it leaves his gun at 300. m/s, perpendicular to Earth's magnetic field. What is the magnitude of the magnetic force acting on the bullet?

Answer: _____

Exercise 2: A wasp accumulates 1.0×10^{-12} C of charge while flying perpendicular to Earth's magnetic field of 5.0×10^{-5} T. How fast is the wasp flying if the magnetic force acting on it is 6.0×10^{-16} N?

Answer: _____

Exercise 3: Kron, the alien freedom fighter from the planet Krimbar, shoots his gun that fires protons at a speed of 3.0×10^6 m/s. a) What is Krimbar's magnetic field if it creates a force of 2.88×10^{-15} N on the protons? b) How does this compare to Earth's magnetic field?

Answer: **a.** _____

Answer: **b.** _____

Exercise 4: The magnetic field in Boston, Massachusetts has a horizontal component to the north of 0.18×10^{-4} T and a vertical component of 0.52×10^{-4} T straight downward. a) What is the magnitude and direction of Earth's magnetic field in Boston? b) If a 2.0-m-long household wire is carrying a current of 15 A in a direction perpendicular to the field, what is the magnitude of the magnetic force experienced by the wire?

Answer: **a.** _____

Answer: **b.** _____

17-2 Electromagnetic Induction

Magnetic Flux and Induced Voltage

Vocabulary   **Flux:** The number of magnetic field lines passing through a given area.

flux = (area)(perpendicular component of the magnetic field)

or $\phi = AB$

The unit for flux is the **weber (Wb)**, which equals one **tesla·meter squared (T·m²)**.

Therefore, if a loop of wire lies perpendicular to a magnetic field, the maximum possible number of lines of flux will pass through the loop. If the loop of wire lies parallel to the field, the flux through the loop will be zero.

Vocabulary   **Faraday's Law:** If the flux through a given area changes over time, a voltage will be induced in the wire and a current will momentarily flow. If the number of turns of wire is increased, the voltage will increase proportionally.

$$\text{potential difference} = \frac{\textbf{(number of turns)(change in flux)}}{\textbf{elapsed time}}$$

or $V = \dfrac{N\Delta\phi}{\Delta t}$

Note: This potential difference is also referred to as the **induced voltage**.

Vocabulary   **Lenz's Law:** An induced voltage always produces a magnetic field that opposes the field that originally produced it.

In other words, if the original magnetic field, and thus the flux, is going toward the north, the induced voltage will produce an opposing field and flux that goes toward the south.

Transformers

Vocabulary   **Transformer:** A device that produces a change in voltage in an alternating current circuit.

A transformer consists of an iron core wound with a primary coil and a secondary coil. An alternating current placed through the primary coil induces a changing magnetic field through the core, which, in turn, induces a voltage in the secondary coil.

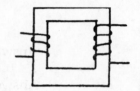

$$\frac{\textbf{voltage in primary coil}}{\textbf{voltage in secondary coil}} = \frac{\textbf{turns in primary coil}}{\textbf{turns in secondary coil}} \quad \text{or} \quad \frac{V_p}{V_s} = \frac{N_p}{N_s}$$

If the primary coil has more turns than the secondary coil, the transformer will step down, or decrease, the incoming voltage. If the primary coil has fewer turns than the secondary coil, the transformer will step up, or increase, the incoming voltage.

Solved Examples

Example 3:   Tyrone is pedaling his bike down the street perpendicular to Earth's magnetic field of 5.5×10^{-5} T. What is the flux through the metal rim of his bicycle wheel, if the wheel has an area of 1.13 m^2?

Given: $A = 1.13$ m^2 *Unknown:* $\phi = ?$
          $B = 5.5 \times 10^{-5}$ T   *Original equation:* $\phi = AB$

Solve: $\phi = AB = (1.13$ m$^2)(5.5 \times 10^{-5}$ T$) = \textbf{6.2} \times \textbf{10}^{-5}$ **Wb**

Example 4:   If the bicycle in Example 3 takes 2.0 s to make a 90° turn onto a northbound street, what is the induced voltage in one metal rim of the bicycle?

Given: $N = 1$ turn   *Unknown:* $V = ?$
          $\phi = 6.2 \times 10^{-5}$ Wb   *Original equation:* $V = \dfrac{N\Delta\phi}{\Delta t}$
          $\Delta t = 2.0$ s

Solve: $V = \dfrac{N\Delta\phi}{\Delta t} = \dfrac{(1 \text{ turn})(6.2 \times 10^{-5} \text{ Wb})}{2.0 \text{ s}} = \textbf{3.1} \times \textbf{10}^{-5}$ **V**

Example 5: While out for a walk with his mother, Lance notices a large, cylindrical gray box high atop a telephone pole. His mother explains that it is a transformer. This transformer takes 6000. V from the power company and steps it down to the 240 V supplied to each of the houses on the street, with the use of a secondary coil containing 100. turns. How many turns are there in the primary coil?

Given: V_p = 6000. V   Unknown: N_p = ?

V_s = 240 V   Original equation: $\dfrac{V_p}{V_s} = \dfrac{N_p}{N_s}$

N_s = 100. turns

Solve: $N_p = \dfrac{V_p N_s}{V_s} = \dfrac{(6000.\ V)(100.\ \text{turns})}{240\ V}$ = **2500 turns**

Practice Exercises

Exercise 5: Patty is driving down the expressway on her way to the office in a town where the horizontal component of Earth's magnetic field is 3.5×10^{-5} T to the north. The driver's side window of Patty's car has an area of 0.40 m^2.
a) What is the magnitude of the flux through the window if the car is moving south? b) How does it differ if the car is moving west?

Answer: **a.** ——————————

Answer: **b.** ——————————

Exercise 6: A medical process called *magnetic resonance imaging* (MRI) replaces X-rays in some instances where pictures are required to study internal organs. Eleanor is undergoing an MRI procedure and is placed inside a chamber housing the coil of a large electromagnet that has a radius of 25.0 cm. A flux of 0.290 Wb passes through the coil opening. What is the magnetic field inside the coil?

Answer: ——————————

Exercise 7: The hood ornament on Abe's sedan is shaped like a ring 8.00 cm in diameter. Abe is driving toward the west so that Earth's 5.00×10^{-5} T field provides no flux through the hood ornament. What is the induced voltage in the metal ring as Abe turns from this street onto one where he is traveling north, if he takes 3.0 s to make the turn?

Answer: _____

Exercise 8: Becky wears glasses whose wire frames are shaped like two circles, each with an area of 2.0×10^{-3} m^2. The horizontal component of Earth's magnetic field in Becky's hometown is 1.9×10^{-5} T. If Becky turns her head back and forth, rotating it through 90° every 0.50 s, what is the induced voltage in the wire frame of one eyepiece?

Answer: _____

Exercise 9: Audrey disassembles the control box of her electric train and finds a small transformer inside. Its primary coil is made up of 600. turns and the secondary coil is made up of 60. turns. a) If the household voltage supplied to the train is 120 V, what voltage is required to make the train run? b) Is this a step-up or a step-down transformer?

Answer: a. _____

Answer: b. _____

Exercise 10: A hydroelectric plant in Niagara Falls sends 3000 V to the transformer in a substation that steps it up to 120 000 V for transmission to homes in New York City. If the primary coil contains 2000 turns, how many turns are there in the secondary coil of the step-up transformer?

Answer: _____

Additional Exercises

A-1: In the giant CERN particle accelerator in Switzerland, protons are accelerated to speeds of 2.0×10^8 m/s through a magnetic field of 3.5 T and then collided with a fixed target. What is the magnitude of the magnetic force experienced by the protons as they are accelerated around the giant ring?

A-2: In Fred's color TV, electrons are shot toward the screen through a 1.0×10^{-3}-T magnetic field set up in the picture tube. a) If each electron experiences a magnetic force of 2.9×10^{-15} N, at what speed is it propelled through the picture tube? b) How does this speed compare to the speed of light?

A-3: A proton shot out of the sun at a speed of 6.0×10^6 m/s during a "sunspot maximum" travels through the strong magnetic field of the sun. What is the maximum magnetic force experienced by the proton at a point where the sun's magnetic field is 0.090 T?

A-4: A 0.90-m-long straight wire on board the *Voyager* spacecraft carries a current of 0.10 A perpendicular to Jupiter's strong magnetic field of 5.0×10^{-4} T. What is the magnitude of the magnetic force experienced by the wire?

A-5: While vacuuming the living room rug, Buster pulls the 4.0-m vacuum cleaner cord so that it is lying perpendicular to Earth's magnetic field of 5.3×10^{-5} T. a) If the cord is carrying a current of 6.0 A, how large a magnetic force is created on the cord by Earth's magnetic field? b) If Buster then pulls the cord so that it lies parallel to Earth's magnetic field, how large is the magnetic force now experienced by the cord?

A-6: At the equator, where Earth's 3.0×10^{-5}-T magnetic field is parallel to the surface of Earth, Donna is spinning her wedding ring (which has a diameter of 2.0 cm) on top of the table. Find the change in flux through the ring if Donna a) slides it horizontally across the table, b) rolls it across the table, c) spins it on its edge.

A-7: Amanda's little brother spins a bar magnet whose magnetic field is 3.0×10^{-2} T over the face of Amanda's electric watch, perpendicular to a circular loop of wire of radius 0.60 cm inside the watch. a) What is the induced voltage in the wire if the magnet is spun over the watch in 0.30 s? b) Why is it a bad idea to put an electric watch too close to a strong magnetic field?

A-8: While Hiroshi sits in his living room, the newspaper carrier rings his doorbell. If a voltage of 120 V passes through the 200-turn primary coil of the transformer, how many turns are needed in the secondary coil to reduce the voltage to the 6.0 V needed to run the doorbell?

A-9: A bug zapper in the Snyders' back yard runs off a 120-V household line through a transformer whose primary coil contains 50. turns while the secondary coil contains 2000. turns. a) What is the output voltage of the transformer? b) Is this a step-up or a step-down transformer?

Challenge Exercises for Further Study

B-1: When Helen turns on the TV set, electrons are accelerated through a 20 000.-V potential difference and deflected by a 1.0×10^{-2}-T magnetic field. What is the average magnetic force experienced by an electron? ($m_e = 9.11 \times 10^{-31}$ kg)

B-2: Captain Kittredge is sailing due north, as indicated by his compass needle, in a location where Earth's magnetic field is 2.0×10^{-5} T. The captain inadvertently places his radio near the compass, allowing the wire from his radio to align in a north-south direction. The 0.80-m-long wire carries a current of 5.0 A and produces a magnetic force on the compass needle of 2.8×10^{-4} N. To what angle will the compass needle turn while the wire is over it?

B-3: A velocity selector is a device that measures the speed of a charged particle by shooting the particle through oppositely charged plates enclosed in a tube. Inside the tube is a constant magnetic field, B. If a particle is to travel, undeflected, down the center of the tube, the magnetic force must equal the electric force. If the magnetic field of 0.630 T is perpendicular to the electric field of 5.00×10^4 N/C, find the speed of an electron sent through the velocity selector.

B-4: An alpha particle (He nucleus) is shot at 5.0×10^6 m/s into a magnetic field of 0.20 T in a device known as a mass spectrometer. What is the radius of the path followed by the alpha particle? (Hint: He nuclei contain 2 protons and 2 neutrons, each with a mass of 1.67×10^{-27} kg.)

18 Modern Physics

18-1 The Atom and the Quantum

Photon Energy

Vocabulary **Quantum:** A packet of energy that exhibits both particle and wave properties.

A quantum of light energy is called a **photon**. The photon's energy is directly proportional to the frequency of its lights. This can be written as

$$\textbf{energy} = \textbf{(Planck's constant)(frequency)} \quad \text{or} \quad E = hf$$

where **Planck's constant, h, is equal to 6.63×10^{-34} J·s.**

Recall from Chapter 13 that $c = \lambda f$. So, the frequency of light can be written as $f = \dfrac{c}{\lambda}$. Therefore, the energy of a photon is

$$\textbf{energy} = \frac{\textbf{(Planck's constant)(speed of light)}}{\textbf{wavelength}} \quad \text{or} \quad E = \frac{hc}{\lambda}$$

The common unit for the wavelength of light is the **nanometer (nm),** which equals 10^{-9} m.

It is important to note that because the energy of a photon is so small, scientists rarely use the unit "joule" when describing this energy. Instead, a smaller unit, the **electron volt (eV)** is more commonly used in equations involving photon energy. Note that the electron volt is a unit of energy and not a unit of potential difference.

$$1 \text{ eV} = 1.60 \times 10^{-19} \text{ J}$$

De Broglie Waves

Vocabulary **De Broglie Wavelength:** The effective wavelength of a moving particle.

Recall that photons of light exhibit both particle and wave properties. According to de Broglie, if a moving particle of matter has a high **momentum**, it exhibits wave properties and has a measurable wavelength.

The de Broglie wavelength of any particle can be found from the equation

$$\text{wavelength} = \frac{\text{Planck's constant}}{(\text{mass})(\text{velocity})} \quad \text{or} \quad \lambda = \frac{h}{mv}$$

Solved Examples

Example 1:   Glenn is a DJ at his high school radio station WPAA, which broadcasts at a frequency of 91.7 MHz. When the station is on the air, how much energy does each emitted photon possess a) in joules? b) in electron volts?

Solution: The term MHz means megahertz or 10^6 Hz. Therefore, 91.7 MHz means 91.7×10^6 Hz.

a. *Given:* $f = 91.7 \times 10^6$ Hz   *Unknown:* $E = ?$
         $h = 6.63 \times 10^{-34}$ J·s   *Original equation:* $E = hf$

Solve: $E = hf\,(6.63 \times 10^{-34}\,\text{J·s})(91.7 \times 10^6\,\text{Hz}) = \mathbf{6.08 \times 10^{-26}\,J}$

b. This energy in joules can be converted into electron volts by dividing by 1.6×10^{-19} J/eV.

$$E = \frac{6.08 \times 10^{-26}\,\text{J}}{1.60 \times 10^{-19}\,\text{J/eV}} = \mathbf{3.80 \times 10^{-7}\,eV}$$

Example 2:   Bart uses a helium-neon laser to align his telescope. The laser emits red light with a wavelength of 633 nm. How much energy, in electron volts, is given off by each photon of laser light?

Solution: First, convert nm to m.   633 nm = 6.33×10^{-7} m.

Given: $h = 6.63 \times 10^{-34}$ J·s   *Unknown:* $E = ?$
        $\lambda = 6.33 \times 10^{-7}$ m   *Original equation:* $E = \dfrac{hc}{\lambda}$
        $c = 3.00 \times 10^8$ m/s

Solve: $E = \dfrac{hc}{\lambda} = \dfrac{(6.63 \times 10^{-34}\,\text{J·s})(3.00 \times 10^8\,\text{m/s})}{6.33 \times 10^{-7}\,\text{m}} = 3.14 \times 10^{-19}\,\text{J}$

This can be converted into electron volts by dividing.

$$E = \frac{3.14 \times 10^{-19}\,\text{J}}{1.60 \times 10^{-19}\,\text{J/eV}} = \mathbf{1.96\ eV}$$

Example 3:   Compare the de Broglie wavelengths for a proton and an electron, each traveling at 3.00×10^7 m/s.

Given: $m_p = 1.67 \times 10^{-27}$ kg   Unknown: $\lambda = ?$
$m_e = 9.11 \times 10^{-31}$ kg   Original equation: $\lambda = \dfrac{h}{mv}$
$v = 3.00 \times 10^7$ m/s
$h = 6.63 \times 10^{-34}$ J·s

For the proton:

Solve: $\lambda = \dfrac{h}{mv} = \dfrac{6.63 \times 10^{-34} \text{ J·s}}{(1.67 \times 10^{-27} \text{ kg})(3.00 \times 10^7 \text{ m/s})} = \mathbf{1.32 \times 10^{-14}}$ **m**

For the electron:

Solve: $\lambda = \dfrac{h}{mv} = \dfrac{6.63 \times 10^{-34} \text{ J·s}}{(9.11 \times 10^{-31} \text{ kg})(3.00 \times 10^7 \text{ m/s})} = \mathbf{2.43 \times 10^{-11}}$ **m**

Therefore, the electron's wavelength is 1800 times larger than the proton's.

Practice Exercises

Exercise 1: The sun is a yellow star and emits most of its radiation in the yellow portion of the spectrum. If the sun's radiation peaks at a frequency of 5.20×10^{14} Hz, how much energy is emitted by one photon of this visible yellow light?

Answer: _____

Exercise 2: After applying sunscreen, Cherie lies in the summer sun to get a tan. The ultraviolet light responsible for tanning has a wavelength over 310. nm, while the burning rays can range down to 280. nm. Which ultraviolet photons emit more energy, those that tan or those that burn? How much more?

Answer: _____

Exercise 3: Gayle cooks a roast in her microwave oven. The klystron tube in the oven emits photons whose energy is 1.20×10^{-3} eV. What are the wavelengths of these photons?

Answer: _____

Exercise 4: During the winter Olympic biathalon trials, Eric is shooting his rifle at a target. What is the de Broglie wavelength of a 10.0-g bullet fired from the rifle at 500. m/s?

Answer: _____

Exercise 5: An electron microscope is observing detail on a virus down to 5.0×10^{-9} m. How fast must an electron in the microscope be moving to observe detail this size? (Hint: Due to diffraction effects, an electron's wavelength must be about the same size or smaller than the object being observed.)

Answer: _____

18-2 The Photoelectric Effect

Because photons of light carry energy, they can cause electrons to be ejected from certain metal surfaces just by being absorbed by the metal and transferring their energy to the electrons. This process is known as the **photoelectric effect**. However, certain conditions must be met in order for photoelectrons to be ejected.

First, the incoming photon must have enough energy to cause the liberation of an electron. The frequency that corresponds to this amount of energy is called the **threshold frequency**. At the threshold frequency, the photon has just enough energy to free the electron from the surface, and there is no excess kinetic energy given to the emitted electron.

The energy required to free the electron is called the **work function**. Any excess energy given to the electron becomes the kinetic energy that puts the electron in motion. Therefore,

photon energy = kinetic energy + work function   or $hf = KE + W$

The photoelectric effect is an interaction of one photon with one electron. The release of electrons from a surface is a function of the energy they receive. Therefore, you are more likely to witness the photoelectric effect by shining dim blue light on a surface than bright red light, because the blue light has a higher energy per photon.

The wavelengths of colors in the visible light spectrum fall approximately in the following ranges.

Violet light	400–440 nm	Yellow light	530–590 nm
Blue light	440–480 nm	Orange light	590–630 nm
Green light	480–530 nm	Red light	630–700 nm

Radiation falling just below 400 nm is called **ultraviolet radiation**, while that falling just above 700 nm is called **infrared radiation**. Generally, the photoelectric effect only occurs with ultraviolet and visible radiation.

Solved Examples

Example 4: When Doug walks through the entrance to the hardware store, a bell in the back of the store rings, triggered by a photocell whose work function is 2.70 eV. a) What is the threshold frequency of the light shining on the photocell? b) What is the wavelength of the light?

a. *Given:* $E = 2.70$ eV
$h = 6.63 \times 10^{-34}$ J·s

Unknown: $f = ?$
Original equation: $E = hf$

Solve: $f = \dfrac{E}{h} = \dfrac{(2.70 \text{ eV})(1.60 \times 10^{-19} \text{ J/eV})}{6.63 \times 10^{-34} \text{ J·s}} = \mathbf{6.51 \times 10^{14}}$ **Hz**

b. *Given:* $c = 3.00 \times 10^8$ m/s
$f = 6.03 \times 10^{14}$ Hz

Unknown: $\lambda = ?$
Original equation: $c = \lambda f$

Solve: $\lambda = \dfrac{c}{f} = \dfrac{3.00 \times 10^8 \text{ m/s}}{6.51 \times 10^{14} \text{ Hz}} = 4.60 \times 10^{-7}$ m = **460 nm**   This is blue light.

Example 5: What is the kinetic energy of photoelectrons emitted when ultraviolet light of 200. nm shines on a photocell whose work function is 2.50 eV?

Given: $h = 6.63 \times 10^{-34}$ J·s
$c = 3.00 \times 10^8$ m/s
$\lambda = 2.00 \times 10^{-7}$ m
$W = 2.50$ eV

Unknown: KE = ?
Original equation: $\dfrac{hc}{\lambda} = KE + W$

Solve: $KE = \dfrac{hc}{\lambda} - W$

$= \dfrac{(6.63 \times 10^{-34} \text{ J·s})(3.00 \times 10^8 \text{ m/s})}{2.00 \times 10^{-7} \text{ m}} - (2.50 \text{ eV})(1.6 \times 10^{-19} \text{ J/eV})$

$= \mathbf{5.95 \times 10^{-19}}$ **J**

Practice Exercises

Exercise 6:   The work function for three surfaces are as follows: mercury = 4.50 eV, magnesium = 3.68 eV, and lithium = 2.30 eV. a) At what threshold frequency are electrons liberated from each of these surfaces? b) What color light corresponds to these threshold frequencies?

Answer: **a.** _____

Answer: **b.** _____

Exercise 7:   Shelley shines her red, helium–neon laser, whose wavelength is 633 nm, on a photocell that has a work function of 2.38 eV. a) Will the photocell function with this wavelength of light? b) If so, what is the kinetic energy of the photoelectrons released? If not, what wavelength corresponds to the threshold frequency?

Answer: **a.** _____

Answer: **b.** _____

Exercise 8:   A classic physics demonstration involves placing a shiny zinc plate on a negatively charged electroscope and shining ultraviolet light on the plate. If the work function of zinc is 4.31 eV and the wavelength of the light is 250 nm, with what kinetic energy are photoelectrons ejected from the zinc plate? b) What will happen to the leaves of the electroscope?

Answer: **a.** _____

Answer: **b.** _____

18-3 Energy Level Diagrams

Each atom has its own characteristic set of "fingerprints" or allowed energy states that its electrons can occupy. An **energy level diagram** is a representation of these allowed energy states. The electrons in an atom cannot occupy any level between these allowed states, but instead "jump" from level to level. This is analogous to a person trying to stand *between*, rather than *on*, the rungs of a ladder. It is impossible to do so!

Generally, electrons are found at the lowest energy level or **ground state**. However, when an electron absorbs a photon from its surroundings, it becomes excited and jumps up to a higher energy level. Since the photon is removed from the incident light, this produces an **absorption spectrum**.

When the electron returns to a lower energy level, it emits one or more photons in the process, producing a bright line or **emission spectrum**. If these emitted photons fall in the visible portion of the spectrum, the characteristic spectral lines of the material are seen.

The energy level diagram for hydrogen is shown. Because hydrogen is the most abundant gas in the universe, the hydrogen spectrum has been studied very closely and names have been given to the transitions between energy levels.

Lyman series: Electrons jump to or from the $n = 1$ level. The electromagnetic radiation emitted or absorbed is characterized as ultraviolet.

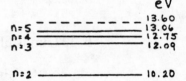

Balmer series: Electrons jump to or from the $n = 2$ level. The electromagnetic radiation emitted or absorbed is characterized as visible light.

Paschen series: Electrons jump to or from the $n = 3$ level.

Brackett series: Electrons jump to or from the $n = 4$ level.

Pfund series: Electrons jump to or from the $n = 5$ level. The electromagnetic radiation emitted or absorbed from these three series is characterized as infrared.

Solved Examples

Example 6: **a.** What wavelengths of light are emitted by an electron jumping from $n = 2$ to $n = 1$, and from $n = 4$ to $n = 3$? b) To what portion of the electromagnetic spectrum do these wavelengths correspond?

From $n = 2$ to $n = 1$

Given: $E_2 = 10.2$ eV   *Unknown:* $\lambda = ?$
$E_1 = 0$ eV   *Original equation:* $\dfrac{hc}{\lambda} = E_2 - E_1$
$h = 6.63 \times 10^{-34}$ J·s
$c = 3.00 \times 10^8$ m/s

Solve: $\lambda = \dfrac{hc}{E_2 - E_1} = \dfrac{(6.63 \times 10^{-34} \text{ J·s})(3.00 \times 10^8 \text{ m/s})}{(10.2 \text{ eV} - 0 \text{ eV})(1.60 \times 10^{-19} \text{ J/eV})} = 1.22 \times 10^{-7} \text{m}$

From $n = 4$ to $n = 3$

Given: $E_4 = 12.75$ eV   *Unknown:* $\lambda = ?$
$E_3 = 12.09$ eV   *Original equation:* $\dfrac{hc}{\lambda} = E_4 - E_3$
$h = 6.63 \times 10^{-34}$ J·s
$c = 3.00 \times 10^8$ m/s

Solve: $\lambda = \dfrac{hc}{E_4 - E_3} = \dfrac{(6.63 \times 10^{-34} \text{ J·s})(3.00 \times 10^8 \text{ m/s})}{(12.75 \text{ eV} - 12.09 \text{ eV})(1.60 \times 10^{-19} \text{ J/eV})} = \mathbf{1.88 \times 10^{-6} \text{ m}}$

b. 122 nm is ultraviolet and 1880 nm is infrared.

Practice Exercises

Exercise 9: Use the energy level diagram for hydrogen on page 239 to determine the shortest wavelength in the Paschen series of hydrogen.

Answer: _____

Exercise 10: The sun's spectrum is made up of many absorption lines called *Fraunhofer lines*. How many electron volts of energy are absorbed in order to produce the H α line whose wavelength is 657.7 nm?

Answer: ⎯⎯⎯⎯⎯⎯⎯⎯⎯⎯

Exercise 11: A stellar spectrum shows three absorption lines of hydrogen produced as electrons move from the $n = 2$ state to higher energy levels ($n = 3$, $n = 4$, $n = 5$). What are the wavelengths and colors of the three lines missing from the continuous spectrum?

Answer: ⎯⎯⎯⎯⎯⎯⎯⎯⎯⎯

Exercise 12: On June 24, 1999, NASA launched FUSE (the Far Ultraviolet Spectroscopic Explorer) to explore the universe using high-resolution spectroscopy in the far ultraviolet spectral region. If FUSE records radiation of wavelength 102.8 nm, between what two energy levels must the electron jump in the hydrogen atom to produce this line?

Answer: ⎯⎯⎯⎯⎯⎯⎯⎯⎯⎯

18-4 Radioactivity

Many atoms that contain large numbers of neutrons are unstable, or **radioactive**. This means that in a given amount of time, the atoms of the substance will decay or change into different atoms with the emission of α, β, or γ rays from the nucleus.

Vocabulary   **Activity:** The rate at which a radioactive sample decays.

If a radioactive sample containing N atoms is allowed to decay for an elapsed time, Δt, there will be a change in the number of atoms, ΔN, which depends upon the **decay constant**, λ, for that particular material. Note: This is not the same λ used to represent wavelength. The decay constant is the probability per unit time that a nucleus will decay. The term $\Delta N / \Delta t$ is called the **activity**.

$$\frac{\text{change in number of atoms}}{\text{elapsed time}} = -(\text{decay constant})(\text{original number of atoms})$$

or $\quad \dfrac{\Delta N}{\Delta t} = -\lambda N$

The SI unit for activity is the **becquerel (Bq)**, which equals one **decay per second**.

The number of radioactive atoms, N, remaining after a time, t, can be found if you know the number of atoms in the original sample, N_o, and the decay constant of the material, λ.

$$N = N_o\, e^{-\lambda t}$$

where e is the base of the natural logarithm and is approximately equal to 2.72.

Another way of examining radioactivity is by looking at the half-life of a sample.

Vocabulary   **Half-life:** The time it takes for half of a radioactive sample to decay.

$$\textbf{Half-life} = \frac{\textbf{0.693}}{\textbf{decay constant}} \quad \text{or} \quad T_{1/2} = \frac{0.693}{\lambda}$$

Solved Examples

Example 7:   Cobalt-60, used in radiation therapy for cancer patients, has a half-life of 5.26 y. A sample of cobalt-60 containing 5.00×10^{12} radioactive atoms sits in a lead case in the medical stockroom of St. Mary's Hospital for 10.0 years. How many cobalt-60 atoms remain after this amount of time?

Solution: First, find the decay constant for cobalt-60.

$$\lambda = \frac{0.693}{T_{1/2}} = \frac{0.693}{5.26 \text{ y}} = 0.132 \text{ y}^{-1}$$

Given: $\lambda = 0.132 \text{ y}^{-1}$ *Unknown:* $N = ?$
       $N_0 = 5.00 \times 10^{12}$ atoms   *Original equation:* $N = N_0 e^{-\lambda t}$
       $e = 2.72$
       $t = 10.0 \text{ y}$

Solve: $N = N_0 e^{-\lambda t} = (5.00 \times 10^{12} \text{ atoms})(2.72)^{-(0.131 \text{ y}^{-1})(10.0 \text{ y})}$
       $= \mathbf{1.33 \times 10^{12} \text{ atoms}}$

Example 8: Radioactive gold-198 is used as a tracer to test liver functions in low-level liver scans. Dr. Rogers uses gold-198 in a liver scan on Otis, who has been exhibiting signs of jaundice. A solution containing 3.00×10^9 gold-198 atoms is injected into his liver and observed after 72.0 h. What is the activity of the gold-198 after this amount of time? (Half-life of gold-198 = 2.70 d)

Solution: First, convert days into hours. 2.70 d = 64.8 h

Next, find the decay constant of gold-198.

$$\lambda = \frac{0.693}{T_{1/2}} = \frac{0.693}{64.8 \text{ s}} = 0.0107 \text{ h}^{-1}$$

Then, find the number of gold-198 atoms remaining after 72.0 h.

Given: $N_0 = 3.00 \times 10^9$ atoms   *Unknown:* $N = ?$
       $e = 2.72$ *Original equation:* $N = N_0 e^{-\lambda t}$
       $\lambda = 0.0107 \text{ h}^{-1}$
       $t = 72.0 \text{ h}$

Solve: $N = N_0 e^{-\lambda t} = (3.00 \times 10^9 \text{ atoms})(2.72)^{-(0.0107 \text{ h}^{-1})(72.0 \text{ h})} = 1.39 \times 10^9$ atoms

Finally, calculate the activity after converting h into s.   64.8 h = 233 280 s

$$\lambda = \frac{0.693}{233\ 280 \text{ s}} = 2.97 \times 10^{-6} \text{ s}^{-1}$$

Given: $\lambda = 2.97 \times 10^{-6} \text{ s}^{-1}$ *Unknown:* $\Delta N / \Delta t = ?$
       $N = 1.39 \times 10^9$ atoms   *Original equation:* $\Delta N / \Delta t = -\lambda N$

Solve: $\Delta N / \Delta t = -\lambda N = -(2.97 \times 10^{-6} \text{ s}^{-1})(1.39 \times 10^9 \text{ atoms}) = \mathbf{-4130 \text{ Bq}}$

Practice Exercises

Exercise 13: Spent fuel rods contain strontium-90 whose half-life is 28.1 y. Josh works at a nuclear reactor and must safely store the spent rods. If a spent fuel rod contains 1.00×10^{27} atoms of strontium-90 when stored in a sealed container, how many strontium-90 atoms will remain if the container is excavated by archeologists 1000. y later?

Answer: _____

Exercise 14: The synthetically manufactured radiopharmaceutical technicium-99 is used to produce a scan of Dale's brain after he suffers a concussion. The half-life of technicium-99 is 6.02 h. What percent of technicium-99 remains in Dale's body 24 h after the scan?

Answer: _____

Exercise 15: In the movie *The Planet of the Apes*, the forbidden zone was an area presumably contaminated by the radioactive plutonium fallout from the detonation of nuclear weapons. If Zera finds a rock in the forbidden zone that is tainted with plutonium-239 whose activity is 100. Bq, how many atoms of plutonium does the rock contain when it is discovered? (Half-life of plutonium-239 is 24 900. y)

Answer: _____

Exercise 16: In Exercise 15, if the explosion occurred 500. y prior to Zera's discovery, how many plutonium-239 atoms did the rock originally contain?

Answer: _____

Additional Exercises

A-1: Gamma rays emitted during the explosion of a nuclear bomb have an energy of 1.2×10^6 eV per photon. What is the frequency of this gamma ray emission?

A-2: An X-ray technician always steps out of the room when the X-ray machine is on. How much energy is carried by each photon of X-ray radiation, if the wavelength of this radiation is 0.0800 nm?

A-3: Mitch is undergoing eye surgery to repair a detached retina. His doctor uses a green laser whose wavelength is 514 nm. How much energy is produced by each laser photon?

A-4: Roy is making holograms with his helium-neon laser. In a helium-neon laser, excited helium atoms collide with neon atoms, raising the neon to an excited state where its energy is 20.66 eV. Stimulated emission then causes electrons in the neon to drop to a lower energy level where E = 18.7 eV. What is the wavelength and color of the light given off by a helium-neon laser?

A-5: At Bell Labs in 1926, Davisson and Germer aimed a beam of electrons at a nickel crystal whose atomic spacing was 0.215 nm. If the electrons had a speed of 4.4×10^6 m/s, calculate the de Broglie wavelength of the electrons to determine whether they would be able to pass through the crystal structure or would reflect back.

A-6: To determine the size of an oxygen nucleus, protons with kinetic energy of 0.100 GeV (1.00×10^8 eV) are shot at oxygen atoms. a) How fast are the protons moving? b) What is the de Broglie wavelength of the proton?

A-7: Three surfaces, sodium, iron, and gold, have respective work functions of 2.46 eV, 3.90 eV, and 4.82 eV. If light, whose wavelength is 300. nm, shines on each of these materials, which ones will show the photoelectric effect, and what will be the kinetic energy of any photoelectrons emitted?

A-8: Use the energy-level diagram for mercury to determine how much energy is needed to ionize a mercury atom in the $n = 4$ level.

A-9: A mercury atom absorbs a photon of wavelength 161 nm. What energy level does it jump to?

A-10: Hal looks at a mercury vapor street lamp through a diffraction grating and measures the wavelength of a spectral line to be 577 nm. Between what two energy levels must the electron jump to produce this line?

eV

- — — — — — — — —10.44
- $n=9$ ————— 8.85
- $n=8$ ————— 8.84
- $n=7$ ————— 7.93
- $n=6$ ————— 7.73
- $n=5$ ————— 6.70

- $n=4$ ————— 5.46
- $n=3$ ————— 4.89
- $n=2$ ————— 4.67

- $n=1$ ————— 0.00

Energy levels for Mercury

A-11: Gloria is testing her basement for radon with a kit she bought at the drugstore. The half-life of radon is 3.83 days and Gloria is informed that 5.00×10^6 radon atoms were present in her basement at the time of testing. Gloria hires a mason to seal off her basement and she runs the test again 30.0 days later. How many radon atoms will now be found in the basement?

A-12: While checking the radioactive tritium levels in the missiles at a Titan missile site, Hugh discovers that it has been 15.0 years since one of the missiles was last inspected. What percent of the radioactive tritium has been depleted? (Half-life of tritium = 12.4 y)

A-13: Nina has a watch whose hands glow in the dark due to a special paint containing radium-226 whose half-life is 1.60×10^3 y. When Nina takes the watch in for a cleaning after 20.0 y, the radium in the hands is found to have an activity of 1.12×10^{14} Bq. How many radium-226 atoms does the watch contain at this time?

A-14: In A-13, how many radium-226 atoms were originally in the watch when it was first purchased 20. years ago?

Challenge Exercises for Further Study

B-1: In Exercise 5, what minimum accelerating voltage of the electron microscope will produce an electron with this de Broglie wavelength?

B-2: Carbon-14 is commonly used to determine the age of organic material. Darlene is on an archeological dig in Mexico and discovers among some ruins what she thinks is an ancient Mayan bone. a) If the bone shows activity of 2.59×10^6 Bq, while the same mass of new human bone shows an average activity of 3.11×10^6 Bq, how old are the excavated bones? (Hint: Half-life of C-14 = 5730 y.) b) Why is carbon-14 a good substance to use for radioactive dating?

B-3: Two containers of radioactive iodine sit on a shelf in Doctor Bailin's supply closet, but the print on the labels has faded and is difficult to read. Dr. Bailin needs some iodine for a thyroid scan but she must only use iodine-131 whose half-life is 8.27 h and not iodione-59 whose half life is 44.6 d. She tests a sample and finds its activity to be 5.00×10^5 Bq. What should the activity be 24.0 h later if Dr. Bailin is testing the iodine-131?

Appendix A:

WORKING WITH NUMBERS

Significant Figures

Addition and Subtraction: When adding or subtracting numbers, your answer cannot have more significant figures after the decimal than the smallest number of significant figures after the decimal in any of the numbers used to obtain the answer.

For example: $25.678 + 3.45 + 67.2 =$ **96.3**   Only 3 significant figures

Multiplication and Division: When multiplying or dividing numbers, your answer cannot have more total significant figures than the smallest total number of significant figures in any of the numbers used to obtain the answer.

For example: $(26.4 \text{ N})(1.2 \text{ m}) =$ **32 N·m**   Only two significant figures

These rules are fairly easy to follow until you begin introducing zeros into your equations. Below are some examples using zeros.

700 has only one significant figure (the 7).
700.0 has 4 significant figures (all 4 numbers).
0.0700 has 3 significant figures (the 7 and the two zeros to the *right* of the 7).
0.007 has only 1 significant figure (the number 7).
7.007 has 4 significant figures (all 4 numbers).

Scientific notation may come in handy when working with significant figures. The number 7000, which has only 1 significant figure, can be written as 7.00×10^3 in order to be written with three significant figures.

You may also make zeros significant by placing a decimal point at the end. For example, 700 has only one significant figure while 700. has three.

Remember, these rules only apply to measured quantities. Quantities that can be counted rather than measured, such as people, coins, etc., are presumed to be an exact number and may be followed by as many zeros after the decimal as needed.

Unit Conversions

Before you solve an exercise, it is important that all units on the ends of the numbers you are using be in the same system. In this book, most quantities have been converted into the SI System (Système International), which is the standard system of units in physics.

Example: Convert 5 years into seconds.

$$(5\ y) \times \frac{(365\ d)}{(1\ y)} \times \frac{(24\ h)}{(1\ d)} \times \frac{(60\ min)}{(1\ h)} \times \frac{(60\ s)}{(1\ min)}$$

Notice that anything you are trying to eliminate in the numerator must be written in the denominator and vice versa. The units appearing in both the numerator and denominator cancel each other out, as shown by the slash marks through them.

Multiplying the numerators gives: $5 \times 365 \times 24 \times 60 \times 60 = 157\ 680\ 000$

Multiplying the denominators gives: $1 \times 1 \times 1 \times 1 = 1$

Final answer: $\frac{157\ 680\ 000\ s}{1} = 157\ 680\ 000\ s$ Note: This number is not written with significant figures.

Some Simple Trigonometry Relationships

The rules of trigonometry are developed with the use of right triangles as shown in the labeled diagram. Using this diagram, you can construct trigonometric equations in the following way.

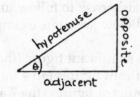

$$\sin \theta = \frac{\text{opposite}}{\text{hypotenuse}} \qquad \cos \theta = \frac{\text{adjacent}}{\text{hypotenuse}} \qquad \tan \theta = \frac{\text{opposite}}{\text{adjacent}}$$

Remember, you can only use the above relationships with *right* triangles. The hypotenuse of a right triangle is always the longest side.

Some Common Prefixes

Mega (M) $= 1 \times 10^6$ centi (c) $= 1 \times 10^{-2}$ micro (μ) $= 1 \times 10^{-6}$
kilo (k) $= 1 \times 10^3$ milli (m) $= 1 \times 10^{-3}$ nano (n) $= 1 \times 10^{-9}$

Appendix B:
SELECTED ANSWERS

Chapter 1
1. 884 m
3. a) 10.7 s
5. -9.00 m/s^2
7. a) 2.2 m/s
9. a) 28.3 m/s
11. 0.36 s
13. 25.9 m
A1. 3.78×10^8 m
A3. a) 16.61 m/s
   b) 37.16 mi/h
A5. Tortoise wins by 47 s
A7. 5 s
A9. $-19\,500$ m
A13. a) 1.11 s
   b) The same
A15. 3.9 m/s^2

Chapter 2
1. 145 km south
3. 50. N forward
5. 175 m/s northeast
7. 6360 km
9. Horizontal: 752 N
   Vertical: 274 N
11. 40.0 m/s
13. 37° to horizontal
15. 465 m
A1. a) 1450 km south
   b) 1650 km
A3. 4.1 m/s
   76° east of north
A5. 14.1 m
   45° north of west
A7. Horizontal: 50. N
   Vertical: 42 N
A9. 4.2 m
A11. 13.4 m/s
A13. 1.2 m (does not clear)

Chapter 3
3. 4500 N
5. a) $-34\,000$ N
7. 102 N
9. a) 78 N
11. 0.20
13. 14.5 N
15. 10 600 N
17. 1860 N
19. Culp: 1.5×10^7 N/m^2
   Vance: 1.0×10^6 N/m^2
21. a) .0079 m^2
   b) 0.050 m
A1. 50. N
A3. -1400 N
A5. 100 N
A7. 0.20
A9. 17.7 N

A11. 625 N
A13. 0.080 N
A15. a) 37 500 N
   b) 75 000 N/m^2

Chapter 4
1. 4.91×10^9 kg·m/s
3. a) 3750 N
   b) 1.5×10^6 N
   c) 400 times as great
5. 11.3 m/s
7. a) 9.0 m/s
9. 10. m/s
11. 215 m/s
13. 9.42 m/s
A1. 1470 kg·m/s
A3. 6080 N
A5. 50 000 N
A7. 1.04 m/s
A9. -0.22 m/s
A11. 17 004 m/s

Chapter 5
1. a) 1430 J
3. 4 N
5. 600 J
7. 17.4 m/s
9. 24.5 m/s
11. 7.7
13. 280 N
15. a) 6.0
   b) 4.4
   c) 73%
A1. 18 800 J
A3. a) 1 610 000 J
   b) 53 700 W
   c) 1 040 000 J
A5. 12 J
A7. a) 1.6 J
A9. 15 200 m
A11. 38
A13. 3

Chapter 6
1. 0.034 s
3. a) 1.6 m/s
5. a) 0.63 m/s
7. a) Jessica: 1.3 m/s
   Julie 0.94 m/s
   b) 0.15 m/s^2
9. 2.5 m/s
11. 1.50×10^{-15} N
13. 0.12 N·m
15. a) 17 N up
17. Anita: 384 N up
   Orin: 246 N up
19. 9.74×10^{37} kg·m^2
21. 5.4×10^{-8} kg·m^2

23. 5.6 m/s
A1. 0.6 s
A3. 3.8 m
A5. a) 2.2 m/s
   b) 35 N
A7. a) 5.9×10^{-3} m/s^2
   b) 3.5×10^{22} N toward sun
   c) 3.5×10^{22} N toward Earth
A9. Outstretched: 12 N·m
   Bent: 5.6 N·m
A11. 1.5×10^{-4} kg·m2
A13. 18 m/s

Chapter 7
1. Twice as large.
3. a) 9.78×10^{-8} N
   b) 1.63×10^{-8} N
5. 4.2×10^{21} m
7. 1.67×10^{-9} m/s^2
9. a) 9.9×10^{30} kg
   b) 5.0 times
11. a) 618 000 m/s
13. a) 2.58×10^{-4} m/s
A1. 1/8100
A3. 4.1×10^{-47} N
A5. a) 1.66×10^{-3} N
A7. a) 4.9×10^{23} kg
A9. 1.33×10^{-9} m/s^2
A11. a) 1340 N
   b) 3560 m/s

Chapter 8
1. 2 m/s
3. 28 h
5. Albert 33 y
   Henry 39.6 y
7. 13.0 m
9. a) 94 450 km
11. 1.0×10^{-3} kg
A1. 15 m/s same direction
A3. 8.3 y
A5. 1390 m
A7. 10^{68} J

Chapter 9
1. a) 710. kg/m^3
3. 1.76×10^{-3} kg
5. 1.3×10^8 N/m^2
7. 5.3×10^{-3} m^2
9. a) 3.0×10^{-6} m
11. 4.2×10^6 Pa
13. 1330 kg/m^3
15. 1.61 N
17. 0.50 m
19. Decreases by 314 m^3
21. 0.015 m^3
A1. 880 kg/m^3

A3. Silver: 10 500 kg/m³
    Earth: 5540 kg/m³
A5. 1.5×10^{-3} m
A7. b) 21 m
A9. a) 9.0×10^3 N
    b) 10. N
A11. a) 3.03 times bigger

Chapter 10
1. 122°F
3. a) −148°C
   b) −234°F
5. 437°C
7. b) 3.96×10^{-4} m³
9. 347 000 J
11. 31.8°C
13. 9630 J
15. 3.9×10^6 J
A1. Hottest: 462°C
    Coldest: −218°C
A3. 2.0×10^{-3} m
A5. 3.1×10^{-4} m²
A7. 1990 cm³
A9. 79.7°C
A11. 0.019 kg
A13. 1300 J

Chapter 11
1. 0.67 s
3. a) 200 N/m
5. a) 0.63 s
7. 2 s
9. a) 3.1 s
11. 0.65 m
A1. 0.0023 s
A3. 20 N/m
A5. a) 0.5441 s
A7. 6.28 s
A9. b) 0.0400 m

Chapter 12
1. 0.013 m
3. 0.4 m/s
5. 188 Hz
7. b) −5.26 m/s
9. 813 Hz
11. 0.300 m
13. 394.0 Hz
A1. 0.0085 m
A3. a) 0.688 m
A5. 40 m
A7. a) Toward: 501.5 Hz
       Away: 498.5 Hz
    b) 3.0 Hz
A9. 15.0 m/s
A11. 20.4 m/s
A15. 628 m/s

Chapter 13
1. 19 700 s
3. 3.80×10^{-7} m
5. 40°
7. a) −36 cm
9. 28.9°
11. 1.39
A1. 260 s

A3. 20°
A5. c) −12.0 cm
A7. a) ∞
A9. b) alcohol: 2.21×10^8 m/s
    water: 2.26×10^8 m/s
A11. 20.7°
A13. a) 42.5°

Chapter 14
1. 11.1 cm
3. a) 0.0508 m
5. a) 20 times
   b) 30 cm
7. 8 times
9. b) 2.7 diopters
11. 0.40 m
13. a) 8.8×10^{-4} m
15. 2.4×10^{-6} m
A1. 12.0 cm
A3. 2.4 cm
A5. 24 cm
A7. 0.17 m
A9. a) −4.0 diopters
    b) 0.29 m
A11. −0.17 diopters
A13. 7130 m

Chapter 15
1. 1.3×10^{-3} N
3. 7.0×10^{-13} C
5. 10. m
7. 1.9×10^{13} N/C
9. 18×10^5 N/C to the right
11. 8800 V
13. 4.0×10^{-3} m
A1. 1.5×10^{-11} N
A3. 4.2×10^{-13} C
A5. a) 0.043 m
A7. 1.3×10^7 N/C
A9. a) 0.14 m
A11. 450 000 J
A13. 600 000 V

Chapter 16
1. 10 800 s
3. 27.5 Ω
5. 1.52 V
7. 2.0×10^4 V
9. 0.8 A
11. a) 240 V
    c) 18 A
13. a) 1.5 A
    b) 80 Ω
15. $8.10
17. a) 3 Ω
    b) 4 A
19. Series: 10. V
    Parallel: 120 V
21. a) 5 Ω
    b) 85 Ω
A1. a) 15 600 s
A3. 100. Ω
A5. 5×10^{-9} A
A7. 14.17 A
A9. $1.2 \times 10^6

A11. 0.25 A
A13. a) 3.0 Ω
     b) 12 A

Chapter 17
1. 4.2×10^{-14} N
3. a) 6.0×10^{-3} T
5. a) Zero
   b) 1.4×10^{-5} Wb
7. 8.4×10^{-8} V
9. a) 12 V
A1. 1.1×10^{-10} N
A3. 8.6×10^{-14} N
A5. a) 1.3×10^{-3} N
    b) zero
A7. a) 1.1×10^{-5} V
A9. a) 4800 V

Chapter 18
1. 2.15 eV
3. 1040 nm
5. 150 000 m/s
7. a) 1.96 eV
   b) 5.22×10^{-7} m
9. 823 nm
11. a) 657 nm Red
    b) 488 nm Greenish Blue
    c) 445 nm Violet
13. 1.85×10^{16} atoms
15. 1.13×10^{14} atoms
A1. 2.9×10^{20} Hz
A3. 2.42 eV
A5. 1.7×10^{-19} m
A7. Sodium: 1.68 eV Yes
    Iron: 0.244 eV Yes
    Gold: −0.676 eV No
A9. 7.72 eV
A11. 2.18×10^4 atoms
A13. 8.18×10^{24} atoms